STRUCTURES FOR MISSION

by

Marvin D. Hoff

The Historical Series of the Reformed Church
in America

No. 14

The Reformed Church in America:

STRUCTURES FOR MISSION

by

Marvin D. Hoff

Wm. B. Eerdmans Publishing Co.
Grand Rapids, Michigan

Copyright © 1985 by Wm. B. Eerdmans Publishing Co.
255 Jefferson S.E., Grand Rapids, MI 49503

Library of Congress Cataloging in Publication Data

Hoff, Marvin D.
  The Reformed Church in America.

  (The Historical series of the Reformed Church in America; no. 14)
  Bibliography: p. 238.
  1. Reformed Church in America—Missions. 2. Reformed
Church—United States—Missions. I. Title. II. Series.
BV2580.H64 1985   266'.5732   85-1585
ISBN 0-8028-0081-5

TO
MARY AND JEAN
DAVID
JOANNE

who bring joy and gladness to my life

The Author

Marvin D. Hoff received his college education at Northwestern, Orange City, Iowa, and Central, Pella, Iowa. He received the B.D. degree from Western Theological Seminary, Holland, Michigan, the Th.M. from Princeton Theological Seminary, and the Doctorandes from the Theologische Hogeschool, Kampen, The Netherlands.

Mr. Hoff is a member of the Society of Biblical Literature, the American Society of Missiology, and the International Association of Mission Studies.

He is an ordained minister of the Reformed Church in America. He has served the Rea Avenue Reformed Church, Hawthorne, New Jersey (1961-65), and the Reformed Church of Palos Heights, Palos Heights, Illinois (1966-69, 1981-85). During a twelve-year period of service on the national staff of the Reformed Church in America, he served as Secretary for Asian Ministries, Secretary for Operations, and Secretary for Operations and Finance.

Since 1969, he has served as a director of the Foundation for Theological Education in Southeast Asia. Most recently, he has served as the part-time executive director of FTE. The FTE maintains program relationships with more than fifty theological education institutions in Southeast Asia; the Association for Theological Education in Southeast Asia; the Program for Theological Education, World Council of Churches; and the newly reopening seminaries in the People's Republic of China.

Marvin D. Hoff became the president of Western Theological Seminary, Holland, Michigan, in 1985.

The Historical Series of the Reformed Church in America

This series has been inaugurated by the General Synod of the Reformed Church in America, acting through its Commission on History, for the purpose of encouraging historical research and providing a medium wherein this knowledge may be shared with the academic community and with the members of the denomination in order that a knowledge of the past may contribute to right action in the present.

General Editor

The Rev. Donald J. Bruggink, Ph.D., Western Theological Seminary

Contents

Foreword

The structures which the RCA has created to carry out her task of mission have invariably been a matter of pragmatic decision rather than of theological reflection. When the Reverend John Henry Livingston translated the Church Order of Dort into English for America's newly-independent Dutch Reformed Church in 1792, he eliminated articles which gave the prince responsibility for the maintenance and expansion of the church, but did nothing to change the articles in the Belgic Confession which had given rise to that polity. This practice of pragmatically adjusting polity to fit the needs of the church, without engaging in theological reflection, discussion and decision, has become habitual for the RCA. Without a theological base to give continuity to polity, a history of our decisions is all the more necessary—especially in an age which seems unwilling to digest one structure before devouring another. It is also to be hoped that such a history of our pragmatic decisions will stimulate us to the reformation of theological reflection to precede our actions of polity.

Marvin D. Hoff has given to the church a much needed history of its structures for mission. As such, this book will be of interest not only to the historian, but to all those who now hold leadership within the mission structures of the Reformed Church in America, as it enables them to understand more clearly where they are, and helps them to move more effectively into the future.

The opening chapter, which covers the church from its inception in 1628 to the end of World War II, should forever put to rest the myth that the RCA has been slow to adapt to new situations. Once the miniscule Dutch Church was free from the control of the Classis of Amsterdam, she exhibited typical American pragmatism—rather than sound theological reflection—in adapt-

ing to her new vision of mission. Experiments followed in be-
wildering succession, and when workable structures were found
(and used), it took the Constitution of the church seventy-five
years to catch up with the practice of the church!

This history of the RCA is made all the more relevant by jux-
taposing the national experience after World War II with that of
the church, with some startling analyses of the impact of the
national scene upon the ecclesiastical scene. Business and professional people in particular will gain insight into the "terrible feast"
of church and nation during this period. Part of the feast enjoyed
by the church took the form of the United Advance, the biggest
and most successful coordinated approach to stewardship of witness and finance attempted to that time. From its success arose
a new structure for mission, the Reformed Church Stewardship
Council, built on the premise (so convincingly demonstrated by
the United Advance) that coordinated stewardship is preferable
to competitive appeals.

While boards had early been established to carry out the mission of the church, the General Synod had itself no continuing
existence between sessions, until the Stewardship Council was
formed. The council's rapid collection of inappropriate referrals
from synod demonstrated the need for a continuing administrative body, which found fruition in the General Synod Executive
Committee.

The General Synod Executive Committee, established in 1961,
by 1962 already had received a referral from the synod to review
the entire program structure of the RCA. Out of that study came
the first full-fledged corporate model for carrying out the church's
business, which found its focus in the General Program Council.

The former boards and agencies concerned with the mission
of the church now operated under a single board, with the result
that for the first time the entire program of the church could be
governed by a single, continuing body. It soon became apparent
that, contrary to popular belief, the majority of funds did not go
to missionary-evangelists proclaiming the gospel, but for the
maintenance of institutions. One of the accomplishments of the

General Program Council was to redress that imbalance and enable a more truly mission-minded approach. Another of its accomplishments was a distribution of staff throughout the church, rather than allowing its continued concentration in the offices in New York.

The General Program Council began its life in the very troubled period of the church when the merger with the Southern Presbyterian Church had just been turned down, and the General Synod of 1969 had entertained a motion toward the dissolution of the Reformed Church in America. Hoff shares the exciting story of creative GPC intervention in that volatile situation.

It should not be supposed that Hoff is simply an enthusiastic promoter of programs and policies with which he was associated. Quite the contrary, he exhibits a tremendous amount of candor in discussing the weaknesses of the General Program Council and, in the Epilogue, its present successor.

Of the GPC, Hoff acknowledges that while enjoying great increases in giving, that support did not keep pace, in terms of percentages, with increases in giving for congregational support. Despite the fact that the Church Growth Fund campaign carried out by the GPC was not only the largest financial campaign in the history of the church, but also the only one to exceed its goal (and by almost a million dollars), Hoff nonetheless sees the GPC as having been unable to maintain its earlier percentage of the parishioner's giving dollar.

The solution of the church was to return to an earlier model of church structure (see Epilogue). Whether or not that earlier structure proves to be any more effective in soliciting the parishioner's dollar is open to question. Has the assumption with which the church has worked since the United Advance been correct? The assumption is that it is better for the church to present a united appeal for its programs than to have various programs presenting their own appeals. These separate appeals were deemed "unseemly," even "unChristian," as several boards and agencies scrambled for funds and "tried to tell the biggest sob story." The success of the United Advance in contrast to the constant financial problems faced by the individual boards seemed to prove that a united appeal was not only more genteel, but more successful. The assertion of Irwin J. Lubbers, president of Hope College (1945-1963), an experienced and successful fund raiser, that specific appeals by specific institutions garner more gifts than general appeals, went unheeded. And indeed, experience appeared to prove him wrong. But as chapter two so dramatically illustrates, those "ineffective" multiple appeals were made in the years of the Great Depression, while the "success" of the United Advance was made during the "feast" of the economic boom after World War II.

Since the United Advance, the one axiom by which the church has lived is its unified appeal for funds. As Hoff points out, the dollar figures kept growing, even though the percentage of the contributor's dollar continued to shrink. It should be acknowledged that there were vested interests in maintaining a united approach to fund raising. The various plans for equalization during the fifties and sixties, followed by the GPC of the seventies, all allowed for those programs not immediately identified as mission (such as education), to obtain a larger share of the budget than they perhaps would have. Foreign missions has always been the big money raiser in the RCA, and a united approach was seen as a way to spread the dollar more evenly. Churches, however, have been marvelously adept at defying such equalization plans— as has been equally true in the most recent reorganization of our structures for mission.

However, it must be asked whether the unified approach to funding has to some extent been a disservice to all programs of the church. The most serious disservice has been in the area of communicating the program! Unified appeals are notorious for their generalized description of both programs and need. Proponents of the unified approach have spoken derisively of "sob stories," but sob stories give an emotional dynamic to specific needs in a way that unified appeals seldom do. This disservice has not only been suffered by foreign missions, but by the other programs of the church, and to perhaps an even greater degree.

Since it wasn't necessary to communicate the need for the program sufficiently clearly to obtain specific dollar support, the program was never really appropriated by the church as its own. Even now, Communication is a separate division from Mission or Social Action.

Appeals are the most effective educational tool the program of the church has. When the appeal is specific, it not only communicates the need, but when there is a gift, the donor has reinforced her or his own awareness of that need in a significant way. Irwin J. Lubbers was both an educator and a fund raiser; all too few people seemed to realize that as he raised funds he also educated people about Hope College. Perhaps as structures continue to shift the attempt should be made to bring those who see the need, and those who communicate to the church, closer together for the actualization and furtherance of the mission of the church.

This volume notes that our structuring for mission has been pragmatic rather than theological. That this is the case is strongly evidenced by the fact that while only one book on church polity has been published by a member of the RCA in the last half century (E. P. Heideman, *Reformed Bishops and Catholic Elders*, Eerdmans: 1970), that book was not once referred to by anyone cited in this volume! However, while structuring for mission remained truly pragmatic, the missiology which guided the Goals for Mission had become increasingly sophisticated. This is evident in the response of the GPC in 1979 when it reiterated that "from the beginning, the mission goals of the General Program Council have been organized around the biblical concept of the Kingdom of God" (p. 205). The commitment of many in the church, however, is to those whose concern is to save souls. Pastors almost automatically translate (often incorrectly) "saving souls" into a concern with increasing the numbers in Christ's church. The biblical concept of the kingdom or rule of God is far broader, encompassing issues of truth and justice, the political as well as the ecclesiastical, dealing with creation as well as redemption. The theological tension between a concern for saved souls and for God's kingdom has not been lessened by a communications process weakened by a lack of specific appeals for funds.

This volume is a rich historical analysis of where we have been. It is further an absolutely essential resource for those who would wish to further examine our past in order to make our future more effective. The church owes a large debt of gratitude to Marvin D. Hoff for this resource.

Donald J. Bruggink
Editor

Acknowledgments

When the 1967 General Synod elected me to membership on the General Synod Executive Committee (GSEC), I didn't realize that I was just beginning a new and exciting turn in my life-long involvment with the Reformed Church in America. The GSEC had been studying the mission structures of the RCA for five years and had just received the responsibility of fine tuning a major restructuring of the RCA's boards and agencies. I spent the summer of 1967 studying and reading, to prepare myself for participation in my new responsibility. The subject gripped me, and I have been hooked ever since. After several years on the GSEC, I was called to join the RCA staff as Secretary for Asian Ministries. My interest in mission structures led to my subsequent call to serve as Secretary for Operations.

A great many sisters and brothers have nurtured me in my Christian pilgrimage, and I want to express my appreciation to them. My thanks go out to:

The members of the Trinity Reformed Church, Orange City, Iowa, who shared the love of Christ with me during my growing years; the members of the Rea Avenue Reformed Church, Hawthorne, New Jersey, who called me to my first ministry and encouraged my growth in pastoral ministry; and the members of the Reformed Church of Palos Heights, Palos Heights, Illinois, who have twice deepened my life through calling me to minister the gospel in their community of faith;

All the persons throughout the RCA who shared their gifts and insights through service on the General Synod Executive Committee, the General Program Council, and the General Synod during the years I was privileged to minister on the staff;

My sisters and brothers who served with me on the national staff of the RCA, for sharing their lives, their wisdom, their faith, and their criticisms;

Dien and Anton Honig, who have shared their hospitality, their encouragement, and their keen insights in the birthing of this book;

Marsha Hoffman, copy editor, and Donald J. Bruggink, editors par excellence;

Jean and Mary, my daughters, David, my son, and Joanne, my wife, for their love and support which bring joy and gladness to my life.

Hegel wrote: "What experience and history teach is this—that people and governments never have learned anything from history. . . ." I share this work in the hope that we may learn something from it so that we may more effectively and faithfully carry on Christ's ministry and mission today and tomorrow.

Marvin D. Hoff
Feast of Epiphany, 1985

The Cover

A green earth globe (a contemporary concept of world) is brack-
eted by a square with four corners (an older concept of world).
Both structures are overlaid by a cross which quarters them and
extends beyond them. The square, circle, and right angle (some
of the most fundamental geometric shapes) combine to symbolize
order, strength, and structure with a global scope.

Rein Vanderhill, Artist

Preamble

Missiology is a relatively new theological discipline. Being new, its role and place amidst the various theological disciplines is not yet clearly defined or identified. Johannes Verkuyl, in his *Contemporary Missiology, an Introduction*, defines missiology as: ". . . the study of the salvation activities of the Father, Son and Holy Spirit throughout the world geared toward bringing the kingdom of God into existence . . . (its) task in every age is to investigate scientifically and critically the presuppositions, motives, structures, methods, patterns of cooperation, and leadership which the churches bring to their mandate" (p. 5). This study will examine the mission structures utilized by the Reformed Church in America (RCA) to carry out its missionary mandate.

The Reformed Church in America has experienced two periods of major structuring for mission in its more than 350-year history. The first period began almost immediately after the final independence of the church from its Dutch ecclesiastical relationships—a 164-year process that was finalized in 1792. Beginning with a report to the 1784 general meeting of elders and ministers on the extension of the church into the new American frontier settlements, this period concluded with the formation of the Board of Foreign Missions in 1832. Throughout this period the RCA experimented with a great many structures for mission, but concluded it with a clear commitment to carrying on its missionary outreach at home and abroad through boards of the General Synod.

Among the experimental structures were: committees or commissions of the General Synod; the deputati of the General Synod; designating a classis to supervise the missionary work of the General Synod; relating to a society of persons organized for missionary endeavors; and establishing a missionary board to serve the General Synod directly.

Some of the major organizations during this period were: a Commission of the General Synod in 1788, a Standing Committee on Missions in 1806, the Missionary Society of the Reformed Dutch Church (all of which were organized to carry on the evangelistic tasks of the church to the American frontiers); and the 1796 formation of the New York Missionary Society, the 1817 formation of the United Foreign Missionary Society, the 1826 merger of the United Foreign Missionary Society with the American Board of Commissioners for Foreign Missions (all of which were organized for missionary work among the American Indians or beyond the American continent).

With the establishment of the Board of Domestic Missions in 1831 and the Board of Foreign Missions in 1832, this period of creative ferment came to a close. The Reformed Church, with the exception of the establishment of the Woman's Board of Foreign Missions in 1875 and the Women's Executive Committee of the Board of Domestic Missions in 1882, carried on its missionary programs through these structures until 1967.

The second period of creativity and ferment began immediately after World War II. As delegates came to the 1945 General Synod, they knew that they faced tremendous challenges in the life of their church. The effects of the Great Depression of the 1930s, the Great Drought of the 1920s and 30s, and World War II had been devastating for the missionary programs of the church. Beginning in 1925, exactly twenty years earlier, the giving of the church for missions had annually declined. Now the church faced massive needs around the world. The war had destroyed many of its missionary programs in India, China, and Japan, and funds were desperately needed to repair buildings and restart missionary programs. The lack of funds had seriously curtailed building programs at domestic mission stations and at the seminaries and colleges of the church.

Rather than compete for desperately needed funds, the leaders of the church proposed a United Advance program. Unknown to all of them, this program became the first step in the second period of Reformed Church structuring for mission. As the United Advance came to a close, its leaders recommended the formation of a Stewardship Council to carry on coordinated budget building and fund raising. The 1952 General Synod formed the Stewardship Council, which carried on its work until 1967. Gradually, the members of the Stewardship Council were assigned responsibilities beyond their mandate (because they were the only continuing body of the General Synod), and they reminded the annual synods of their more narrow tasks. In addition, people throughout the church were discussing the need for a continuing body to represent the General Synod between its annual sessions. These discussions produced the General Synod Executive Committee in 1961. The final structural change for this period took place in 1967 with the creation of the General Program Council through a merger of the Board of North American Missions, the Board of World Missions, the Board of Education, and the Stewardship Council.

Our story broadly sketches the developments of mission structures in the first period, and then focuses on the period from 1945 to 1980. Our story shows that 1. The Reformed Church has always been pulled into new missionary structures by its commitment to the missionary task. As persons in the church have received new visions of the missionary tasks to be carried out, they have begun to develop and design structures for carrying out their new visions of the biblical tasks. 2. The Reformed Church did not, and could not, use the missionary structure which had produced its beginnings in the United States. When the Reformed Church established its separate existence from its mother church in the Netherlands, it adopted (with some minor adaptations) her polity, with the exception of the Dutch church's relationship to the Dutch government. Because state and church were separated in America, the American church had to remove the section on magistrates from its adaptation of the Dutch polity. Having made this change in its polity, it could not employ the Dutch missionary structure model which incorporated close cooperation between church, state, and commerce. The American scene made it necessary for the Reformed Church in America to develop its own structures for mission. 3. Though ready to experiment with a variety of mission structures (such as committees and commissions of the General Synod, the designation of a classis for the task, societies), the church always kept the General Synod involved in the missionary responsibility. After several decades of experimentation, the church decided to place the General Synod at the center of the missionary task and structure through the creation of boards. This placed the highest judicatory of the church in the central position of carrying out the missionary task through the preaching of the gospel and the building of the church of Christ. 4. The church quickly (by 1828) learned that persons were necessary to carry on the day-to-day responsibilities for implementing the missionary task. Early efforts were made to use pastors of local churches for itinerant missionary preaching and doing the administrative work for the mission structure. By the 1830s the church had set aside persons for the special tasks of missionary work and staff work. Although the RCA has never revised its theology (or liturgy) for the offices in the church to include staff positions, the staff has carried the major responsibilities for the missionary task of the church. 5. The Reformed Church has always maintained a separation between the responsibilities of its highest judicatory (the General Synod) and the mission/program tasks of the church. Although there was some discussion in the 1960s about linking them more closely, the final decision was to keep them separate through the continuation of the General Synod Executive Committee and the establishment of the General Program Council. While maintaining General Synod control of, and responsibility for, the denominational mission structure, the RCA has also maintained a functioning separation.

Our story includes a chapter on the American experience from 1945 to 1980. The major purpose of the chapter (2) is to provide a taste of the shifts in American life that affected the missionary structures of the church.

The Reformed Church in America, after a struggle of more than 150 years to establish herself and gain her independence, began to wrestle with her calling to be a missionary community. Through this wrestling, she designed her structures for mission. With them, she has been faithful to Christ's mandate to share the gospel to all the world.

I

The Reformed Church in America From 1628 Through 1945

The Reformed Church in America had two quite distinct beginnings in the United States. The first took place in 1628 in the colony of New Amsterdam—now New York. The primary purpose of the immigration which produced this beginning was commercial and economic. The second took place in Holland, Michigan, and Pella, Iowa, between the years 1847 to 1854. The purposes of this second immigration were both religious and economic.[1]

THE FIRST BEGINNING

Henry Hudson, an Englishman sailing for the Dutch East India Company, established the first contact with the New World for the Dutch. In 1609 he sailed his eighty-ton *Halve Maen* up the river which has been named after him. He traveled approximately 150 miles up river, engaged in some small trade with the Indian tribes, and returned to the Netherlands in October.

After Hudson's return to the Netherlands, the Dutch claimed all the land from the Delaware to the Connecticut rivers. Several small trading posts were established in New Amsterdam and Fort Orange (the present day Albany, New York), and trading was conducted with the various Indian tribes. As the benefits of the newly-claimed land became more obvious, the Dutch West India Company was organized. Formed in 1621, this company was authorized to colonize, defend, and govern the possessions claimed for it in the New World. The first settlers began arriving in 1623 and established the colony of New Amsterdam. They came to carry on trade in the new colony and make a profit for the Dutch West India Company.

Two years after the formation of the company the Consistory of Amsterdam noticed that the charter failed to provide for the spiritual needs of the new colony. They called this to the attention of the company's directors, who then committed themselves to support "religious services both on shipboard and on land." It was agreed that the church would select the ministers and teachers for the colony, and the company would provide for their financial support. When the company adopted new articles on March 28, 1624, the second article stated:

> Within their territory they shall only worship according to the true Reformed Religion, as it is done within this country at the present, and by a good Christian life they shall try to attract the Indians and other blind persons to the knowledge of God and his Word, without, however, committing any religious persecution, but freedom of conscience shall be left to every one, but if one of them, or if any one within their territory shall intentionally curse or speak blasphemy against the name of God and our Saviour Jesus Christ, he shall be punished by the Commander and his Council according to circumstances.[2]

Late in 1623 the company asked the consistory to recommend spiritual leaders for the new colony. Bastian Jansz Krol, a "comfortor of the sick,"[3] arrived in New Amsterdam on March 8, 1624. As a lay worker, the "comfortor of the sick" could read prayers, passages of Scripture, sermons prepared by others; catechize the children; and, with special permission in unusual circumstances, administer baptism and perform marriages. Jan Huygens, a second "comfortor," arrived in May of 1626 with his brother-in-law, Peter Minuit, the first director general of New Amsterdam.

The first worship services must have been held in the open air because there would not have been a room large enough for them. Francios Molemacker erected a horse mill at 32 and 34 South William in 1626. It had a large second floor room which became the place of worship for the church. The first ordained minister to serve in New Amsterdam, the Rev. Jonas Michaelius, arrived on April 7, 1628. He immediately organized a church,

and Minuit and Huygens were appointed elders and Krol a deacon. In an August 11, 1628, letter to a friend in Amsterdam,
Michaelius described the first Lord's Supper in the new church:

> At the first administration of the Lord's Supper which was ob-
> served, not without great joy and comfort to many, we had fully
> fifty communicants, Walloons and Dutch, a number of whom made
> their first confession of faith before us, and others exhibited their
> church certificates. Others had forgotten to bring their certificates
> with them, not thinking that a church would be formed and estab-
> lished here; and some who brought them had lost them unfortu-
> nately in a general conflagration, but they were admitted upon the
> satisfactory testimony of others to whom this was known, and also
> upon their daily good deportment, since one cannot observe strictly
> all the usual formalities in making a beginning under such
> circumstances.[4]

Michaelius, who returned to the Netherlands in 1632, was
replaced by the Rev. Everardus Bogardus in 1633. During his
time the congregation grew to more than 300 people. The third
minister, the Rev. Johannes Megapolensis, arrived in 1642 to
serve at Fort Orange, making him the first minister outside New
Amsterdam. He served the manor of Patroon Kiliaen Van Rensselaer. The patroon system had been introduced in 1629 to encourage settlement in the New World. If a person promised to
settle his tract with fifty persons over fifteen years of age in four
years, the company gave him a large tract of land. The patroon
had extensive rights over his settlers and the land given to him.
Megapolensis moved to New Amsterdam in 1649 and ministered
there until his death in 1670. Between 1628 and the conquest by
the British in 1664, fifteen ministers served the thirteen churches
established in the colony.[5]

Although the Dutch West India Company had agreed in 1623
to provide support for ministers and teachers needed by the colony, remuneration for the ministers was a chronic problem. When
the Consistory of Amsterdam became more responsible for providing ministers in 1636, the company gave less financial support

to the church. In 1649 the people appealed directly to the States General because the company had failed to adequately endow the church with property to provide for its material needs. After a number of fruitless attempts to gain funds for supporting the civil servants, both military and clergy, Peter Stuyvesant gave the excise on the wine and beer consumed in New Amsterdam to the burgomasters with the proviso that they use the proceeds to pay the salaries for the civil servants and ministers.[6]

In one of his letters Megapolensis lamented:

> On Sunday we have many hearers. People crowd into the church, and apparently like the sermon; but most of the listeners are not inclined to contribute to the support and salary of the preacher. They seem to desire that we should live upon air and not upon produce.[7]

The company regularly demonstrated that it considered New Amsterdam an economic, not a spiritual, venture. Since the colonists were not accustomed to providing the financial support required by their schools and churches, both suffered greatly.

CAPTURED BY THE BRITISH

With the restoration of the Stuart family to the monarchy in England, the territory given to the Dutch West India Company was deeded to James, Duke of York, brother of the new king, Charles II. The situation in New Amsterdam became precarious because of this move by the British against their Dutch commercial competitors. The colony was surrounded by British settlements, with New England on the north and Virginia and Maryland on the south. With a population of approximately 8,000, it was greatly outnumbered by the more than 50,000 residents of New England. In August of 1664 four British frigates anchored off Coney Island. On September 4 they aimed their guns at the fort and demanded the surrender of New Amsterdam. Although greatly outnumbered by the 1,000 soldiers on the frigates, Peter Stuyvesant, the director general, was determined to defend New

Amsterdam. Dominie Samuel Megapolensis convinced him to surrender in order to spare the colony from devastation.

The Rev. Samuel Megapolensis was one of the Dutch commissioners who negotiated the terms of surrender. More than likely he was the person responsible for protecting the rights of the Dutch church under the new government. Article 2 of the surrender agreement allowed the continued use of the church in the fort. Article 8 stated: "The Dutch here shall enjoy the liberty of their consciences in Divine Worship and church discipline."[8] In spite of the surrender agreements, the new Governor, Nicolls, was told that it would be highly desirable to have "one faith" and worship in New York. He was also urged to "proceed very warily and not enter upon it, till you have made some progress in your less difficult business."[9] As the pressure increased to establish the Anglican church at the expense of the agreements with the Dutch church, local congregations sought royal charters. The New York Church, probably because of the efforts of Dominie Henry Selyns, received the first charter on May 11, 1696.[10] Similar charters were procured by other local churches.

A great many things changed for the Dutch church with the change of governments. The most notable was the end of immigration. The church was now dependent upon internal growth. One practice did not change—Dutch remained the language of the church. Although English became the language of education, government, and commerce, the church retained Dutch. The first English-speaking minister did not come until 1764—100 years after the surrender to the British. He was Archibald Laidlie, a Scotsman who arrived from the Netherlands in 1764. One year before this the Collegiate Church had introduced De Ronde's English abridged catechism in New York. The majority of Reformed churches continued to use the Dutch language into the early 1800s.

Although the political government of New Netherland changed from the Dutch to the British, the Classis of Amsterdam continued to carry out its responsibility for supervising the life and work of the Dutch church in the New World. As early as 1662 Dominie

Polhemius had written: "In relation to the general state of the church, which by the blessing of God, is constantly increasing, I will only say that we stand in need of communication with one another in the form of a Classis, after the manner of the Father-land. It is desirable that this be begun, although I do not know of much business to be transacted."[11]

It was not until 1737 that serious efforts began to establish a classis for the church. In 1736 the Consistory of Schoharie, New York, asked for permission to ordain Johannes Schuyler. Since several promising young persons had lost their lives at sea while traveling to the Netherlands for theological training and ordina-tion, the consistory desired to ordain Schuyler themselves. When the classis delayed in responding to the request, Dominie Haeg-hoort encouraged the Consistory of New York to call a meeting of representatives of the various churches. At this meeting on September 5, 1737, he presented his plan for a coetus or eccle-siastical assembly. The plan was adopted and sent to the Classis of Amsterdam for its approval. When the classis adopted the plan in April of 1739, it removed the power to examine and ordain candidates for the ministry. The organizational meeting of the coetus was not held until 1747. Each church sent minister and elder delegates, and the coetus organized three particular bod-ies—New York, Jersey, and Albany.

When the coetus organized into an independent classis in 1755, a great deal of opposition occurred. A minority, located mainly in New York City, opposed the move because they wanted to retain their ties to the Classis of Amsterdam, and they organized themselves into the Conferentie. By 1764 the Conferentie had become "An Assembly Subordinate to the Classis of Amsterdam." The conflict in the church was intense. It split families and churches. In Hackensack there were two consistories and two churches using the same sanctuary. As the Coetus began to func-tion more independently of the Classis of Amsterdam through examining and ordaining candidates for the ministry, obtaining a charter for Queen's College in 1766 and organizing it in 1770 in New Brunswick, the Conferentie sent strong letters of denunciation to the Classis of Amsterdam. The deep split was finally healed in 1771 through the efforts of John H. Livingston.

After serious reflection, Livingston had decided to join the ministry of his family church. Although he spoke English and had received training in America, he finished his theological work at the University of Utrecht, the Netherlands. During his time in the Netherlands he met with members of the Classis of Amsterdam and the Synod of North Holland and developed a plan to unite the rival factions in the American church. Upon his return he became the minister of the second English-speaking church in New York and presented his plan of union. The plan called for one general body, with five particular bodies. The new school at New Brunswick was to be under the general body. By 1772 everyone had agreed to Livingston's plan of union, and the future looked brighter for the reunited church. The Revolutionary War, however, made it impossible to implement the plan.

After the war, the citizens of the newly independent nation determined to be ecclesiastically independent also. The Livingston "Plan of Union" was now implemented. The general and particular bodies became synods and classes. Livingston translated the rules of government of the Synod of Dort into English, and these, along with explanatory articles, were declared to be the "ecclesiastical rule of the Dutch Reformed Church in North America." Thus, in 1794 the body that had been functioning as the general body since 1771 became the General Synod of the Dutch Reformed Church in North America, and the five particular bodies became its classes. After 176 years, the church had an independent existence and could fulfill all of the acts and responsibilities of a church, reformed according to the Word of God.

THE SECOND BEGINNING: MICHIGAN AND IOWA

After Napoleon and the French troops had been defeated, the Netherlands was reorganized not as a republic but as a monarchy under the House of Orange. The Church Reorganization Law promulgated by King William I on January 7, 1816, changed the name of the church from the Gereformeerde Kerk to the Hervormd Kerk. The new law made it possible for the king to appoint the officials and ministers in the church, allowed for the introduction of songs (in addition to the Old Testament Psalms) into worship, and altered the confessional standards permitting a more liberal and rational interpretation of the creeds of the church. As the result of a religious awakening, people began to advocate a return to the earlier theological and practical commitments of the church.

A group of theological students at the University of Leiden began to meet for worship and theological reflection. Included in the group were Henrik Pieter Scholte and Albertus Christiaan Van Raalte, both of whom led migrations to the United States in the late 1840s. By 1834 the leaders of the separation, Hendrik De Cock, H. P. Scholte, A. Brummelkamp, S. Van Velzen, A. C. Van Raalte, F. Gezelle Meerburg, and Louis Baehler, were either suspended from the ministry or disciplined. This led to the formation of the Christlica Gereformeerde Kerken. The members and leaders of the new church were mocked and considered to be a part of an illegal church.

Since most of the members of the Christlica Gereformeerde Kerken were quite poor, and farmers, the economic dislocations of this period affected them greatly. Taxes were very high. More than sixteen percent of the Dutch people were on the poor rolls. The farmers experienced periodic floods, disease among their livestock, and a severe potato disease which became most intense in 1845 and 1846. It was just at this time that a schoolmaster visiting Holland spoke with Van Raalte and Brummelkamp about the great opportunities in America. Van Raalte responded by writing a letter, entitled "To the Believers in the United States of North America," which came into the hands of Dr. Isaac N. Wyckoff, a Reformed Church minister in Albany, New York. He had it published in *The Christian Intelligencer* (presently, *The Church Herald*), which led to the formation of a society to help the immigrants. When Van Raalte and his group of fifty-three arrived on November 17, 1846, they were met by Dr. Thomas De Witt of the Reformed Church.

On February 9, 1847, they established their colony in western Michigan. As a part of their life in the new land, they organized the Classis of Holland. In 1848 the Western Department of the Board of Domestic Missions reported to the General Synod that ". . . a large colony of Hollanders, consisting of three thousand souls . . . have located themselves in this vicinity (Grand Rapids) . . . other denominations are using active measures to bring (Van Raalte's colony) under their influence, while we, who are of the same origin, springing from the same branch of the Reformation . . . are doing nothing but exposing them to be swallowed up by men of every name and every creed."[12] One year later Dr. Isaac Wyckoff visited the new immigrants and invited the Classis of Holland to join the Reformed Church. During his visit the classis prepared the following request:

> Considering the precious and blessed unity of the Church of God and the plainly expressed will of our Savior that all should be one, and also the need which the separate parts have of one another, and especially remembering how small and weak we ourselves are, therefore, our hearts have longed for intercourse with the precious Zion of God ever since our feet first pressed the shores of their new World . . . all God's children, of whatever denomination are dear to us; but in the management and care of our own religious affairs we feel more at home where we find our own standards of faith and principles of church government . . . We have, therefore, resolved to send one of our brethren, Rev. A. C. Van Raalte, a minister of the church of God, as a delegate to your church Judicatory, which is soon about to meet in Albany or vicinity. We authorize him in our name to give and to ask all necessary information which can facilitate the desired union.[13]

The Synod of Albany voted to accept the Classis of Holland in 1850.

Scholte and his fellow immigrants had settled in Pella, Iowa. Through Drs. Wyckoff and De Witt, the Reformed Church provided financial support to the Iowa colony and also invited them to join the church. Although Scholte chose to remain independent, the First Reformed Church of Pella joined in 1856. Additional Dutch immigrants settled in western Michigan, Wisconsin, northwest Iowa, and the Paterson, Passaic areas of New Jersey. Many of them also joined the Reformed Church.

The new immigrants had been influenced by the new missionary spirit sweeping nineteenth-century Christendom prior to leaving the Netherlands. Shortly after establishing the First Reformed Church of Holland, the consistory voted to use fifteen percent of their offerings for "foreign missions" and fifty percent for "domestic missions." On June 24, 1851, four short years after their arrival on the shores of Lake Michigan, the new colonists laid the keel for a "missionary ship." The Rev. Philip Peltz, secretary of the Board of Foreign Missions, and the Rev. John Van Nest Talmadge, pioneer missionary to Amoy, China, were present for the inspiring event. The ship was never finished, and gradually the keel rotted away in the waters of Lake Macatawa. Nonetheless, the keel symbolized the community's commitment to mission, and the realities of this commitment were lived out through the gifts of money and sons and daughters for the world mission of the Reformed Church.

Prior to the Dutch immigration of the mid-nineteenth century the Reformed Church had begun work in the Midwest, but it did not flourish. By 1849 there were ten congregations in Wisconsin and seven in Michigan. They were organized into the classes of Michigan and Illinois. The second immigration provided major growth for the Reformed Church. In his report to the 1882 General Synod the secretary of the Board of Domestic Missions reported that one-sixth of the churches and one-eighth of the membership of the church was in the Holland Classis.[14] The vast majority of these people came into the Reformed Church because of their immigration from the Netherlands, and not through the evangelistic efforts of the church—either in the East or Michigan. The second beginning provided the Reformed Church with the numerical, financial, and theological strength to carry on its ministry in the United States. The first beginning came at a time of great geographic and commercial expansion in the Netherlands. The second beginning arose during a time of great religious ferment. The descendants of the two migrations have provided the United States of America with a vibrant church.

MISSION TO AMERICA: THE AMERICAN INDIANS AND THE NON-DUTCH

The "Provisional Regulations" of the Dutch West India Company issued in 1624 stated in Article 2: "by their Christian life and conduct [the settlers shall] seek to draw the Indians and other blind people to the Knowledge of God and His Word."[15] The Dutch settlers in New Netherland had many contacts with the various Indian tribes through trading, especially for furs, but the period from 1624 through 1796 did not produce a great deal of organized mission effort to the Indians. Several pastors, most notably Johannes Megapolensis and Bernardus Freeman, did learn the Indian language and culture and brought numerous Indians into their churches.

The first minister to New Netherland, Michaelius, sent the following description of the Indians to a friend in Amsterdam: "As to the natives of this country I find them entirely savage and wild, strangers to all decency, yea, uncivil and stupid as garden poles, proficient in all wickedness and godlessness; devilish men, who serve nobody but the devil, that is, the spirit, which, in their language, they call Mennetto. . . ."[16] Because of his assessments of the Indian culture and religion, Michaelius suggested the following plan for evangelizing the Indians: "It would be well then to leave the parents as they are, and begin with the children who are still young. So be it. But they ought in youth to be separated from their parents; yea, from their whole nation. For, without this, they would forthwith be as much accustomed as their parents to their heathenish tricks and deviltries. . . ."[17] There are no indications that either Michaelius or his successors tried to implement this strategy for mission to the Indians (although it came to be employed by a great many in subsequent years).

The first minister to serve outside of New Amsterdam, and thus live more closely to the Indians, conducted a noble ministry among them. The Rev. Johannes Megapolensis was called to "perform the duty of the Gospel to the advancement of God's Holy Name and the conversion of many poor blind men . . . (and) to proclaim Christ to Christians and heathens. . . ."[18] Megapolensis carried out this part of his call through learning the Mohawk language and culture and preparing a lengthy tract describing them. His intimate knowledge of, and personal relationship with, the Mohawks made it possible for him to mediate the release of Father Isaac Jogues, a French Jesuit missionary, who was held captive for more than a year. In spite of his efforts, which began several years before those of the more widely-known John Eliot, Megapolensis's work among the Indians, both in Fort Orange and later in New Amsterdam, produced few converts. When the Classis of Amsterdam appeared confused about the results, the Dominies Megapolensis and Drisius wrote to set the record straight.

> . . . you mention in your letter, that you have gathered from our letters, that the knowledge of the Gospel is making great progress among the Indians here . . . We greatly wish indeed, that such were the state of things . . . It is true that a sachem of the Indians has sojourned for a length of time among us at the Manhattans, who was diligent in learning to read and write, which he learned to do tolerably well. He was also instructed in the principal grounds of the Christian faith, and publicly joined in recitations on the catechism by Christian children. We gave him a Bible that he might peruse it and teach his own countrymen from it. We hoped that in due time he might be the instrument of accomplishing considerable good among the Indians. But we acknowledge that he has only the bare knowledge of the truth, without the practice of godliness. He is greatly inclined to drunkenness, and indeed, is no better than the other Indians.[19]

With the exception of the work in the North, most notably that of Freeman, mission work among the Indians completely lapsed after the conquest of New Netherland by the British. A great many factors, most notably the lack of ministers for their own churches, led the Dutch in America to retreat from mission to the Indians.

The Rev. Bernardus Freeman served as the second minister of the First Reformed Church of Schenectady. The Earl of Bellomont, Governor of the Provinces, wrote to the five Indian nations declaring: "for the present I shall settle Mr. Vreeman, an able good minister, at Schanectade, who I intend shall be one of those that shall be appointed to instruct you in the true faith. He will be near the Mohawks . . . and will take pains to teach you. He has promised to apply himself with all diligence to learn your language, and doubts not to be able to preach to you therein in a year's time."[20]

During his five years in Schenectady, Freeman learned to write and preach in the Mohawk language. Five years after he left Schenectady for a new parish in Long Island the Mohawks petitioned Governor Hunter to appoint Freeman "to live (with us) at our Castle and not at Schinnectady nor Albany."[21] Freeman translated the first three chapters of Genesis, the Gospel of Matthew, several chapters from Exodus, several Psalms, and most of the biblical passages relating to the birth, passion, resurrection, and ascension of Jesus into the Mohawk language, but unfortunately his work was not printed because of lack of funds.

The mission efforts of the Dutch Reformed Church in relationship to the American Indians were very limited. A few ministers carried on programs in addition to their ordinary parish work, but there were no organized efforts between 1624 and 1796. Not even the period of the "Great Awakening" under the leadership of Theodorus Jacobus Frelinghuysen produced a spirit of Christian concern for the various Indian tribes.

The Dutch Reformed Church's lack of a sense of mission can also be seen from its relationship to the English speaking people. With the fall of New Amsterdam to the British in 1664, English became the language of the American colonies. Immediately, some of the leaders of New Amsterdam began attending the Anglican Church and maintaining their standing in the new community through participating in its various "English" organizations. The leaders of the Dutch church did not make the shift to English until 1764, a century after the British conquest. During this entire period the church preserved its Dutch language and culture and did not reach out to the new people populating New York and the middle colonies.

From 1624 through its "declaration of independence" in 1792, the Reformed Protestant Dutch Church in America sought to maintain its various ministries and churches. The hardships encountered in this task kept the church, like many other Protestant churches in the New World, from carrying out the missionary spirit of the New Testament.

THE REFORMED CHURCH: ITS THEOLOGY AND POLITY

With the adoption of the Articles of Union in 1771, the Reformed Dutch Church in America adopted for itself the government of the Reformed Church in the Netherlands. The constitution included its doctrines, its mode of worship (Liturgy), and its government. The doctrines were contained in the three standards of unity, the Belgic Confession, the Heidelberg Catechism, and the Canons of Dort.

The Belgic Confession was written by Guido de Bres, who patterned it after the Gallican Confession of 1559. Its main heads of doctrine include: God, God's revelation, the Trinity, Creation, Providence, the Fall, Election, Salvation through Jesus Christ, the Church, Magistrates, and the Last Judgment. Our interest is in the portrayal of the church in the confession. Article XXVII is "Of the catholic christian church" and states: ". . . This church hath been from the beginning of the world, and will be to the end thereof . . . this holy church is not confined, bound or limited to a certain place, or to certain persons, but is spread and dispersed over the whole world. . . . "[22] The marks ". . . . by which the true church is known, are these: If the pure doctrine of the gospel is preached therein; if she maintains the pure administration of the sacraments as instituted by Christ; if church discipline is exercised in punishing sin. . . ."[23] The magistrates have included in their charge ". . . . to promote the kingdom of Jesus Christ, and to take care that the word of the gospel be preached everywhere, that God may be honored and worshipped by everyone, as he commands in his word. . . ."[24] Thus, the strongest challenge to mission in the Belgic Confession is made the responsibility of the magistrates, not the leaders of the church. This assignment of the biblical task of mission seemed natural in the context of Christendom, when everyone, including the magistrates, were baptized members of the church. As the Reformed Church carried on its ministry in the pluralism of the United States, there was no possibility for the magistrate to carry out the mission task.

The Heidelberg Catechism is probably the best known, and most loved, of the three standards of unity. It was written by Zacharias Ursinus and Caspar Olevianus in the city of Heidelberg in the Lower Palatinate and was first published in 1563. The Heidelberg Catechism is divided into 52 Lord's Days and 129 questions and answers. Its three major parts are: of the misery of man, of man's deliverance, and of man's thankfulness. Question 54 asks: "What believest thou concerning the 'Holy Catholic Church' of Christ? The answer declares: That the Son of God from the beginning to the end of the world, gathers, defends and preserves to himself by his Spirit and word, out of the whole human race, a church chosen to everlasting life, agreeing in true faith; and that I am, and forever shall remain, a living member thereof."[25] This answer contains seeds for the development of a biblical theology of mission, but they did not come to fruition in the Reformed Church in America, nor other Reformed bodies for that matter. To confess that God uses "his Spirit and word" to gather a church ". . . out of the whole human race . . ." should have stirred the church to missionary outreach. One searches in vain for persons who were motivated to missionary endeavor through this simple, and biblical, portrait of the Holy Catholic Church.

The Canons of Dort were written in the years 1618 and 1619

by the "great" Synod of Dort. The major heads of doctrine are: of divine predestination, of the death of Christ, and the redemption of men thereby, of the corruption of man, his conversion to God, and the manner thereof, and of the perseverance of the saints. Article III under the first head of doctrine declares:

> And that men may be brought to believe, God mercifully sends the messengers of these joyful tidings to whom he will, and at what time he pleaseth; by whose ministry men are called to repentance and faith in Christ crucified. "How then shall they call on him, in whom they have not believed? And how shall they believe in him of whom they have not heard? And how shall they hear without a preacher? And how shall they preach except they be sent?" (Rom. 10:14, 15).[26]

The October, 1771, meeting of ministers and elders declared the Rules of Church Government adopted by the Synod of Dort in 1618 and 1619 to be the government of the Reformed Dutch Church in America. The General Synod of 1792 adopted a series of Explanatory Articles that specifically applied the Rules of Church Government to the situation in America. The only major change from the Dutch Rules of Church Government related to the magistrate.

> Whatever relates to the immediate authority and interposition of the Magistrate in the government of the Church, which is introduced more or less into all the national establishments in Europe, is entirely omitted in the Constitution now published. Whether the Church of Christ will not be more effectually patronised in a civil government where full freedom of conscience and worship is equally protected and insured to all men, and where truth is left to vindicate her own sovereign authority and influence, than where men in power promote their favourite denominations by temporal amoluments and partial discriminations, will now, in America, have a fair trial.[27]

This revision in the church's government did not revise the theology of the Belgic Confession which continued to assign the missionary task to the magistrate.

The Rules of Church Government are divided into four sections: of the offices, of ecclesiastical assemblies, of doctrines, sacraments, and usages, and of Christian discipline. The responsibilities of the various offices are: minister, "to persevere in prayer, and the ministry of the word; to dispense the sacraments; to watch over his brethren the Elders and Deacons, as well as over the whole congregation; and lastly, in conjunction with the Elders, to exercise christian discipline, and to be careful, that all things be done decently and in order"[28]; elders, in addition to the responsibilities common to the ministers, to "instruct and comfort the members in full communion, as well as to exhort others to the regular profession of the christian religion"[29]; and the deacons, "to collect the alms and other monies appropriated for the use of the poor, and with the advice of the Consistory, cheerfully and faithfully to distribute the same to strangers, as well as to those of their own household . . . to visit and comfort the distressed, and to be careful that the alms not be misused. . . ."[30] Prior to his ordination, a minister had to have a call to serve a congregation unless "he was sent as a Missionary to churches under persecution, or employed to gather congregations, where none have as yet been established."[31]

The ecclesiastical assemblies were the consistorial, the classical, the particular synod, and the General (national) Synod. "A greater Assembly shall take cognizance of those things alone which could not be determined in a lesser, or that appertain to the churches or congregations in general. . . ."[32] The only provision made for the continuing work of the synods was the establishment of deputies. "Every Synod shall depute some of its members to put in execution whatever has been ordained by such Synod. . . ."[33]

Neither its theology, nor its polity, nor the model of its own beginnings in the United States adequately prepared the Reformed Dutch Church for the mighty movements of the Holy Spirit in the early nineteenth century. Its theology had been shaped in reaction to the sixteenth-century theological stances of the Roman Catholic Church and failed to reflect the missionary spirit of the New Testament, the early Christian church, and the church that spread the gospel from the center of Rome to the vast reaches of Europe. Its polity reflected the settled situation of post-feudal Europe, with offices and assemblies needed by a geographically-based church. Neither the responsibilities of the various offices, nor the individual offices, reflect the New Testament outreach tasks of the disciples, evangelists, and apostles. Unlike the Roman Catholic Church, which had developed religious orders for the evangelizing task of the church, churches of the Reformed persuasion had no governmental provision for participating in the missionary mandate of the gospel. In fact, the Belgic Confession assigned this task to the magistrate.

The Reformed Church could not look back upon its founding in America as a model because this was accomplished through very close links between the state, commerce, and the church. The Dutch West India Company, through provisions in its charter at the urging of the Classis of Amsterdam, carried the burden of providing spiritual sustenance in New Netherland. Although its heritage did not provide it with theological or governmental guidance for the new outburst of missionary awareness in the nineteenth century, the Reformed Church began to participate with other Protestant communions in this new outpouring of the Spirit.

BEGINNINGS IN MISSION: 1784-1832

The nineteenth century produced the greatest flowering of missionary enterprise in the Christian church since the acts of the apostles. Kenneth Scott Latourette, in his monumental series on the advance of Christianity, called it "the great century" and devoted three of his seven volumes to it. The seeds had been sown by persons like George Whitefield, Jonathan Edwards, and others, but William Carey crystallized the movement in Great Britain. With the 1793 formation of "A Society for Propagating the Gospel Among the Heathen," organizing for the missionary task had begun. Seven new mission organizations were begun in Great Britain by the first year of the new century.

The 1784 "General Meeting of ministers and elders delegated

by the respective Particular Bodies of the Dutch Reformed Churches" received a draft report "Respecting the State of the Outstanding Congregations and of the Churches" which provided the stimulus for extending the church. After dealing with specific problems in a few of the local churches, the report goes on to portray the state of the whole church and the challenges before it.

The new settlements which are now occurring in the respective States of this land, and will daily increase, present the most favorable opportunities for the extension of our churches and the diffusion of the pure doctrines of grace . . . if we had Ministers who could be employed by the Rev. Body among them as Missionaries . . . some popular and reasonable measures . . . should be, in the speediest and best manner, taken for the supply of the existing need, and the extension of the borders of our Church.[34]

Since the committee was not prepared to recommend specific measures for meeting the challenge, they resigned.

Two years later the "Extension of the Church" had become a regular article of business at the General Body, and a committee was appointed to carry forward the challenge described in 1784. Each of the four ministers on the committee were to prepare a plan "in which he shall state the appropriate means by which the above salutary object, the extension of the Church, shall . . . be attained . . . and these plans shall be upon the table at the next Synod. . . ."[35] The plan presented to, and adopted by, the 1788 General Synod called for each church to take offerings for the missionary extension of the church, the offerings to be presented at meetings of the classis, and by representatives of the classis to the meeting of the General Synod. The synod was to use these funds "to employ . . . such licentiates and ministers . . . appointed and sent by this Rev. Synod to collect said dispersed persons to the unity of the faith and discipline . . . into our churches; and that such missionaries shall yearly give account of their labors to this Rev. Body."[36]

The classes were also exhorted to employ all means for forming new congregations in their areas. The 1789 General Synod received the collections of the previous year, and appointed a commission of three ministers (including Dr. John H. Livingston who earlier negotiated the Articles of Union) and three elders to engage and supervise one or more missionaries.

The 1791 General Synod "having taken this matter into mature consideration, resolve(d) to commit its execution . . . to the Deputati Synodi, to whom the missionaries or ministers employed therein shall from time to time and yearly make a particular report. . . ."[37] The deputati were expected to employ the missionaries, disburse the collected funds, and report to each meeting of the General Synod. The 1794 General Synod appointed a committee of two ministers and two elders "to obtain missionaries and make arrangements for supplying the pulpits of those missionaries while absent from their congregations."[38]

By 1800 the General Synod decided "considering the nearness of the Classis of Albany to the missionary region in the North and West, that they be directed to assume the superintendence (under the direction, however, of the General Synod) of the missionary business in those quarters, and annually report their progress to the Particular Synods. . . ."[39] When informed that Miss Sarah De Peyster had provided funds in her will for the missionary efforts of the Reformed Dutch Church, the 1804 General Synod instructed Dr. Livingston, its president, "to inform the executors . . . that the standing committee for missions is the Classis of Albany, which has been hitherto and still is considered by the Dutch churches as the only missionary society of said churches."[40]

Based on a request from the Particular Synod of New York, the 1806 General Synod appointed a Standing Committee of Missions for the Reformed Dutch Church in America. The members were to be four ministers and four elders from within the bounds of the Particular Synod of Albany, and their task was to implement the missionary programs of the church. The 1809 General Synod invested ". . . the Committee on Missions with power to supply any vacancy which may happen in their body by death or otherwise, by their own vote, during the recess of General Synod."[41]

Since the 1784 General Synod received a report on the state of the church, a new article entitled "Extension of the Church" was added to the regular meeting agenda. Successive General Synods changed the title of this agenda item to: "Church Extension, Missionaries, and Missions." Church extension work was carried on in Hardy County Virginia, on the upper Salt River in Kentucky, and in upper Canada (Ontario).

In addition to employing several persons for full-time missionary work to evangelize those unrelated to the church and gather Christians into the church in their new home on the frontiers, ministers installed in regular congregations carried out missionary tours, the committee providing pulpit supply for their churches during their absence. After a missionary tour of northern and western New York in 1800, the Rev. Peter Stryker reported to the General Synod: "The Lord in the Course of his Providence is opening a large Field in the Western Territory for the Extension of his Church and the Spread of the Gospel . . . The Period is not far distant when the Fullness of the Gentiles shall come to the Knowledge of divine Truths as they are revealed to us . . . to insure Thousands and Millions all temporal, Spiritual, and heavenly Blessings."[42]

None of the specific missionary endeavors of this period provided growth and increase to the Reformed Church. Because of the great distances and the lack of regular ministerial leadership, most of the congregations begun through these efforts either transferred to other denominations or disbanded. The most important contribution of this experiment in "mission" was the final structure determined most appropriate for implementing the missionary task of the church. After experimenting with carrying out its missionary task through a commission of the General Synod, the Deputati Synodi, and the Classis of Albany, the 1806 General Synod appointed a Standing Committee for the task. The committee had the power to appoint missionaries, receive and disburse the mission funds, and even appoint additional members if necessary. The Government of the Church did not provide for such a Standing Committee (the Deputati Synodi were to "execute" the actions of synod), but the challenge of the missionary task called for it. The Reformed Church would not amend its government to provide for this new vehicle of mission until the early twentieth century, by which time its mission boards had become mighty arms of the church for the mission of Christ.

Between 1809 and 1819 the General Synod did not take any major acts regarding its Standing Committee on Missions. In fact, the 1814 General Synod received no report for its review, and "enjoined on the standing committee on Missions to make an annual report to the General Synod."[43] The 1819 General Synod voted to locate the Standing Committee on Missions in New York, elected a completely new committee, and expressed its thanks to the members of the old committee located in Albany.[44] The 1820 report regrets that "very little Missionary effort has been performed . . . (because the Committee) were not furnished with the means necessary to carry on Missionary operations. . . ."[45] Since matters had not improved by 1821, it was resolved to appoint "a Committee of three ministers and two elders . . . to draw up a plan for Missionary operations, and report to the next General Synod."[46]

Although no plan was presented to the 1822 General Synod, the delegates did learn about the formation of the "Missionary Society of the Reformed Dutch Church" by a number of mission-minded persons in New York. The General Synod resolved "that hereafter the Board of Managers of the Missionary Society of the Reformed Dutch Church, be the Standing Committee on Missions, and that they be required to give a digest of their proceedings, annually, to General Synod."[47] All ministers and consistories were encouraged to form auxiliaries for this new society, plus the United Society, in their local congregations. With the designation of the Missionary Society of the Reformed Dutch Church as the missionary arm of the General Synod, the Reformed Church had taken a major step toward carrying out the missionary mandate of the gospel through a board controlled by the General Synod. The 1806 decision to appoint a Standing Committee for the missionary task moved the church in this direction, but the designation of the new missionary "society" as a "board" of the General Synod made it more permanent.

The missionary program of the church prospered under the society, which saw its primary task to be the establishment of new churches in the frontier communities springing up in the United States. In many of these communities the work related to persons who had been members of the church in their old communities, and were challenged to join the church in their new communities. Missionaries were appointed to serve vacant churches in New York City, Long Island, New Jersey, and upper New York State.

The 1828 report on missions summarizes the efforts from 1809 through 1828. Between 1809 and 1815 not more than two or three missionaries had been appointed, and the annual contributions did not exceed $400. By 1828 twenty-one missionaries were serving twenty-eight vacant churches, and the annual contributions had risen from $1,943 in 1822 to more than $5,000 for 1828.[48] When the members of the General Synod's review committee learned about the many gains made in "domestic" missionary work through the efforts of the New York Society, the committee recommended, and General Synod approved, a request to the Board of Managers of the Missionary Society to organize a board or agency in the region of the Synod of Albany. The new board was organized on September 9, 1828, but reported to the 1830 General Synod that it was hampered in carrying out its mandate because of too limited power and authority. A second matter of concern to the Albany board was the dismissal by the New York Society of the mission agent, the Rev. John Schermerhorn. He had been appointed in 1828, the first staff appointment in the Reformed Church, and had served with distinction. Nonetheless, he had been dismissed by the society.

The General Synod made several landmark decisions in response to the communication from the Albany board. First, they voted to reconstitute the Board of Managers of the Missionary Society of the Reformed Dutch Church.

Your Committee are free to declare, that the Missionary Society of the Reformed Dutch Church has been of essential service to the church . . . The difficulty appears to be, that this society is not so entirely under the control of General Synod as could be wished. We find that collision between it and the ecclesiastical bodies has occurred, which, under its present organization cannot easily be prevented. Why should not the missionary operations of our church be under the control of General Synod, and the persons conducting them accountable to the Synod for all their proceedings? If it be objected that such a body as is contemplated, has formerly existed in our church, and was characterized by comparative inertness and inefficiency, it may be asserted that the spirit of the age, and the appointment of a General Agent, possessed of the requisite qualifications, and conducting an energetic and systematic plan of operations, may perhaps have the effect to produce different results. We believe that such a system would be distinguished for simplicity, unity, harmony, power and effect.[49]

The General Synod recommended that the New York Society amend its constitution to reduce the membership on its board to fifteen and to provide for their election by the General Synod, rather than the members of the society. The synod also employed "the Rev. J. F. Schermerhorn . . . (as) General Agent of the Church, at a salary of $1300 . . . to prosecute the plan for raising funds in behalf of the Missionary Society, the Education Society, and the Theological School. . . ."[50]

Delegates to the 1831 General Synod learned that Mr. Schermerhorn's work had been very effective, but that his salary had not been paid because of a conflict between Schermerhorn and the directors of the New York Society. More importantly, it was reported that the New York Society had refused to amend their constitution to provide for General Synod election of the Board of Managers and had once again elected their own board. Thus, it was the "painful duty" of the Committee on Missions to prepare recommendations to end the strife. After rescinding the actions of the 1830 synod, a new Board of Missions of the General Synod of the Reformed Dutch Church was established. ". . . to which

shall be confided all the missionary concerns of the Church
. . . the said Board shall consist of thirty-four members, of whom
one-half at least, and not more than two-thirds, shall reside in
the city of New York . . . said Board . . . to take all proper and
necessary measures to further the cause of missions, subject at
all time to the direction and control of the Synod. . . ."[51] The
synod also transferred all the missionaries and properties of the
New York and Albany societies to the new board. With its actions, the General Synod disbanded both the New York and the
Albany societies.

With the establishment of this new General Synod Board for
Missions, almost five decades of creativity and ferment in structures for domestic mission came to a conclusion. The Reformed
Dutch Church had experimented with various methods of carrying out its "domestic" missionary task, and, in the end, concluded that a board directly accountable to the synod would be
the best.

The "state of the church" report to the 1784 General Synod
stimulated one strand of organizing to carrying out the missionary
mandate of the gospel within the Reformed Church, and the
formation of the New York Missionary Society initiated another
strand. The Presbyterian, Reformed, and Baptist churches of New
York City formed the New York Missionary Society for the purpose of evangelizing the American Indians. Dr. John H. Livingston was vice president of the society which introduced several
new features for promoting the cause of missionary work among
the Indians, including a monthly prayer meeting rotating among
the churches, a magazine that printed reports on various missionary efforts, including those of the London Missionary Society,
and the preaching of missionary sermons to stimulate a missionary spirit among the people. Dr. John H. Livingston preached
two famous sermons, "The Glory of the Redeemer" and "The
Triumph of the Gospel," under the auspices of the society.

"Christ is all and in all" (Col. 3:11) was the text for "The Glory
of the Redeemer." After describing the glory of Christ in the
Scriptures, in the religion of sinners, and in providence, Liv-

ingston concluded with a stirring challenge to engage in missionary efforts for this Christ.

> Had the Missionary Society any temporal pursuits in view; did the
> prospects of gain, of policy or ambition, mingle with the motives
> which have associated us; some other topic would have been cho-
> sen this evening . . . what is our work, what our object? Is it not
> to honour the divine Redeemer—to make known to the heathen
> that a Saviour reigns—to extend the kingdom of righteousness,
> peace and truth to idolatrous savages—and change the habitations
> of ignorance and cruelty into enlightened dwellings of purity and
> comfort?[52]

"The Triumph of the Gospel," preached on April 3, 1804, ex-
pounds a millennial theme from the Book of Revelation. Using
as his text Revelation 14:6 and 7: "And I saw another angel fly
in the midst of heaven, having the everlasting Gospel to preach
unto them that dwell on the earth, and to every nation, and
kindred, and tongue, and people, saying, with a loud voice, Fear
God, and give glory to Him; for the hour of his judgment is come:
and worship Him that made heaven and earth, and the sea, and
the fountains of waters," Livingston identified the Reformation
as the first stage, the present missionary age as the second stage,
and the fall of Babylon as the third and final stage leading to the
Millennium. He expected the fall of Babylon to take place in the
year 2000.

> Every motive which stimulates to vigorous efforts in propagating
> the Gospel, derives additional force and energy from this word of
> prophecy . . . Let missionary societies ascend the prophetic mount,
> and enjoy the vast prospect laid open to their view . . . They are
> employed by him, in the midst of the churches, to accomplish his
> blessed purposes, and fulfil his word. By their agency the preach-
> ing angel commences his flight, and through their instrumentality
> the treasure of the Gospel will be brought to all the nations of the
> earth.[53]

This sermon, which was printed and widely distributed, had an
extensive and profound influence.

The Rev. Joseph Bullen became the first missionary of the society. He was commissioned for work among the Chickasaw tribe in western Georgia on March 21, 1799. The service was held at the New Dutch Church. Sometime later Deacon Ebenezer Rice was commissioned to serve as a catechist and general mechanic.

The Northern Missionary Society, patterned after the New York Society, was organized in January and February of 1797. It too included members from the Presbyterian, Reformed, and Baptist churches. Its first president was the Rev. Dirck Romeyn, minister of the First Reformed Church of Schenectady. This society sent missionaries to Indians in central and western New York.

The American Board of Commissioners for Foreign Missions was created by the General Association of Massachusetts on June 27, 1810. Four divinity students, Adoniram Judson, Samuel Nott, Samuel J. Mills, and Samuel Newell, appeared before the association and stated ". . . our minds have been long impressed with the duty and importance of personally attempting a mission to the heathen . . ." and asked ". . . whether they might expect patronage and support from a Missionary Society in this country, or must commit ourselves to the direction of a European society. . . ."[54] The commissioners formed the board on September 5, 1810, and included in its constitution the following: "The object of this Board is to devise, adopt and prosecute, ways and means for propagating the gospel among those who are destitute of the knowledge of Christianity . . . The appointment of missionaries, their destination, appropriations for their support, and their recall from service, when necessary, shall be under the exclusive direction of the Board."[55]

After examining Adoniram Judson, Samuel Nott, Samuel Newell and Gordon Hall, and endorsing them for missionary service, a committee of the board dispatched Judson to London to inquire about the possibilities of cooperation with the London Missionary Society. Upon his return, the board determined to carry on its own missionary program and appointed the four to serve in India.

This was the beginning of the first overseas missionary program from the United States.

Members of the Reformed Church, including John Schermerhorn, had various contacts with the persons whose call to mission stimulated the formation of the American Board. The most significant contact came through the appointment of Dr. John Scudder to serve in Ceylon under the board. Dr. Scudder was a member of the Reformed Dutch Church on Franklin Street in New York during the pastorate of the Rev. Christian Bork, who had been converted through the preaching of Dr. John H. Livingston. While carrying a personal concern for evangelism within his local church, he read the tract "The Conversion of the World, or the Claims of Six Hundred Millions," in the home of a patient. Feeling called to the mission field, he learned of an advertisement placed by the American Board for a physician for India. He volunteered to go and was appointed by the board in 1819 to serve in Ceylon, becoming the first foreign missionary of the Reformed Church.[56]

The 1816 General Synod received a letter from the General Assembly of the Presbyterian Church in the United States inviting them to join with the Presbyterians and Associate Reformed Church in the formation of a "Society for Foreign Missions." The synod appointed five ministers and two elders to serve on the Joint Committee, which reported to the 1817 General Synod that the Presbyterian and Associate Reformed churches had already adopted the proposed constitution and formed the United Foreign Missionary Society. The constitution stated that the

> object of the society shall be, to spread the gospel among the Indians of North America, the inhabitants of Mexico and South America, and in other portions of the heathen and anti-christian world . . . The business of the society shall be conducted by a board . . . annually chosen by the society . . . The board shall present their annual reports to the highest judicatories of the three denominations for their information . . . Any person paying three dollars annually or thirty dollars at one time, shall be a member of the society . . . Missionaries shall be elected from the three

churches indiscriminately. This constitution may be altered by a vote of two thirds of the members present, at an annual meeting, with the consent of the highest judicatories of the three denominations.[57]

The General Synod approved the constitution, and appointed the Rev. D. Philip Milledoler and Elder Stephen Van Rensselaer to implement the plan. In addition, the United Missionary Society was "recommended to all ministers and churches to give the measure their active support."[58] The 1818 General Synod recommended the society "to the patronage and support of the several judicatories and congregations . . . (and approved) all the amendments of the Constitution suggested by the Board of Managers, excepting the second, which they consider to be improper and dangerous."[59] This General Synod also began the practice of including a special missionary sermon at each annual meeting.

The United Foreign Missionary Society, in its first annual report, stated that the New York Society had agreed to transfer all "their books, and papers, their missionary stations, their Missionary and Teacher, and all their funds,"[60] providing the new society would honor its mission covenant and contracts. The United Society agreed, and the New York Society concluded its existence in 1821.

After two years of organizational preparations, the first missionary group was appointed at the 1820 meeting. It consisted of eight males, nine females, and several children. They were appointed to establish a mission among the Osage Indian Tribe in Missouri. Although the society periodically discussed establishing a mission program in South America, notably Venezuela, its programs were limited to the American Indians. Missions were also established among the Tuscarora, Seneca, Cataraugus, Chippewa, and Machinaw tribes. The work of the society was furthered through the organization of auxiliary societies, of which there were 68 in 1821 and and 189 by 1824. The treasurer reported receipts of $15,263 for 1820 and a decrease to $14,486 by 1824.

The most serious aspect of the decrease was a decline from $4,225 to $1,086 from local congregations.

The Reformed Church participated actively in the United Foreign Missionary Society, and had several of its members as prominent officers. Elder Stephen Van Rensselaer was president, Dr. John H. Livingston, one of the vice presidents, and the Rev. Philip Milledoler, corresponding secretary. A number of factors, financial difficulties being a major one, led the society to merge with the American Board in 1826. This merger produced the second link between the Reformed Church and the American Board.

The 1826 General Synod consented to the merger of the American Board and the United Board because ". . . it is expressly declared, that no pledge of support or recommendation to the patronage of our Churches, is understood to be implied in the consent of this Synod. . . ."[61] In addition to commending the efforts of the Missionary Society of the Reformed Dutch Church to the members of the Reformed Church, the General Synod encouraged its society to ". . . consider the propriety of taking measures to begin missionary operations among the aborigines of our country, and elsewhere."[62]

The next year's General Synod Committee on Missions reported:

> While we say, God speed to the system of Foreign Missions, for it is great, splendid and eminently successful in bringing forward the latter day glory, yet it is believed that the cause of Domestic Missions should go hand in hand with it, and indeed among ourselves should have the precedence . . . The Committee are not aware, what considerations led the last Synod to recommend a Foreign Mission, by our Church in her individual capacity . . . as the Board have made progress in preparatory steps . . . they feel themselves so delicately situated, as to be unable to suggest any measures in relation to it; though as a committee, they conceive it (a) matter of very doubtful expediency.[63]

The next reference appears in the 1831 report of the Committee on Missions:

Your Committee are gratified to learn that there is a desire in some of the churches, that a foreign mission should be established under the auspices and direction of our own denomination. It is undoubtedly and lamentably true, that in many of our congregations no contributions are made for the support of foreign missions. This arises not so much from want of ability or inclination, as the want of a definite object to which our benevolence may be profitably directed. The establishment of a mission of our own would probably obviate some of the objections that are now made to contributing aid to foreign missions. It would be under our own direction— we would have confidence in our own agents, and be satisfied that our charities were faithfully dispensed. We believe that the desire for the establishment of a foreign mission is a growing desire in the churches; and trust that the time is not far distant when it may be undertaken with good prospects of success. But the Committee are of opinion that the time has not yet arrived. It cannot be concealed, that in regard to the subject of our domestic missions, there are some difficulties now existing in the church, which should, if practicable, be obviated and removed before any new operations are undertaken.[64]

The 1832 General Synod, in a move that no doubt surprised the 1831 committee, established a new Board of Foreign Missions.

With the establishment of the Board of Missions in 1831 and the Board of Foreign Missions in 1832, the Reformed Dutch Church concluded almost five decades of creative experimenting with various structures for implementing its missionary mandate. The General Synod had entrusted its missionary tasks to a commission, to the Deputati Synodi, to the Classis of Albany, to a Standing Committee, and to various voluntary societies comprised mainly of members of the church. None of them were deemed adequate for the task, so the synods of 1831 and 1832 created boards directly accountable to the General Synod. The government of the church did not provide for this new vehicle for mission, but the movement of the Spirit in this time produced a new structure for the church. It was not until the opening decades of the twentieth century that this new phenomenon in Reformed Christianity was incorporated into the government of the church. A second major innovation had taken place—the Reformed Church had hired a "general agent." The Rev. John Schermerhorn became the first of a long line of persons serving the church in positions of executive responsibility. In effect, they replaced the Deputati Synodi in "executing" the decisions of the synod and its boards. A third shift, though not radical or new, was the engagement of missionaries by the church. The "offices" of the church did not call for missionaries or staff, and the responsibilities of the four offices did not include the evangelistic task, but the movement of the Spirit in the opening decades of the nineteenth century reintroduced this biblical task and function into the life of the church.

BOARDS FOR DOMESTIC MISSION

The newly-appointed Board of Missions had a difficult first year. Although the Northern Board had turned over its funds and mission programs to the new board, the New York Board had refused to do the same. Thus, the new board had received the cooperation of the Albany area, which had the greatest mission need and the smallest amount of money for meeting the need, but not of the New York area, which had the greatest resources for the challenges facing the board. By 1834 the Missionary Society of the Reformed Dutch Church had become an auxiliary of the Domestic Mission Board, had agreed to pay receipts to the synod's board, and had ceased appointing missionaries. The society retained ". . . the right of nominating for appointment, Missionaries, and of aiding weak Congregations to the amount of all such moneys as they may pay into the Treasury of your Board."[65]

The 1832 General Synod also faced a crisis with regard to the general agent. Although it is possible that the controversy between the Northern Board and the New York Society (Schermerhorn was from the north) and some other personality conflicts clouded the issue, many seemed to feel that the General Synod should not have employed an agent for its work. The Committee on Missions presented an exceptionally long report on the beneficial aspects of engaging a general agent. The report extols the many benefits that arose from the agent's work in the previous year, cites the use of agents by many other Christian causes, and emphasizes the urgency of pursuing the church's work. It acknowledges that a general agent is

> . . . a new office, unknown to the Constitution, it seems, like the office of deacon, to take its rise from circumstances. It is not an office of the Constitution of the Church of Christ as he gave it, nor do we pretend it is a part of the "pattern exhibited"—there is no ordination to it, nor is it viewed as a standing department in his house, nor is it any thing more than a means of concentrating, in one person, the acts of the whole company of ministers, and prosecuting a given object by a system of operations.[66]

The synod concurred and reelected Schermerhorn its general agent. He declined the appointment, and the Rev. A. Henry Dumont was elected. Even though the work of Mr. Dumont produced $5,201 for the Board of Missions and a total of $7,074 for all the causes of General Synod, ". . . a large portion of the Church earnestly desired the discontinuance of the agency. . . ."[67] Therefore, the synod voted to discontinue the general agent and use another "mode for obtaining the Churches charities."[68] Within one year the receipts dropped fifty percent—from $5,000 to $2,400. Several years of financial struggle led the 1842 General Synod to appoint the Rev. Ransford Wells to supervise the work of the Foreign and Domestic boards, the Board of Education, and the Sabbath School Union. Within several years his efforts increased the funds for domestic missions to $9,500 annually.

The board, renamed the Board for Domestic Missions during the 1840s, continued its major focus on beginning new churches. During the 1830s and 1840s approximately forty churches per year received aid from the board. The Church Building Fund, established by the board in 1854, became fully operational by 1861. The fund, from an original capital of $25,000, lent money for the construction of church buildings, and, in the early years, did not charge interest. The 1901 report of the board stated that it had provided financial support to 230 churches and missions, was aiding 164 missionary pastors, and had total (not including the Women's Executive Committee) receipts of $51,681.

Since the board's original charter limited its work to "aiding weak and founding new churches of the denomination," it appealed to the General Synod for a broadening of its task. The 1900 General Synod amended the mandate of the board to read: "to allow its missionaries to engage in evangelistic work which may not immediately eventuate in the founding of new churches."[69] The broadened mandate made it possible for the board to begin evangelistic work among "the hordes of aliens pouring into our country."[70] The board, comparing its new program among the immigrants with the historic missionary programs of the Foreign Board, declared to the 1907 General Synod:

> More than a million immigrants come thronging into our country every year. Vast hordes of these are without any religious faith or connection whatever . . . It is high time we were doing Foreign Missionary work within our own borders. America is being heathenized as fast as we are Christianizing Asia . . . Why should not some of our young men and women who wish to be missionaries acquire one of these languages and get to work in a foreign colony, without going more than a half-hour's trolley ride from their own home?[71]

The work began among the Japanese in New York City, and expanded to Italian communities in New Jersey and Chicago and Hungarian communities in Peekskill, New York. By 1913, only seven years after its illustrious beginnings, the interest of the church had waned in this domestic "foreign" mission program. The whole program had been terminated by 1945.

Although the Foreign Board had been unable to respond to a request from Mexico for missionaries in the 1880s, the Domestic Board was able to begin a work in Chiapas in the 1920s. In cooperation with the Presbyterian Church of Mexico and the

Presbyterian Church in the USA, the board assigned Mabel and John Kempers to the work. During the 1930s the Mexican government imposed severe restrictions on the religious efforts of "foreigners," but the Kempers were able to continue the work. A second couple, Ruth and Garold Van Engen, joined them in 1943.

BOARDS FOR FOREIGN MISSION

The Reformed Church had three links between itself and the American Board of Commissioners for Foreign Missions: through Dr. John Scudder, through the merger of the United Board for Foreign Missions with the American Board in 1826, and through the Rev. David Abeel. Abeel had been sent by the Seamen's Friend Society to the Dutch West Indies and soon became a missionary of the American Board. Abeel's personal purpose was to prepare himself for an eventual mission to China. He assumed that contact with the various Chinese communities would make it possible for him to learn their language and culture in preparation for mission work to China. The Particular Synod of New York, which joined with the Particular Synod of Albany in petitioning the 1832 General Synod to establish a foreign mission board, stated as a reason for beginning a new board ". . . one of her own sons . . . is now engaged in exploring hopeful fields of labor, will probably soon return to this country and might for a season be happily employed in rousing the attention and energies of the church and enlisting the hearts of our pious young men in the work."[72] A joint committee of the synod and the American board developed a report on this referral and reported to the October, 1832, meeting of the General Synod. Because the American Board had previously agreed to the report, the General Synod could proceed to establish its own board for cooperation with the American Board. The synod voted to appoint

. . . the Board of Foreign Missions of the Reformed Dutch Church, whose special duty it shall be, to correspond with the American Board of Commissioners for Foreign Mission on the subject of the contemplated co-operation in the selection of stations, etc. concert and carry into effect measures for the collection of funds, and transmit them to the aforesaid Board, appoint agents, and facilitate their operations, assist in the formation of Missionary families, and report their doings annually to General Synod. [73]

The board was to be composed of fifteen members, seven of whom had to reside in the city of New York. The first meeting was held in the consistory room of the Nassau Street Reformed Church in early November of 1832.

Through the urgings of David Abeel, the Board of Foreign Missions began a new work in Borneo (the Dutch East Indies—present day Indonesia). It was assumed, wrongly, that the Netherlands would look favorably upon this endeavor by a sister church. Four graduates (Elihu Doty, Elbert Nevius and William Youngblood from the class of 1836 and Jacob Ennis from the class of 1837) of New Brunswick Seminary began the mission, but a number of factors made it necessary to abandon the work by 1849.

Several years after the Opium War concluded, Britain opened a number of Chinese coastal ports to foreigners. David Abeel was able to realize his goal for mission work in China because of this opening and arrived in Amoy in 1842.

Since the Reformed Church had been cooperating with the work of the American Board for a number of years, the cooperative agreement was not radically new. The two new provisions were that the Reformed Church would work through its own board, and that it would have the right to form "a distinct mission, or distinct missions . . . with an ecclesiastical organization and public worship according to their own views and wishes."[74] After twenty-five years of this cooperative effort, the 1857 General Synod decided to dissolve the cooperative agreement and "take charge of these missions." The major reason given was "that this action will tend to call out far more largely and promptly the resources of our denomination."[75] The American Board graciously concurred in the dissolution and transferred the mission programs in Amoy and Arcot to the Reformed Church. Since individual missionaries had been appointed by the American Board, the board allowed them to determine their personal course. All of them chose to transfer to the Board of Foreign Missions of the Reformed Church. With the conclusion of the cooperative agreement with the American Board, the Reformed Church, like almost all the other American denominations, had its own foreign mission board and program.

The 1857 General Synod, in addition to dissolving the relationship with the American Board, had before it an extensive communication from its missionaries in Amoy. By this time the work in Amoy consisted of six churches, three of which had been organized by Reformed Church missionaries and three by English Presbyterian missionaries. Rather than being organized under either the English Presbyterian Church or the Reformed Church, the six had established their own Chinese association. Since missionaries of the Reformed Church had always been expected to develop churches ". . . approaching, as nearly as possible, that of Reformed Protestant Dutch churches in our own land . . . the converts at Amoy, as at Arcot and elsewhere, are to be regarded as an integral part of our Church . . . and the missionaries were directed to apply to the Particular Synod of Albany to organize them into a Classis."[76] The missionaries would not comply because of their relationship to the English Presbyterians, and because, more importantly, they believed in establishing a Chinese church independent from both foreign countries.

The Rev. John Van Nest Talmadge carried on most of the correspondence for the Amoy missionaries. When his wife died, it became necessary for Talmadge to spend time in the USA. Because of this personal tragedy, he was present at the 1863 meeting of the General Synod. His boyhood pastor, Dr. Talbot W. Chambers, declared to Talmadge ". . . our missionaries, who carry to the heathen the doctrine of Christ as we have received it, must also carry the order of Christ as we have received it . . . It is not enough to have genuine Consistories, we must have genuine Classes . . . our polity must be reproduced in the mission churches established by the blessing of God upon the men and means furnished by our Zion."[77] A letter from the missionaries in Amoy presented to the 1864 General Synod declared, "We conscientiously feel that in confirming such an organization we should be doing a positive injury and wrong to the churches of Christ established in Amoy, and that our duty to the Master and His people here forbids this . . . ."[78] The missionaries went on to declare that they should be recalled and replaced by persons of other convictions if the synod persisted in its determination to form a Classis of Amoy. The delegates avoided a showdown by declaring

> . . . while the General Synod does not deem it necessary or proper to change the Missionary policy defined and adopted in 1857, yet, in consideration of the peculiar circumstances of the Mission of Amoy, the brethren are allowed to defer the formation of the Classis of Amoy, until, in their judgment, such a measure is required by the wants and desires of the Churches gathered by them from among the heathen.[79]

The brethren in Amoy never formed a Classis of Amoy and thus began a significant new policy in mission for the Reformed Church. The policy did not affect the Classis of Arcot, which had been formed in 1854. The Reformed Church, however, did not again form a classis outside the United States and Canada.[80]

With the separation of the Board of Foreign Missions from the American Board, all the missionaries, real estate, and property for the programs in Amoy and Arcot were transferred to the RCA.[81] The programs in Amoy and Arcot remained at the center of the missionary outreach of the Reformed Church until the middle of the twentieth century. With the exception of new work in Japan, which was begun in 1859 and Arabia, which was begun in 1889 and transferred to the Board of Foreign Missions in 1894, the Reformed Church found it necessary to decline other invitations to expand its missionary involvement—primarily because of the lack of funds. Invitations to Syria, South Africa, Mexico, and work among the American Indians (as in the early days of the United and American boards, work among the American Indians was considered the task of the "foreign" board) were all declined.

The Amoy mission began with the arrival of David Abeel in 1842. The Revs. Elihu Doty and William Pohlman arrived from Borneo prior to Abeel's leaving in 1844. The work was carried out in close cooperation with personnel from the London Missionary Society and the English Presbyterian Church. Its focus was evangelistic, educational, and medical. Evangelistic tours were conducted by the various missionaries with the expectation of gathering a congregation of people into a chapel and then a church. By 1900 there were twelve self-supporting churches, forty-one preaching stations, twelve native pastors, and thirty native evangelists. At the same time there were ten Reformed Church missionaries present in Amoy.

The educational work led to the formation of a middle school and the Charlotte W. Duryee Bible School for women. Each of the mission stations engaged in informal educational work with the persons related to the mission program. Although David Abeel had commented upon the desperate need for medical services by the persons living in the Amoy area, the first hospital, the Neerbosch Hospital in Siokhe, was not opened until 1889. Hope Hospital, Kolongsu, was opened in 1899.

Since General Synod "deferred" the organization of the Classis of Amoy, the work there continued in close cooperation with the London Missionary Society and the English Presbyterians. Each group had a geographical area assigned to them for their missionary efforts, but the emerging churches were all yoked in one classical organization. By 1919 this Chinese church had merged with the Congregational Union to form the South Fukien Synod of the Church of Christ in China. In 1934 the South Fukien Conference of the Methodist Episcopal Church joined the synod, making all Protestant work in the Amoy area part of one Chinese church.

The second major area of Reformed Church missionary endeavors was Arcot, South India. Dr. John Scudder had been transferred from Ceylon to South India by the American Board in 1836. In 1847 the Prudential Committee of the American Board asked the Reformed Church "to consider the expediency of undertaking a mission among the Tamil-speaking people of southern India and in the neighborhood of its Madras Mission, to be composed entirely of missionaries from the Reformed Protestant Dutch Church."[82] The board responded positively at its November meeting, and the link between the Reformed Church and South India was established.

Dr. Scudder's sons Henry, William, and Joseph joined him in the new endeavor. By 1853 they had petitioned the Particular Synod of New York for permission to form the Classis of Arcot. Having received the permission of the particular synod, they formed the classis in 1854—the first, and ultimately only, classis of the Reformed Church outside the North American continent. The mission quickly became responsible for Christian work in Arcot, Arni, Chittoor, Coonoor, and Vellore. A missionary community was established at each major city, and the missionaries with their native assistants toured the villages in the area. If persons responded positively to the gospel message, they were baptized and a church was organized. By 1901 there were 24 organized congregations in the Classis of Arcot, and more than 150 village preaching stations.

The Arcot Mission had the principle of "evangelize first, educate afterward." In carrying out this principle, the various mission stations devoted their first efforts to evangelistic tours of the villages. If it became possible to organize a church in a village, a school was organized (generally by the wives of the missionaries) in the village. A more comprehensive area school was organized at the mission stations located in the central cities, such as Vellore. Boarding schools of a still higher educational standard were established in eight of the largest cities.

Theological education began almost immediately and gradually led to the formation of the Arcot Theological Seminary. During the late 1880s the General Synod authorized the formal organization of "The Theological College of the Arcot Mission" and endorsed the establishment of an endowment for the school. Dr. Jacob I. Chamberlain collected over $55,000 for the endowment, and the 1889 General Synod received the first report from the Board of Superintendents. The General Synod continued to appoint professors of theology, the fourth office in the Reformed Church, for the Arcot Seminary until 1962 and listed the professors in the directory of the General Synod, just as it did the professors serving at Western and New Brunswick seminaries.

The Classis of Arcot had participated in the various discussions on church cooperation from the very beginning of its formation in 1854. By 1875 the Presbyterian Alliance had been formed, and the Classis of Arcot joined with twelve other Presbyterian groups in five council meetings. As the twentieth century began, the Classis of Arcot invited the Free Church of Scotland and the Church of Scotland to a merger creating one, new church. The Free Church concurred and in 1902 joined with the Classis of Arcot to form the Synod of South India. The Classis of Arcot presented its last report to the General Synod of the Reformed Church in America in 1902, almost fifty years after its formation. When the British and American Congregational missions joined the synod in 1908, it became the South India United Church. By 1919 the United Church had begun the conversations with the Methodists and the Anglicans that produced the historic Church of South India in 1947. Through this pilgrimage a church that began as an organic part of the Reformed Church in America became a part of the most ecumenical church in Christendom.

Almost from the beginning the work in the Arcot area included a medical program. Several of the missionaries had received their physicians' certificates. A large hospital was developed in Ranipett, with a smaller dispensary in Wallajapett. A major thrust forward in medical missionary work came through Dr. Ida Scudder, granddaughter of pioneer missionary, John Scudder. While on a visit to her parents' home in India, Ida Scudder witnessed the death of three Indian women in a single night because no male doctor was allowed to attend an Indian woman. Because of this experience she dedicated herself to medical missionary work and founded the Vellore medical program, one of the premiere missionary medical complexes in the world.

The Board of Foreign Missions began its first new work in 1859, two years after its separation from the American Board. When the treaty of 1858 opened Japan to foreigners, the Revs. Guido F. Verbeck and Samuel R. Brown were sent by the Reformed Church. Verbeck settled in Nagasaki and Brown in Yokohama. Since the Japanese government forbade the acceptance of Christianity by the Japanese people, the early years presented great difficulties to the missionaries. They spent their time learning the difficult language and culture of the Japanese. Gradually, they were able to locate persons to assist them in translating the Bible into Japanese and to study the Bible with them. By March of 1872 eleven men had been baptized and were ready to organize the first church in Japan. They called themselves "The Church of Christ in Japan."

All the churches carrying out missionary work in Japan wanted to establish one church, and in 1876 the missions of the Presbyterian Church in the United States of America, North, the United Presbyterian Church of Scotland, and the Reformed Church in America formed a council for the one, Japanese church. The local churches related to the council called themselves "The United Church of Christ in Japan." The doctrinal standards for the new church were the Westminster Confession of Faith and Shorter Catechism, the Heidelberg Catechism, and the Canons of the Synod of Dort. The council was joined by the Presbyterian Church in the United States of America, South, in 1885 and the Reformed (German) Church in the United States in 1886. This church continued to minister in Japan until the 1940s when the government of Japan, because of the wartime emergency, merged all Christian churches into a United (Kyodan) Church. After the war, the Anglicans and the Lutherans left to return to their former denominations, but most of the others have remained in the Kyodan.

The various missions functioning in Japan created a unique organization for evangelistic work. Rather than each mission carrying on its own work, an Evangelistic Committee was formed. Because it carried out its work from Tokyo, the work centered in the south (Nagasaki) did not at first come under its review. Later, evangelistic committees were organized in the local areas to function under the Mission Board in Tokyo. This approach brought the closest linking between the indigenous church and the evangelistic programs of the missions.

Educational work played a central role in the mission program in Japan. In fact, Mr. Verbeck so impressed the Japanese government with his educational leadership abilities that he was called to Tokyo to provide guidance to the educational program of the government. Schools like Meiji Gakuin (1886) and Ferris (1870) were organized to carry forward the educational task. Meiji Gakuin included a theological department that provided training for Japanese persons desiring to enter the ministry.

The fourth, and final, major mission field of the Reformed Church in America between the years 1857 and 1946 was Arabia. During a time of great missionary interest at New Brunswick Seminary, three students committed themselves to missionary service. James Cantine, Philip T. Phelps, and Samuel Zwemer pledged themselves to pioneering missionary work on a foreign field. Under the influence of their professor of Old Testament, James Lansing, they determined to begin work in Arabia. Their motto came from the Old Testament text: "O that Ishmael might live before Thee!" (Gen. 17:18, KJV). They developed a plan which called for five-year subscriptions to support the beginning of the mission, after which the work would become the responsibility of the Board of Foreign Missions. The 1888 General Synod referred the plan to the board, but financial pressures kept the board from becoming involved. Undaunted, the group incorporated the mission in New Jersey, and Cantine and Zwemer began explorations for their pioneering work.

The first station was established at Busrah and the second at Bahrain. A third station was opened in Oman in 1893. By 1894 it became obvious that the independent program was encountering too many administrative difficulties, and it was transferred to the Board of Foreign Missions. For a number of years it was maintained as a separate corporation, which was composed of the members of the Foreign Board.

The Reformed Church in America had functioned with "boards" for mission for more than a century before they were officially incorporated into her formal constitution. When the Committee on the General State of the Church reported to the General Synod of 1900, they recommended a significant amendment to the constitution. They prefaced their amendment with the following statement:

> The time has come for the church to declare in unmistakable terms that the conquest of the world for Christ is the fundamental argument of the church's existence; that the command "evangelize all nations" is not subsidiary work . . . As the constitution now stands, reference to this sacred trust appears only incidentally . . . To give all the present and prospective missionary enterprises at home and abroad full constitutional recognition and support, the following amendment to the Rules of the Church Government is recommended for adoption: . . . To the General Synod also belongs the power and duty to institute and organize such general agencies as shall best enable the church to fulfil the command of the Lord Jesus Christ by which he has enjoined on all His disciples the duty of teaching all nations and preaching the Gospel to every creature; to maintain, supervise and direct such agencies when erected in the conduct of missionary operations at home and abroad; and to recommend such methods in the churches as shall effectively sustain such agencies and tend to secure the largest dissemination of the Gospel.[83]

The classes passed the amendment, and the Reformed Church had finally changed its polity to reflect its century-long practice of carrying out the mission of the church through "boards" of the General Synod. Practice, rather than the careful statement of theological principles, had produced this shift in polity.

The American historian, Arthur Schlesinger, Sr., has remarked that ". . . American history was singularly poor in ideas, deficient in political theory, in philosophic system, in abstractions of all sorts."[84] The Reformed Church carried out this American spirit in its establishment of mission boards and did not enter into thorough theological reflection before adding this new, nineteenth-century phenomenon to its polity. Because there had not been significant theological reflection when the "boards" were created, nor at the time of their incorporation into the church's official polity, the persons conducting the revisions in the structure in the mid-twentieth century did not inherit a theological tradition for the place of the "boards" in the life of the church.

WOMAN'S BOARD OF FOREIGN MISSIONS

The Rev. David Abeel's influence had stimulated the organization of the first women's foreign missionary society. As he passed through London on his way back to the United States in 1834, Abeel spoke on the needs of the various fields, and the women of London responded by forming the "Society for Promoting Female Education in China and the East." At a similar meeting in the United States the women were dissuaded from organizing by Dr. Rufus Anderson, secretary of the American Board. One of the ladies, Mrs. Bethune, asked "What! is the American Board afraid the ladies will get ahead of them?" Mrs. Thomas Doremus reported "Some were for going on; others, out of respect for Dr. Anderson, were willing to wait; and Dr. Abeel, with tears rolling down his face exclaimed: 'What is to become of the souls of those who are ignorant of the offers of mercy and of the Bible?' "[85]

Mrs. Doremus, who remained personally active in the foreign missionary cause, helped form the first American women's organization in 1861, the Woman's Union Missionary Society of America for Heathen Lands. As its first, and long-time, president she provided leadership to the new organization and the women of the Reformed Church in the missionary cause. Although a number of denominations organized their own woman's boards, the Congregational in 1868, the Methodist in 1869, the Presbyterian in 1870, and the Baptists in 1871, the women of the Reformed Church did not organize until 1875. An 1883 statement declares:

The women of our Reformed Church were almost the last to establish a Woman's Board of Foreign Missions. This was not that
they were less zealous advocates of the cause, but hitherto their
personal interest had been directed through the channel of the
Synod's Board and their individual gifts absorbed into those of the
customary church collections . . . But the interest of many of our
church members was becoming dissociated from the work of our
own Board and their gifts diverted into the channel of the Woman's
Union Society.[86]

As declared by its constitution, the purpose of the new board
was to "aid the board of Foreign Missions in the Reformed Church
in America by promoting its work among the women and children
of heathen lands." During the early years the efforts of the women
were focused on programs at home to support the missionary
thrusts of the Foreign Board. Gradually, especially because of
the financial crisis faced by the Foreign Board in the early 1880s,
the Woman's Board accepted financial responsibility for the foreign efforts involving women and children. After 25 years of service the women could report that the number of missionary
auxiliaries had grown from 19 (after the first year) to 555. The
financial contribution of the Woman's Board was $2,891 in 1875;
and this had grown to $33,029 by 1899. During the first twenty-
five years of its existence the Woman's Board had contributed
$447,000 to the overseas work of the Reformed Church.[87]

During the early years men provided the leadership for the
board. At the first meetings "All the remarks were made and all
the reports were read by men," and the women did not influence
the missionary programs of the Foreign Board. Gradually the
women assumed the leadership roles in their board and also influenced the policies of the Foreign Board. During their first
decade the women were urged to provide female medical personnel for China, but they declined. Fifteen years later they were
ready to support Dr. Ida Scudder in her commitment to carry
on medical missionary work in India.

Through the organization of missionary auxiliaries, through
providing financial support for the women sent into mission by

the Foreign Board, and through providing the financial support for the board's programs for women and children, the Woman's Board supplemented the work of the Foreign Board. The board did not begin new fields or programs by itself but undergirded the programs of the Reformed Church's Foreign Board.

WOMEN'S BOARD FOR DOMESTIC MISSIONS

The 1881 General Synod, taking notice of the very effective work of the Woman's Board for Foreign Missions, urged the organization of a similar board for the domestic missionary work of the church. At the semi-centennial of the Board of Domestic Missions in 1882, a group of women gathered and formed the new board. In addition to forming auxiliaries in local churches for the support of the domestic mission program, the Women's Board provided the funds to build parsonages for ministers seeking to establish new congregations in the West. For the first years of their existence, the provision of parsonages formed the major work of the board.

Gradually the Women's Board sought new endeavors for themselves and expanded into other missionary efforts within the United States. The first new effort involved missionary work to the American Indians. For several years they had a Committee on Indian Mission but no specific program of their own. A visit by Mrs. John Bussing, president of the board, and Mrs. Charles A. Runk, chairwoman of the Committee on Indian Mission, to the Rev. Frank Hall Wright, a Choctaw Indian minister recovering from tuberculosis in New York City, led to his appointment to begin specific work among the Indian tribes. He carried out his work in southwestern Oklahoma and organized churches among the Cheyenne near Colony, among the Commanche near Lawton, and among the Apaches imprisoned at Fort Sill. Later the Women's Board supported churches in Mescalero, New Mexico, and in Winnebago, and Macy, Nebraska. Interestingly, the General Synod did not form classes for these churches, as had been done in the nineteenth century for the work in Arcot and had been demanded for the work in Amoy, but rather made these churches members of the Classis of New York. New York was probably chosen because it was the location of the board offices. The American Indian churches remained members of the Classis of New York until 1957,[88] when they were finally transferred to classes in their own geographical areas.

Two other missionary programs were begun by the Women's Board. The first, located in Jackson County, Kentucky, began with the sending of Cora A. Smith and Nora L. Grant in 1900. Smith was a Bible teacher and nurse, and Grant a teacher. They initiated educational, medical, and evangelistic work. Gradually the work grew into a hospital, schools, and a boarding school. Churches were also established in the various communities (belonging, like the American Indian churches, to the Classis of New York). The second program was in Brewton, Alabama. Mr. James Dooley, director of the Southern Normal and Industrial School, had interested a number of midwestern congregations in the work of the school. As local Reformed churches became more involved in the program, the Particular Synod of Chicago overtured the 1919 General Synod to assume control of the program. The Women's Board was similarly inclined, and it became responsible for Southern Normal School.

As the Executive Committee of the Women's Board for Domestic Missions became directly responsible for major mission programs in the Reformed Church, their organizational structure was reviewed and revised. In 1909 the board adopted a new name and decided to incorporate. The purposes of the newly incorporated Women's Board of Domestic Missions of the Reformed Church in America were: "To assist the Board of Domestic Missions of the Reformed Church in America in the promotion of the growth of said church, by building parsonages, furnishing churches and supporting missionaries . . . This organization shall also work for the evangelization of America by establishing missions and through educational work."[89]

The Women's Board, in distinction from the Woman's Board for Foreign Missions which did not carry out mission programs of its own, maintained a variety of mission programs separate from the denomination's Board of Domestic Missions. By 1915 it became necessary to establish a joint committee of the boards to consider their areas of mutual concern. Based on the recommendation of the Joint Committee, the boards adopted three principles for their mutual actions in the domestic mission program of the Reformed Church. "1. A United Budget to list the needs of the work of both Boards. 2. A joint appeal to the churches and their organizations for all needs listed in the Budget. 3. A joint responsibility for the maintenance of all the work of Domestic Missions."[90]

ADDITIONAL BOARDS OF THE REFORMED CHURCH IN AMERICA

A delegate to the 1945 General Synod of the Reformed Church in America would have received printed reports from six boards. Our survey has sketched the formation and initial programs of four of them: the Board of Domestic Missions, the Board of Foreign Missions, the Woman's Board of Foreign Missions, and the Women's Board of Domestic Missions. Because our major focus is on the mission program of the church, the Board of Education and the Board of the Ministers' Fund did not enter into the story. Since they will be a part of the story from 1945 to 1980, a brief description of their beginnings and programs is required.

The Board of Education began in 1828 through the efforts of a number of prominent ministers in New York City. The purpose of the board was "to aid indigent, pious young men, who are preparing for the Gospel ministry, to be educated in the Theological Seminary at New Brunswick."[91] The 1831 General Synod established its own board, and it continued the work of aiding students for the ministry. During succeeding years the work of the board was expanded to aiding RCA college students, and in 1865 the General Synod empowered the board to aid classes in the establishment of academies. Aiding students for the ministry and relating to the colleges (Central, Hope, and Northwestern) and the seminaries (New Brunswick and Western) remained the major role of the Board of Education until 1933. In that year the

General Synod greatly expanded the work of the board by consolidating into it the work of the educational department of the Board of Publication and Bible School Work, the Department of Missionary Education, the Commission on Evangelism, and the Department of Stewardship Education. With this consolidation, the Board of Education retained its responsibilities for the educational institutions of the Reformed Church and also became responsible for the denomination's various programs in Christian nurture.

The Ministers' Fund, later to become the Board of Pensions of the Reformed Church, was established by the 1923 General Synod. This new board became responsible for the Widows' Fund, the Disabled Ministers' Fund, and the Ministerial Pension Fund. The Ministerial Pension Fund had just been established and was conducting a drive for a one-million-dollar endowment. The drive was successfully concluded a few years later and provided the major retirement benefit for Reformed Church ministers for many years. The work of the Ministers' Fund was expanded by the establishment of the Contributory Annuity Fund in the 1930s and continued without major changes until 1945.

SUMMARY

The Reformed Church in America began as an extension of the Reformed Church in the Netherlands. Its planting in the New World resulted from the cooperative efforts of the magistrate (the government), commerce, and the Classis of Amsterdam. After the Reformed Church gained its independence from its Dutch roots, it began to carry out its responsibility for spreading the church of Jesus Christ within the United States and throughout the world.

Having deleted the responsibilities of the magistrate from its adaptation of the Dutch Rules of Church Government (although the Belgic Confession continued to charge the magistrates with the tasks of promoting the kingdom of God and preaching the gospel) because of the American separation of church and state, and lacking a close link with the emerging commercial interests in America, the RCA experimented with new vehicles for extending the church. After testing committees of the General Synod and societies of committed Christians, the RCA followed a number of other American denominations and established boards of the General Synod. Each of the boards was charged with a specific portion of the task of extending the church. Each maintained its own life, independent of, but in cooperation with, the other boards of the church. The Reformed Church did not amend its polity to provide for this addition to the structure of a reformed church until almost seventy-five years after the formation of its first board. Nonetheless, the boards became a major factor in the church's life. The annual General Synod reviewed their work and appointed their new members. Because they continued their work throughout the year, the boards came to have a prominent place in the life and work of the church; almost more prominent and influential than the General Synod itself.

With the addition of boards to its life, the Reformed Church soon faced the need to provide personnel for implementing the programs of the boards. When John Schermerhorn was employed as the general agent of the Missionary Society of the Reformed Dutch Church, a second major addition entered the Reformed Church. Staff to implement the programs of the church, though not called for by the offices of the church, were engaged. The boards and their staffs provided major leadership to the church and new additions to her life and work.

In addition to establishing boards of the General Synod for implementing her mission in the world, the Reformed Church in America made another major mission structure decision in the nineteenth century. When it began missionary work in India, it followed the pattern of its own beginnings in the United States and established a classis for the newly-organized churches—the Classis of Arcot. As its new work in Amoy, China, led to the formation of churches, the General Synod called for the establishment of the Classis of Amoy. The missionaries to Amoy refused to extend the Dutch Reformed Church of America to China and resisted the establishment of a classis. In cooperation with the missionaries of the English Presbyterian Church, they established the Church of Christ in China. When the missionaries threatened to resign if they were forced to form a separate classis, the General Synod of 1864 affirmed the missionary policy of establishing a classis for the new churches in Amoy but deferred the implementation of the policy until a classis was "wanted and desired" by the new converts in China. A Classis of Amoy was never established, even though the General Synod never revised its missionary policy. Because of the stand of the Amoy missionaries, the Reformed Church in America, with the exception of the Classis of Arcot, never extended itself and its organizational structure into the foreign mission fields. The Classis of Arcot, no doubt because of the missionary leadership pioneered by the Amoy missionaries, was one of the first to work cooperatively with other churches in the Arcot area.

Although it followed the other American denominations (such as the Presbyterians, Methodists, and Episcopalians) in establishing mission boards, the Reformed Church in America charted its own direction in the establishment of the churches produced through the efforts of its missionaries. It followed neither the pattern of its beginnings in the United States, which included more than 150 years of membership in the Classis of Amsterdam, nor the pattern of other American denominations which established extensions of themselves in the countries of their missonary endeavors. The Reformed Church, although reluctantly and under the threat of its missionaries to Amoy, planted indigenous churches through its overseas missionary efforts. These churches did not have a dependent organizational relationship to the RCA, but lived their new life of service to Christ organizationally independent of an overseas church.

II

The American Experience: 1945-1980— "A Troubled Feast"

"A Troubled Feast" . . . The "troubled" aspects may well be the more familiar—the frightful assassinations of public men, the malignant effects of two Asian wars, the endemic violence, the persistence of social ills. Acknowledgement of the reality of the "feast"—that is, the widespread affluence made possible by the prodigious expansion of the economy—has often been more grudging. Yet in these years millions were lifted out of poverty, millions more into the ranks of the middle class. And it was the abundance that shaped many of the contours of American society in the nearly three decades since 1945, especially the consumer culture in its multifarious ramifications, and that exerted a decisive influence upon not only the troubles of this era but the too little noticed advance.[1]

Our story focuses on 35 years in the history of the Reformed Church in America. William E. Leuchtenburg, who has written one of the few historical surveys on this contemporary period, sets the tone for our vignettes of this period. During these almost four decades Americans experienced rapid and radical change. Some of these changes had a beneficent effect on the life of the church—the rapid spreading of affluence made it easier for the members of the church to give money for its mission programs. Some of them had a directly negative effect on the life of the Reformed Church—the flight of middle class whites from the urban population centers of the nation to the new suburbs deprived the church of many members and severely weakened most of its largest and strongest churches.

Several peaks dot the sweep of these years in the American experience. The presidential political slogans moved from the

"Fair Deal" to the "New Frontier" to the "Great Society." Two Asian wars, the Korean and the Vietnamese, challenged the country's resources, both material and moral. Violence reared its ugly head in the assassinations of President John F. Kennedy and Senator Robert F. Kennedy and in the unsuccessful attempts on Presidents Truman, Ford, and Reagan; in the student riots of the sixties, with the killing of four Kent State University students on May 4, 1970; in the mob violence responding to the movements among the blacks to gain their "civil rights," most vividly carried out in the assassination of their spiritual leader, Martin Luther King, Jr.; and in the "long hot summers" of the late sixties in the teeming ghettos of the American cities. Corruption crept into the highest levels of the American government, as demonstrated by Watergate, and the highest levels of American business, as shown by the "kickback" scandals of the seventies. The population of the nation exploded through the post-World War II baby boom but sought "zero growth" because of a new sense of ecological pressure on the world's resources. The "troubles" were deeply felt.

As Leuchtenburg states, the "feast" was not as readily acknowledged. Major technological advances relieved a great many laborers of dangerous work in the mills and factories of the nation. Medical advances removed the scourge of many diseases, such as polio, and brought increased life expectancy and better health to millions. Leisure time, available for recreation and travel, greatly increased as the 40-hour week moved from dream to reality and vacations extended from one week up to four or five for many employed persons.

Drs. Thomas Ludwig and David Myers, members of the psychology department at Hope College, Holland, Michigan, have identified several principles from psychological research which shed light on the American experience from 1945 through 1980. In an article entitled "Poor Talk" they share the principles.

> The first principle is the "adaptation-level" phenomenon . . . The basic point is that success and failure, satisfaction and dissatisfaction are relative to our prior experience . . . Material progress does not

sustain a sense of increased well-being, since our experience is recalibrated so that what was formerly seen as positive is now only neutral and what was formerly neutral becomes negative . . . This is why, despite the increase in real income during the past several decades, the average American today reports no greater feeling of general happiness and satisfaction than was the case 30 years ago . . . The second insight from psychological research is the "relative-deprivation" principle . . . the relative-deprivation principle is based primarily on comparison with other people. The basic point is that success and failure, happiness and discontent are also relative to what we observe others like ourselves experiencing . . . If our rewards are greater than those received by others whom we perceive to be of a similar background, education, or occupation, we experience happiness and contentment; on the other hand, if our rewards fall below some weighted average of the rewards accruing to our peers, we feel a sense of righteous indignation, . . . dissatisfactions . . . are compounded by a second psychological phenomenon—the principle of "upward comparisons" . . . when people are given the opportunity to compare themselves with various other people, they generally choose to measure themselves against those whose performance or rewards have been superior rather than inferior to their own.[2]

Ludwig and Myers do not apply their insights from psychology to the effects of the experiences from 1945 to 1980 on the American culture, nor do they extend their insights to the effects on an institution, like the Reformed Church. Nonetheless, their insights from the discipline of psychology shed significant light on the inability of the American people to perceive the "feast" aspects of these 35 years. Having "adapted" to the new affluence and experienced "relative deprivation" through comparisons with the more affluent and endowed, the American people continually made "upward comparisons." Rather than remember the past, with some of its deprivations and difficulties, the American people have focused on the future, expecting new and better gifts from it.

The Reformed Church, as an institution swept along by the American milieu during these 35 years, has also shown the same characteristics. The more the denomination quantified the measures of success—a larger mission budget next year, greater giving for mission/education programs, more members this year than last, a larger number of children in Sunday school this year—the more the phenomena of "adaptation," "relative deprivation," and "upward comparisons" shaped her self-perceptions as a church, both locally and denominationally. The unprecedented gains of the fifties and the early sixties, which included growth in financial resources for denominational programs, growth in the number of members and churches, growth in every measurable area, caused an "expectation" of growth. The seventies, for reasons which will be described in succeeding paragraphs, did not produce results to meet these expectations. The church found itself more "troubled" than "feasting" because of its expectations.

Our story can only examine a few slices of the American experience from 1945 through 1980. Because they have had the largest impact on the experiences of the RCA, we will examine: the perceived role of religion, the impact of population, the economic boom, the trends in philanthropy, and a few impacts of technology. Our objective will be to set a stage for understanding the subsequent story of the Reformed Church told in this book.

RELIGION

Writing in the early nineteenth century, Alexis de Toucqueville declared ". . .there is no country in the world where the Christian religion retains a greater influence over the souls of men than in America. . ."[3] If de Toucqueville had been able to visit America at the midpoint of the twentieth century, he would have discovered a major growth in the influence of the Christian religion over the American experience. One indicator, the percentage of the population belonging to the church, portrays the growing influence of the church in the life of the nation. In the early 1700s approximately 4% of the population belonged to a church, and this had risen to 10% by the early 1800s—the time of de Toucqueville's visit. The percentage kept rising—it was 16% by 1850, 36% at the beginning of the twentieth century,

50% by 1940, and an astounding 62% by 1976. The American people increasingly have placed participation in a religious institution at the center of their lives. The growth trend in participation in religious institutions peaked in our period, 1945-1980, and, for the first time in the American experience, showed a time of decline.

Will Herberg, in his classic *Protestant-Catholic-Jew*, written in 1955 and revised in 1960, aptly describes the state of religion in the fifties:

> . . . Americans, by and large, do have their "common religion" and that "religion" is the system familiarly known as the American Way of Life . . . what is being designated under the American Way of Life is not the so-called "common denominator" religion; it is not a synthetic system composed of beliefs to be found in all or in a group of religions. It is an organic structure of ideas, values, and beliefs that constitutes a faith common to Americans and genuinely operative in their lives . . . (it) is not merely a civic religion to celebrate the values and convictions of the American people as corporate entity. It has its inner, personal aspects as well . . . there has developed, primarily through a devitalization of the historic faiths, an inner, personal religion that promises salvation to the disoriented, tormented souls of a society in crisis. This inner, personal religion is based on the American's "faith in faith."[4]

The mood of the fifties toward religion shows powerfully in the actions of Congress in 1954 to add "under God" to the pledge of allegiance and in 1955 to place the phrase "In God We Trust" on all American currency.

Toward the end of the fifties, or early in the sixties, a significant shift occurred. Although the precise time or the underlying causes for the shift cannot be identified, the results became clear throughout the decade. Religious institutions no longer experienced growth in participation and membership. People's attitudes toward the religious side of life shifted. Polls began to show a significant decline in the areas most important to religious organizations—membership, attendance, contributions. Although the formal religious organizations of America experienced major declines (attendance, membership, resources) in the sixties, William L. O'Neill observed at the close of the decade:

> American religious life was probably more fertile and diverse in the sixties than at any time since the nineteenth century. If all this did not quite amount to an age of faith, it certainly seemed so compared with the 1950's which now looked like merely an age of churchgoing. The old religious revival declined; religion itself did not. The established churches became more secular, unchurched youth more religious. Anti-communism excepted, the 1950's was a time when rational, scientific, and secular ideas dominated. In the sixties romantic, millennial, chiliastic, and utopian impulses undermined them.[5]

The seventies brought renewed energy and commitment from the formal religious institutions of the country. Through explorations on *Why Conservative Churches are Growing* and institutes on church growth, significant segments of Protestantism sought to understand the decline experiences of the sixties and revitalize their relationship to the American people. Along with these new efforts, the American people shifted their perceptions of the role of religion and its institutions.

The Princeton Religion Research Center, using the results of the various Gallup polls, publishes the most comprehensive and scientific analyses of the American population's perceptions on religion. Through citing three of their reports, on the influence of religion, church membership, and church attendance, the attitudes of the American people to religion are portrayed. The financial commitment of the American people to their churches is portrayed in our paragraphs on philanthropy.

The 1979 Gallup Poll[6] showed 65% having "a great deal" or "quite a lot" of confidence in the church or organized religion. The percentages for the other 10 key institutions were: banks, 60%; military, 54%; public schools, 53%; newspapers, 51%; U.S. Supreme Court, 45%; television, 38%; organized labor, 36%;

Congress, 34%; and big business, 32%. The answers to the question, "At the present time do you think religion as a whole is increasing its influence on American life or losing its influence?" portray the shifting mood of the people toward religious institutions during this period.

	Increasing	Losing
1978	37%	48%
1977	36	45
1976	44	45
1975	39	51
1974	31	56
1970	14	70
1969	14	70
1968	18	67
1967	23	57
1965	33	45
1962	45	31
1957	69	14

The persons perceiving religion to be increasing its influence dropped from a 1957 high of 69% to a 1969 low of 14%, from which it began to rise to 37% by 1978. Most American religious institutions probably reached their peak of influence and acceptability between the years 1955 and 1960.

The Gallup Poll also asked people to indicate their religious preference. The results show an increasing preference for Roman Catholicism and a decline for Protestantism.

Religious Preference	Protestant	Roman Catholic	None
1978	60%	29%	8%
1976	61	27	6
1974	60	27	6
1971	65	26	4
1966	68	25	2

Although the increasing significance given to religious institutions is a positive factor, Protestants have become concerned about the declining percentage of the population preferring to live out their religious experience through the Protestant churches.

A second indicator of the place of religious institutions in the life of the nation comes from church or synagogue attendance. The statistics for attendance peaked at 49% in 1958 and then began a continued decline to 40% by 1971. After several years at 40%, attendance increased slightly to 41% in 1976 and continued at 40.5% for 1977 and 1978.[7]

A third indicator from the Gallup polls shows the percentage of persons claiming membership in the church. The graph for the years 1936 through 1979 shows steady declines in the percentages, with a marked plateau from 1952 through 1965. In 1936 77% claimed membership in a church; this had dropped to 73% by 1952. Between 1952 and 1965 it remained constant at 73% but dropped to 71% by 1975 and 69% by 1979. With the exception of the membership statistic, all the other indicators show a resurgence of interest in, and importance for, the religious experience in American life at the beginning of the 1980s.

The Reformed Church grew through the period 1945 to 1980, and its growth rate almost mirrored the place of religion in the life of the American people. In 1945 there were 742 churches with 173,975 adult communicant members.[8] By 1980 the RCA had grown to 923 churches with 214,389 members.[9] The growth peak had been reached in 1965 when there were 927 churches and 233,000 members.[10] The 35-year growth rate was 24% for churches and 23% for members. While this steady growth pattern may seem adequate, it compares with a 62% growth rate for the population of the United States.

George Gallup, the president of Gallup Polls, has written:

Evidence is mounting that the U. S. may be in an early stage of a profound religious revival . . . The observations of both laity and clergy, as well as behavioral measurements, indicate an upturn in religious interest and activity . . . Among the various factors which could be pointed to as accounting for the increased activity in the religious and spiritual climate of the U. S. are the following: a turning inward to seek refuge from the pressures of everyday existence; a search for nonmaterial value in light of the disappointments of the material world and the fading of the "American dream"; President Carter's open discussion of his own personal religious beliefs, which has focused new attention on religion in the U. S. and particularly the evangelical movement; a normal upswing following a decline in religious interest and activity . . . (and) the efforts of the nation's clergy in response to the need to make religion more appealing to young people and to satisfy their apparent spiritual hunger.[11]

POPULATION

Between 1945 and 1980 the population of the United States increased rapidly, and then returned to a more stable growth pattern by the end of the period. After several decades of a declining growth rate for the American population, a major upturn was experienced in 1950 and continued through approximately 1970. The following chart presents the results of the decennial census:

Total Population
(in Millions)

1910	92,407
1920	106,461
1930	123,077
1940	132,594
1950	152,271
1960	180,671
1970	204,879
1978	281,548[12]

Between 1945 and 1978 the population of the United States came very close to doubling. The major source of growth was a tremendous increase in the annual birthrate. The 1947 live birth-

rate was 113 per 1,000 females of childbearing age, which compared with 77 for the year 1935 and 88 for the year 1944. After
a few years of decline following the 1947 peak, the birthrate
began to climb again. By 1952 it again reached 113; it reached
a peak of 122 in 1957.[13] The 1960 births totaled 4,307,000, but
births had declined to 3,328,000 by 1978.[14] The tremendous increase in the birthrate, linked with a decline in the death rate
because of medical advances, fueled an unprecedented period of
population growth in the United States. At the beginning of the
twentieth century, and again during the Great Depression, people had worried about the lack of growth in the population of the
United States. With the geometric growth of the mid-twentieth
century, people became concerned about a too rapid growth for
the nation.

Because the growth rate of the population came primarily from
the rapid rise in the birthrate, more and more persons became
"native" Americans. The 1960 census shows:

	Foreign Born	Native of Foreign Born	Native of Native Born
1900	15.3	23.4	61.3
1920	14.5	23.9	61.6
1940	9.6	19.5	70.9
1960	5.9	15.0	79.2

Immigration, which had produced major growth for the Reformed Church in America between 1845 and 1875, no longer
provided a natural growth pool for the church. Growth, if it were
to be experienced, had to come from the persons already living
in the United States.

The Reformed Church in America did not grow in proportion
to this tremendous increase in the population of the United States.
When the United States had a population of approximately
140,000,000 people, the Reformed Church had an adult membership of 175,000 people. By the time the population had grown
to 218,548,000 people—an increase of 56%—the Reformed

Church had only grown to 215,000—an increase of only 22%. Three demographic factors had a negative impact on the growth pattern of the Reformed Church during this period: the major shift of the United States population to the Southwest; the movement of people from the cities to the suburbs; and the rapid decline in rural population.

The Reformed Church in America had its major membership base in the Northeast. More of its members lived in New York State than any other in the nation. Between 1960 and 1970 (the census bureau estimates sometime in 1964) California surpassed New York as the most populous state in the nation. The tremendous migration affected the entire Southwest: the population of Phoenix alone jumped from 65,000 in 1940 to 439,000 in 1960! The states showing the largest population gain from 1950 to 1960 were: Florida, 79%; Nevada, 78%; Alaska, 76%; Arizona, 74%; California, 49% (it had been 53% from 1940 to 1950); and New Mexico, 40%.[15] When the 1950 to 1960 migration is analyzed by color, the results are:

Regions	White	Non-white
Northeastern	−206,000	+541,000
North Central	+679,000	+558,000
The South	+ 52,000	−1,457,000
The West	+3,518,000	+1,321,000

During this period the South grew 17%, the Northeast, 16%; the North Central, 13%; and the West, 39%.[16]

The westward movement of the Reformed Church had an impact on the leadership of the denomination. Several indicators could be used to show this, but a review of the membership of the executive committees of the various boards will suffice. The 1945 membership on the executive committees of the Boards of Education, Domestic Missions, Foreign Missions, Ministers' Fund, and Direction included 40 persons: 38 persons from the New York area and two persons from the three western particular synods. Because of the speed of air travel and the shifting population center of the RCA, this had changed radically by 1980. In that year the executive committees had 34 members, with 16 living in the three eastern particular synods and 18 living in the three western particular synods.[17]

The second migration factor which negatively affected the Reformed Church was the movement of people from the cities to the suburbs of the nation. Around 1948 there were 35 million people in the suburbs of the United States; this had doubled by 1968. During this period the annual migration to the suburbs exceeded the previous peaks of immigration from European countries. Although most of the new suburbs were linked to the great cities of the nation—in 1940 48% lived in metropolitan areas and by 1969 64.5% lived in metropolitan areas, people no longer lived in the cities and utilized their services. For the Reformed Church this meant a serious decline of its membership base in the cities, especially its major city, New York. Suburbs were typified by shopping centers, private homes, a network of superhighways, ownership of automobiles (increasingly, two per family), transportation to the city, and political structures separated from the city itself. Although New York only lost 110,000 people to suburban flight from 1950 to 1960, the racial composition of the city shifted radically. The non-white population of the city grew from 10% in 1950 to 14% in 1960.

A comparison of Reformed Church membership in selected cities shows the following:

	1945	1980
Albany, New York	1,877	1,190
Chicago, Illinois	5,594	713
Grand Rapids, Michigan	8,458	8,479
Jersey City, New Jersey	2,558	511
Newark, New Jersey	1,027	269
New York, New York	19,727	9,772
Schenectady, New York	3,658	1,940
Total	42,899	22,844[18]

Our sample clearly shows the shift of membership in the Reformed Church from the urban centers of the USA to the suburbs. A delegate to the 1945 General synod would have learned that 24% of the membership of the RCA lived in the sample cities (11% living in New York City alone), and a delegate in 1980 would have seen this decline to 10% (below 4% in New York City).[19] In 1945 the Reformed Church was an urban/rural church; by 1980 it had become a suburban church with small percentages remaining in the urban/rural areas of the country.

Previously, Reformed churches had moved to a new section of New York City when the population shifted—from the Battery to the lower east side, to Twenty-ninth and Fifth, to Forty-eighth and Fifth, and to the upper east side. The political and geographical boundaries of the city made it impossible to continue this pattern of following a migratory people. Now it became necessary to follow the people to the suburbs, through the establishment of new churches, and seek to maintain the city churches in the midst of "changing" neighborhoods.

The third migration which negatively affected the Reformed Church was the rural exodus. As World War II came to a close a large minority of RCA membership was in the rural areas of upper New York State, Michigan, Illinois, Iowa, and the Dakotas. Between 1940 and 1950 more than 7.5 million people left the farms of the nation. This exodus increased to 9.9 million people between 1950 and 1960, producing a net loss of 17.4 million people and leaving only 15 million people on the farm. As mechanization radically increased the size of the farms—the number of farms declined from 5,380,000 in 1950 to 3,703,000 by 1959 (a 30% decrease in nine years)—people were forced to leave the rural areas of the nation.[20]

With the close of World War II the numeric strength of the Reformed Church was in the urban areas of the Northeast and the rural areas of upper New York State and the Middle West. Although the 35 years from 1945 to 1980 brought rapid and radical growth to the United States, the areas of Reformed Church membership strength experienced decline and major population shifts through the dominant migratory trends of the period.

ECONOMY

As World War II drew to a close, a great many people began to fear the economic consequences which might be brought about by the ending of the war. Although World War I had been followed by the tremendous boom of the twenties, the boom was followed by the international bust of the thirties. The Great Depression had only been cured by the tremendous tooling up for World War II. The historian Richard Hofstadter later commented: "We were surprised by the fact that instead of having a tremendous depression after the war, which those of us who were mature in the '30s thought surely was coming, we entered upon one of the great boom periods of history." The economist John Kenneth Galbraith, as he portrayed the American experience, called it "The Affluent Society." When he wrote, the median family income had just topped $4,000 per year. By 1968, when Galbraith issued a revised edition of his book the median family income had risen 85%. The 30 years between 1945 and 1975 produced the greatest economic boom in the history of the United States, perhaps even in the history of the world.

Several statistical indicators will demonstrate the radical economic increases experienced by Americans during this time. For example, the gross national product (GNP) indicates the total economic output of the nation. Between 1900 and 1960, expressed in current dollars, it had grown from $17.3 billion to $503.7 billion.

GROSS NATIONAL PRODUCT IN CURRENT DOLLARS
(billions)

1900	17.3
1920	88.9
1932	58.5
1945	213.6
1960	503.7

A more detailed examination of the period of our study shows:

	Current Dollars (Billions)	1972 Dollars (Billions)
1946	209.6	475.7
1950	286.2	533.5
1955	399.3	654.8
1960	506.0	736.8
1965	688.1	925.9
1970	982.4	1,075.3
1975	1,573.2	1,217.4[21]

The radical growth in the gross national product, even though three or four recessions were experienced during this period, was paralleled by a massive growth in personal income. In 1946 the Department of Commerce placed personal income at $177.3 billion, and it had grown to $1,294.8 billion by 1975. More significantly for the mission of the church dependent on the giving of its people, there was a similar increase in disposable personal income.

DISPOSABLE PERSONAL INCOME

	Current Dollars (Billions)	1972 Dollars (Billions)
1946	158.6	332.4
1950	205.5	361.9
1955	273.4	425.9
1960	349.4	487.3
1965	472.2	612.4
1970	685.9	741.6
1975	1,114.4	868.4[22]

The Reformed Church in America has always raised its annual budgets for the mission of its local congregations, as well as its classical, particular synod, and General Synod programs, from the freewill giving of its people. During this period RCA members and friends had a rapidly-increasing personal income from which to give.

A second view of the rapidly-increasing financial resources of the American family comes from charting the growth in per capita income.

PER CAPITA INCOME: 1950-1978

Year	Current Dollars	1977 Dollars
1950	1,138	2,865
1955	1,434	3,245
1960	1,769	3,620
1965	2,210	4,245
1970	3,177	4,958
1975	4,818	5,425
1978	6,455	5,999[23]

During these 35 years the median family income increased in current dollars from $3,031 in 1946 to $17,640 in 1978. If constant 1977 dollars are used (to adjust out the inflationary factor) the growth is from $8,223 in 1946 to $16,394 in 1978.[24] This is almost a 100% increase in 35 years. In 1965 *Fortune* magazine conducted a study of the distribution of families by income group. Using constant 1965 dollars, they discovered that three out of five families had a 1950 income of less than $5,000, and only one in five had an income of $7,000 or more. By 1965 (using constant dollars so inflation did not affect the fifteen-year comparison) almost half the families had incomes over $7,000 and only one-third had incomes less than $5,000. The percentages were:

	1950	1965
Under $3,000	30%	17%
$3,000 to 4,999	30	16
$5,000 to 6,999	20	18
$7,000 to 9,999	13	24
Over $10,000	7	25[25]

Although this great economic boom was not enjoyed by all segments of society and a great many people experienced deprivation because others gained excessive economic benefits, the number and percentage of people living below the poverty line also declined during this time. In 1959 it was estimated that 39,490,000 persons (22.4% of the total population) lived below the poverty line. By 1978 this figure had declined to 24,497,000. Some of the decline came from an adjustment to the poverty line, but the persons living in poverty did show a "real" numerical and percentage decline in this twenty-year period.

A final statistic, unemployment, shows the experience of the time. As World War II came to a close there were 12,123,455 persons employed by the military, compared with a total labor union membership of 14,796,000. By 1960, military employment had declined to 2,476,435, and labor union membership had grown to 18,117,000 (the growth of the labor unions was stunted by the radical shift from "blue" collar to "white" collar workers during this period). In 1945, defense spending consumed 40% of the gross national product; this had declined to 10% by 1960. The United States had been able to shift from a wartime employment situation to a peace-time situation without radical unemployment (the Korean War in the fifties and the Vietnam war in the sixties also helped reduce unemployment). The percentage of unemployed persons moved from 3.8 in 1948 to a high of 6.8 in 1957 and remained in the four to six range for most of the period. This changed radically in 1975 when it jumped to nine percent, and did not drop back below eight for several years.[26] For most of the 35 years, Americans were able to find employment and participate in the "feast."

PHILANTHROPY

The real, and inflation-fueled, growth of the American economy between the years 1945 and 1980 had a radical impact on the life of American churches, including the Reformed Church.

For much of recorded history, the church served as the main motivator and institutional channel of philanthropy, and this was so

as much in early America as in medieval Europe. Church groups
in the new settlements of the New World served as the principal
recipients of alms and as dispensers, to the worthy, of goods, services and advice. With four out of ten philanthropic dollars still
going to, or through, religious groups, religion continues to play
a major role in both the motivations and dispensations of philanthropy. The course of modern giving, however, can be seen largely
as a process of secularization and of institutionalization outside of
organized religion.[27]

Several trends in the decades of the fifties, sixties, and seventies
provided major warnings to philanthropical organizations, especially those in the religious sector. Although all of them received
more money, in total dollars, than had ever been given before,
the cumulative effect of the trends would create major difficulties
for them as they entered the eighties. ". . . there are profound,
and in some areas, troubling, shifts happening in the interrelated
realms of voluntary organization and philanthropy, changes that
reflect, as these quintessential elements of American society must,
broad churnings in the society as a whole."[28] Thus, although the
Reformed Church in America experienced astronomical increases
in the dollars contributed to it for mission on all levels (local
congregations, classical, particular synod, General Synod, and
other missions), the giving trends boded ill for providing the
necessary financial resources for the continuing programs of the
church.

CONTRIBUTIONS

The American people gave $6.6 billion to philanthropic causes
(religion, education, social welfare, health and hospitals, arts and
humanities, civic and public, and other areas) in 1955. By 1979
this had grown to $43.31 billion, an astounding growth of 556%
in 24 years. A comparison of this growth rate with the gross
national product for the years 1968 through 1979 shows that,
instead of a significant growth in philanthropy, giving in the United
States had actually declined during these 12 years.

Year	Total Giving	Gross National Product	% of GNP
1968	$17.56	$ 865.2	2.03
1969	19.57	930.3	2.10
1970	20.75	977.1	2.12
1971	22.84	1,054.9	2.16
1972	23.30	1,158.0	2.01
1973	25.60	1,306.3	1.96
1974	27.71	1,406.9	1.96
1975	29.68	1,499.0	1.98
1976	32.54	1,691.4	1.92
1977	36.02	1,887.2	1.91
1978	39.63	2,106.9	1.88
1979	453.31	2,368.8	1.83[29]

A study by the economist Ralph Nelson has shown that giving, as a proportion of personal income, had dropped 15% from 1960 through 1972. When compared with government spending, the shift becomes more significant. In 1960 private giving was one-ninth of government spending (not including defense spending), but it had dropped to less than one-fourteenth by 1974.[30] The American people, because of the ravages of inflation and a shift in their personal priorities, became less and less philanthropic during the decades of the fifties, sixties, and seventies.

RECIPIENTS

Several categories have been used to describe the recipients of the American philanthropic dollar. In one study, the categories were: religious institutions, health and welfare, education, civic and cultural, and all others. Using these categories the study charted the percentage of total giving going to the five categories. In 1940 religious institutions were receiving 57% of the philanthropic dollar; this had declined to 46% by 1974. Health and welfare began at 20% in 1940, increased to 26% by 1950, declined to 20% by 1960, and grew to 25% by 1974. Education had declined from 1940 to 1950, increased from 1950 through 1970, and declined from 1970 to 1974. The major gainer was civic and cultural, which followed a steady growth pattern from one percent in 1940 to eight percent by 1974. Thus, although religious institutions increased their receipts from $3.33 billion in 1955 to $20.14 billion in 1979, they received a smaller percentage of the American philanthropic dollar at the end of the period than at the beginning. From almost 50% at the beginning of the period, its percentage declined to 41% at the beginning of the seventies. Although the percentage had climbed back to almost 46% by 1979, the major benefactors were the new religious movements (such as "electronic church"), rather than the historic religious institutions. Religious institutions, faced with a society that has reduced its philanthropic giving, are also faced with receiving a declining share of the dollars contributed.

CONTRIBUTORS

A third area of statistics, that of the contributors, sheds additional light on the situations confronting religious institutions in America as they seek support from the voluntary sector. The University of Michigan, in a study for the Commission on Private Philanthropy and Public Needs, determined the shares of giving and percentages of households compared to the 1973 total household income.

1973 Income	% Households	% Giving less
$4,000	16%	2%
4,000-7,999	19%	4%
8,000-9,999	13%	10%
10,000-14,999	23%	20%
15,000-19,999	16%	18%
20,000-29,999	10%	17%
30,000-49,999	3%	8%
50,000-99,999	.67%	11%
100,000 and up	.016%	10%

The survey shows that most of the giving in America (54%) comes from the 87% of the households having an annual income of less than $20,000. Additionally, the survey demonstrated that the "higher-income givers give more of their monies to educational and cultural organizations and hospitals while lower-income donors give above all to religion."[31] Thus, the religious institutions of America face a third challenge: as inflation raises the annual income of the population, they must fight the trend of higher-income people giving less to religion and more to other philanthropic causes seeking their support.

> All told, the prevailing financial pattern of the nonprofit sector has become one of uncommonly higher costs, more resources required for old problems and new solutions, more uses needing greater aggregate subsidies for traditional services and new, less traditional groups adding their claim to the philanthropic pie. And it has been, in terms of private support, a barely growing pie all this time, not growing at all of late in terms of the real purchasing power of private contributions. This is the pattern that underlies the very real financial difficulties—"crisis" is no hyperbole here— of the philanthropic world.[32]

The giving of individuals, the source of most of the philanthropic dollar, had declined by 15% from 1960 through 1972. In 1960 the figure represented 1.97% of personal income; it had declined to 1.67% by 1972.[33]

The Reformed Church faced special challenges because of these changes in giving patterns by Americans. As inflation increased the annual income of its members, they moved from lower middle class on through to upper middle class. This changed the focus of their giving from predominantly to the church to include educational and civic groups. Thus, the church, in addition to receiving a smaller percentage of its members' personal income, also received a smaller percentage of their personal giving. All the while, inflation greatly increased the costs for maintaining the local programs of the church and also made a negative impact on the denomination's mission and education programs.

The apparent increases in American philanthropy provided similar affluence to the Reformed Church. As delegates gathered at the 1945 General Synod, they could reflect on 15 or 20 lean years in the life of their church. As they gathered at the 1980 General Synod, they could look back on 35 years of apparently astounding increases in giving to their church. A comparison of the financial information reported to the 1945 and 1980 General Synods shows:

LOCAL CHURCH REPORTS	1945	1980
Congregational Purposes	4,773,776	64,308,641
Denominational Mission	1,209,518	7,282,289
General Synod Mission		
Special Fund Drives	485,149	
Classical, PS	3,092,746	
TOTAL	5,983,294	76,003,545[34]

The Reformed Church benefited from the tremendous increase in American philanthropy and the inflation of the dollar. In just 35 years the annual income to local churches increased $70,020,251. No one, projecting the income of the church in 1945, ever would have expected this tremendous surge, but, on the other hand, no one would have projected the tremendous impact of inflation which severely limited the purchasing power of this giving.

TECHNOLOGY

Alvin Toffler, who alerted people to the tremendous psychological impact of the mid-twentieth century's massive changes in *Future Shock*, went on in the *Third Wave* to call the technological revolution the third wave of major human change. The first two waves were the agricultural revolution and the industrial revolution. The "third wave" made a profound impact on the life of the Reformed Church and its members, but only two small segments will be described in our story.

The first is the revolution in transportation brought about by the jet airplane. Prior to the airplane, the fastest a person could travel from Chicago, the nearest midwestern point, to New York City was 24 hours by train. With the arrival of the propeller airplane, travel time was reduced to 10 or 12 hours. With the jet plane, it became possible to make the trip in less than three hours. Before this technological advance, the leadership of the Reformed Church had to live near New York City. In fact, the 1848 reorganization of the Board of Domestic Missions added Jersey City to New York City as a place of residency for members of the board. Although constitutional restrictions limiting membership on the church's boards no longer existed in the forties and the fifties, travel limitations forced the church to select its leadership from the greater New York area. The jet plane changed that geographical restriction. People could travel from California to New York for a one-day meeting. The technological advance of the jet plane made it possible for the church to respond to "democratizing" tendencies and elect people from the various sections of the nation, rather than just those living close to New York.

A second technological advance, the computer, affected the business milieu more than it directly affected the work of the church. Business people found it possible to carry out more and more complex operations through the utilization of the computer. Larger and larger businesses could be operated and controlled through this technology, making it possible for smaller units to be merged into larger units. New economies and efficiencies were gained through the mergers. These gains, which were sought for the church in the 1967 creation of the Office of Administration and Finance, were increasingly the experience of business persons in the late fifties and early sixties. When elected to leadership positions in their church, the business people sought to bring the same efficiencies to the work of the church.

CONCLUSION

As the Reformed Church in America, through its members and leaders, participated in American life through the exciting years from 1945 through 1980, it participated in the "terrible feast." Because her leaders unconsciously adapted their levels of expectation from the church, especially in the area of financial support, the "feast" sides of American life came to be the expected. With the rapid increases in financial support experienced into the late 1950s, the annual General Synod regularly increased the mission/education budgets. For a time, the budgets were almost met, but then the "terrible" sides of the American experience began to be felt. The annual budgets were not met. The church stopped growing.

Since the leaders of the Reformed Church did not perceive the societal trends taking place in religion, population, economy, and philanthropy, they did not adequately prepare the church for these trends. As religion became less important in the life of the American people, the Reformed Church was doubly hit with the population shift away from its historic urban centers of strength. As the American people began to give a smaller percentage of their income to religious institutions, the Reformed Church also experienced a loss of its historic economic base. While the Reformed Church had experienced great abundance during the first years following World War II, the social trends following 1955 brought complex problems into the life of the church.

Donald Luidens, an associate professor of sociology at Hope College, has drawn a 1977 portrait of the membership of the Reformed Church. Based on a scientifically developed and circulated questionnaire, he was able to paint the following portrait of the membership of the RCA toward the close of our thirty-five-year period.

> . . . over 98 percent are Caucasian; only a small fraction of the members come from Asian, American Indian, Mexican or African backgrounds . . . over half the entire membership claims Dutch

heritage . . . Well over a majority of each midwestern synod's members claim Dutch heritage. By contrast, a quarter or less of the members from the eastern synods have Dutch backgrounds . . . the Reformed Church lay membership is an especially elderly one. Half of the active communicants are over 50 years old . . . only one quarter of the communicants are between 16 and 34. In contrast, about one-third of American adults are over 50, and fully 43 percent are between 16 and 34 years old . . . While 52 percent of all Americans are women, 55 percent of the members of the Reformed Church are females . . . While barely a quarter of the American people have completed more than a high school degree, over half of the Reformed Church lay membership has had some form of post-high school education; another 24 percent have completed high school . . . The RCA is an upper-middle class denomination . . . A quarter of the members are involved in professional and managerial occupations; another quarter are employed in sales positions and in skilled and semiskilled labor; a third quarter are housewives and homemakers; and the final quarter are . . . retirees (15 percent), students (five percent), and farmers (six percent) . . . Reformed Church membership, regardless of particular synod, is primarily a small-town enterprise. Over half of our members are from communities of under 20,000 people. On the other hand, barely five percent of our members are in cities larger than 250,000 . . . An especially large number (four out of ten) of active communicants are participants in congregations which have fewer than 250 members.[35]

Since a similar study was not carried out in 1945, no comparisons to determine the shifts between 1945 and 1977 can be made.

III

The United Advance: A Coordinated Fund-Raising Program

As delegates gathered for the 1946 General Synod of the Reformed Church in America, they came with a new sense of hope and optimism for the future. The wars in Europe and the Pacific had finally concluded. The American economy, which had suffered a devastating crash in 1929 and had been further disrupted by the 1930 droughts in the major agricultural areas of the nation, seemed to be moving out of the wartime focus on the military and into a peace-time opportunity to provide for the long delayed needs of the people. The leaders of the Reformed Church had been preparing for this new day of challenge and opportunity. The Staff Conference, an unofficial group composed of the staff executives of the boards of the church (Board of Foreign Missions, Board of Domestic Missions, Woman's Board of Foreign Missions, Women's Board of Domestic Missions, Board of Education, and the Ministers' Fund), had been surveying the major program needs of the church. As they reviewed the domestic and international needs of the mission programs of the church, they developed a proposal unprecedented in the life of the Reformed Church. Because the needs and opportunities were so overwhelming and engaged every aspect of the church's life, the Staff Conference prepared a proposal for a "united approach" to the church. Rather than have each board present its urgent and large needs for new financial resources to the individual congregations, the Staff Conference submitted a proposal that sought to minimize competition for the resources of the church and maximize the possibilities for the members of the RCA to meet the massive challenges of the post-war period.

78

BACKGROUND

The denominational programs of the church had suffered through a long financial drought. Beginning in 1930, when contributions for the national programs of the church declined from $1,291,576 in 1929 to $986,387, the members of the church had decreased their giving six straight years. The lowest point was reached in 1935 when giving declined to $521,550—a loss of more than fifty percent in six short years. Gradually the giving of the church had increased, but by 1945 it had not even reached the 1929 level (a total giving for 1945 of $1,209,518 was reported to the participants in the 1946 General Synod). As important for the leadership of the church, the percentage given for denominational programs had declined from a high of twenty-seven percent in 1921 to a low of fifteen percent in 1935. By 1945 the percentage had climbed back to twenty percent, but congregations in the Reformed Church were already being required to spend more and more of their financial resources on maintaining their local church programs.

All of the programs of the church had suffered greatly from these years of financial "drought." The Board of Foreign Missions had been forced to keep missionaries in the United States because there were no funds to send them to the field. New missionaries could not be appointed, and candidates were encouraged to seek ministries in the United States until funds became available for their appointment. New building programs in Japan, China, India, and the Middle East had to be canceled, and greatly-needed maintenance was deferred from year to year. The Board of Domestic Missions did not have funds for beginning new churches, nor could it maintain its missionary thrusts among the new immigrants to the United States. The educational institutions of the Reformed Church; its colleges: Hope, Central, and Northwestern; and its seminaries: New Brunswick and Western; had delayed desperately-needed maintenance and building programs. The church faced major challenges in all areas of its life and work as it sought to recover from the devastating effects of the Great Depression and World War II.

Similar, though less extensive, challenges faced the Reformed Church at the conclusion of World War I. At that time a special "progress" campaign was developed to meet the needs. The goal of the campaign, for the denominatioal benevolent program, was annual giving of $1,000,000 by 1923. The goals for local churches were: double church membership; one candidate for the ministry; efficient teacher training classes for Sunday school teachers; training classes for young people in service; an every-member canvass; preaching on proportionate giving; a "live" men's missionary society; a "live" women's missionary society; a community church; pro rata giving to all the boards; and one-fifth of the members subscribing to the denominational weekly.[1] The campaign was conducted through establishing organizations at the classical, the particular synod, and the General Synod levels. The goal of $1,000,000 per year was met in 1921, and then again in the years 1925 through 1929. The 1923 General Synod formed the "Progress Council" to carry through the work of the campaign. Its major function was to promote the work of the national boards throughout the life of the church.

PROPOSAL

The Staff Conference proposal called for a special "united approach" to the church for a total of $2,300,000. The proposal described the many programs that would benefit from the funds. Included were: rebuilding churches, schools, and hospitals destroyed by the war in China and Japan, providing relief for war-devastated Europe, carrying out maintenance programs at New Brunswick and Western seminaries, building dormitories at Central and Hope and a classroom building at Northwestern, establishing ten new churches in the growing areas of the United States, and providing a special emergency fund for evangelism and church extension. Because of the importance and scope of the proposal, the General Synod appointed a special committee to review it. Five elders and eleven ministers spent many hours during the sessions of synod thoroughly studying the proposal.

Based on its study, the committee reported to its fellow delegates:

> We have thoroughly considered the report of the Staff Conference which proposes a United Advance and we realize the importance of such a program . . . We highly commend the Boards of our Church for submitting to our General Synod this splendid program which gives evidence of vital unity . . . We also took into account that if the Boards did not appeal to the Church in unity, they would appeal separately. It would then be a free-for-all. Whichever Board could tell the biggest "sob-story" or whichever presented the best "salesmen" would garner in the lion's share of the gifts . . . Underlying this request for funds is the realization that if our Church is to succeed in this, we must be a revitalized Church. We must seek first to be a purified people. The promise is that if we seek first the Kingdom of God and His righteousness all other things shall be added unto us.[2]

The General Synod adopted the recommendations of its special committee that a united appeal be conducted. Specifically, it called for a recognition of "the imperative urgency of evangelism, church revitalization, and church extension; and that we recommend that this program seek to be first a spiritual advance; and that the Committee be instructed to make evangelism the underlying purpose."[3] After passing various implementing actions, the General Synod requested ". . . the entire Denomination to be much in prayer, so that with God's blessing and the deepening of our spiritual lives this crusade may be a blessing to His Glory."[4]

PROGRAM

Writing to the ministers and consistories of the Reformed Church, Marion de Velder, the newly-appointed director of the United Advance, declared the ". . . heart of the United Advance is stewardship and evangelism; complete dedication of self to God and outreach for Christ. We believe it is God's clear call to our

Church and people. We ask you to answer this call by thought and prayer which shall result in enthusiastic support and fuller participation as this movement goes forward."[5] Evangelism and stewardship—these were the two aspects of the Christian life which received continued focus during the United Advance program.

Dr. Jacob Prins, who had been appointed to the new executive staff position of minister for evangelism by the Board of Domestic Missions in 1944, was the associate director of the United Advance program. He carried direct responsibility for its evangelistic phase. A new organizational structure was proposed which called for committees on evangelism at the congregational, the classical, and the particular synod levels. The department of evangelism of the Board of Domestic Missions served as the national evangelism committee. Each local church was challenged to:

> Careful, prayerful planning for a minimum of a "WEEK OF WIT-
> NESSING" . . . By lay leaders chosen and trained in the task of
> winning men to faith in Jesus Christ as Savior and Lord . . . Special
> Evangelistic services in the Fall and early Spring to inspire our
> own people . . . to greater concentration in witnessing to Christ
> by life and lip . . . Plans for possible Rural Church evangelistic
> crusades in churchless and pastorless communities using tent,
> school-house, hall, empty country store-building or open air . . .
> One afternoon and evening set aside each week for visiting, by lay
> men and lay women and youth, the unsaved, and those unrelated
> to any local church and for personal soul winning.[6]

The objective of the evangelism portion of the United Advance was "To win more men to Christ, to build them up in Christ, to direct them into service for Christ." Its goal was "Every believer winning others to faith in Christ."[7]

Stewardship, the second main "spearhead" of the advance, was "understood as the complete committal to God on the part of every Christian."[8] Through the literature developed for the advance, the members of the Reformed Church were challenged to make this commitment. As a symbol of their commitment of themselves and their resources to God, they were called to make a major financial commitment to the United Advance programs.

The United Advance included mission programs in five areas: relief, foreign missions reconstruction, home missions, evangelism and extension, and educational institutions. The specific programs within the five categories were:

Relief: Overseas relief and reconstruction (primarily in Europe), chaplains, orphan missions, war prisoners, American Bible Society; $550,000.

Reconstruction in Foreign Mission Fields: China: $257,000; Japan: $114,000; Miscellaneous: $9,000; for a total of $380,000.

Home Missions: Ten new churches: $100,000; Trade School and Expansion, Brewton: $75,000; Indian Fields: $47,000; Kentucky: $21,000; Miscellaneous: $7,000; for a total of $250,000.

Evangelism and Extension: larger evangelistic programs and general extension of the RCA: $200,000.

Educational Institutions: Hope (for dormitories): $320,000; Central (for a dormitory): $300,000; Northwestern (for a classroom building): $200,000; New Brunswick Seminary (restoring campus buildings): $100,000; and Western Seminary (new classroom building): $200,000; for a total of $1,120,000.

The grand total for the United Advance Fund was $2,500,000.[9] This was an unprecedented financial challenge for the Reformed Church. To seek to meet this challenge, a highly-organized plan was developed for the "fund-raising" side of the United Advance.

ORGANIZATION

The United Advance was the most comprehensive evangelism and stewardship program ever to be undertaken by the Reformed Church in America. In order to accomplish this new challenge, special plans were developed. A General Committee composed of representatives of the forty-two classes, plus fourteen other persons, was established. This committee appointed a Central Committee to act as an executive group. The members of the

Central Committee were: chairman, Bernard J. Mulder; director, Marion de Velder; associate director, Jacob Prins; associate director, Daniel Y. Brink; and representatives from the nine geographical areas (upper New York State, central area, Michigan area, west central area, north Jersey area, south Jersey area, lower New York area, mid-Hudson area and far west area) of the Reformed Church. The Central Committee provided guidance and counsel to the directors of the advance. Under the area committees, each classis formed a committee and each church within each classis was expected to form a committee.

United Advance Director Marion de Velder carried out his responsibility while serving as the pastor of the Hope Reformed Church of Holland, Michigan. The consistory of Hope Church released de Velder to provide the "staff" services for the advance. The major responsibilities of Jacob Prins, as the advance's associate director, were for the spiritual aims of the advance, with a special focus on the evangelism programs. The second associate director, Daniel Y. Brink, pastor of the Trinity Reformed Church, West New York, New Jersey, supervised the campaign in the eastern synods. Bernard J. Mulder, who had recently become executive secretary of the Board of Education after having served as editor of the denomination's weekly magazine, was the chairman of the Central Committee. These four clergymen provided the major organizational leadership for the advance.

After describing the organization of the program, an early brochure concludes:

The successful prosecution of the Advance program rests upon: 1. A thorough understanding by *all* of the need for United Advance and the causes of the Advance Fund. 2. The numbers of people mobilized, including all the constituency—adults, youth and children. 3. The cooperation of all avenues—directors, area chairmen and committees, classis committees, pastors, consistories, local church committees. 4. The enlistment of *every* member of the Reformed Church in praying, working and giving.[10]

The Central Committee developed an "equal shares" program which assigned a portion of the total $2,500,000 goal to each of the nine areas, and then expected that the area, because it knew the local situation best, would assign the appropriate portion of its goal to the classes and the local churches. The equal shares were based upon the membership of the churches and their past record of giving to benevolences. Classical visitors met with local consistories and asked them to accept the "equal shares" goal for their church. The "equal shares" were not more than eighteen dollars nor less than twelve dollars per member.

After the local consistory had accepted its "equal share," the local committee was expected to visit every family within the congregation. The purpose of the visit was to share information about the United Advance program and to solicit a pledge from the family. Not all the local churches conducted an every-family visit, but those that did had the most success in meeting their commitment to their "equal share."

The organization and style for the United Advance program borrowed heavily from other denominations and secular organizations (such as the Community Chest) which were conducting similar programs. Several times in the advance's literature references are made to these secular groups. Through the incorporation of the fund-raising strategies of these other groups, the leadership of the United Advance secured the largest commitment ever made by the members of the RCA to their denominational mission and educational programs.

RESULTS

Marion de Velder presented a progress report on the financial results of the United Advance to the 1948 General Synod. He was able to report that by April 30, 1948, a total of $1,694,898 had been received toward the goal of $2,500,000. The money had been disbursed to:

RELIEF:

Church World Service	$525,397
American Bible Society	$10,028
War Prisoners Aid	$5,000
German Relief	$3,938
Holland Relief	$923
Miscellaneous	$3,319
TOTAL	$548,605

FOREIGN MISSIONS:

Board of Foreign Missions	$258,000
Foreign Missions Conference	$3,685
International Missionary Council	$1,315
TOTAL	$263,000

HOME MISSIONS:

Board of Domestic Missions	$153,232
Women's Board	$57,276
TOTAL	$210,508

EDUCATIONAL INSTITUTIONS:

TOTAL	$611,298

PROMOTION AND ADMINISTRATION

TOTAL	$ 46,508

The final report was presented to the 1949 General Synod. By that time the total receipts had reached almost $2,000,000.

Although the fund-raising portion of the United Advance did not reach its goal of $2,500,000, the Reformed Church, through the advance, took a signficant step forward in financing its mission and education programs. In 1945 the average per-member gift for the denominational benevolent program in the Reformed Church was $6.95. The goal of the United Advance program was to produce double that amount for a special program, while maintaining the regular giving, in the short time of twenty months. Twenty-six classes, which had averaged $3.73 per member in

1945, were asked to raise an additional $12 per member, and sixteen classes, which had raised $12.04 per member, were asked to raise an additional $18 per member. The denomination was asked to raise more than double its 1945 benevolent giving through the twenty-month campaign. By 1948, because of the efforts of the United Advance, the average per-member giving to benevolences had risen from the $6.95 of 1945 to $13.70. In 1945, 75% of local congregational monies were used for their own purposes, and 25% were given for the mission/educational programs of the General Synod. By 1948, these figures had changed to 62% for local congregational purposes and 38% for the benevolent causes of the denomination. Through the efforts of the United Advance, the benevolent giving of the church had doubled in three years—from $1,209,000 in 1945 to $2,400,000 in 1948.

The United Advance had demonstrated conclusively that the Reformed Church could link its spiritual commitments to evangelism and stewardship with the secular fund-raising techniques emerging in American philanthropy. The evangelistic thrusts of the United Advance had not only brought new awareness of evangelistic responsibility within the church, it had also produced growing churches and the planting of new churches.

CONTINUATION

The United Advance, through the efforts of the General Committee, the Central Committee, and the three directors, brought the greatest focus on stewardship for mission and evangelism that the Reformed Church had ever experienced. Prior efforts had been made to stimulate more faithful stewardship throughout the church, but none had been as intensive. As the first year of the advance program drew to a close, the benefits derived from an intensive program in stewardship became increasingly clear. Based on this experience, the advance recommended to the 1947 General Synod that it

. . . give careful consideration to the appointment of a permanent committee on stewardship, to replace the present standing committee (a standing committee only met during the sessions of General Synod) on systematic beneficence. This committee on stewardship would have as its goal to do all possible to stimulate benevolent giving, both on the individual level by enlistment in tithing or any other income deduction plan, and on the church level by helping local churches to raise the proportion of benevolent gifts to that raised for local needs to a respectable proportion. This permanent committee could gear into the United Advance now and carry on beyond 1948 with a long term emphasis.[11]

The General Synod adopted the recommendation and appointed a new, permanent committee on stewardship.

After its first year of work in close cooperation with the leadership of the United Advance, the committee reported to the 1948 General Synod: "While others are charged with the responsibility of shaping the policy of the church for benevolent appeals, this Committee regards its work of long range importance in cultivating the joy of Christian giving in the membership of the Churches."[12] The committee recommended that a full-time "minister of stewardship" be employed by the Board of Direction (the permanent committee of the General Synod) for promoting the cause of stewardship. The General Synod defeated this recommendation.

The permanent committee did not have a successful second year. Its report to the 1949 General Synod laments its lack of laymen, budget, and progress. The lamentation closes with the recommendation that the committee be dissolved because of the recommendation contained in the report of the United Advance Committee. A later General Synod dissolved the committee—with thanks for their efforts.

In closing their final report to the General Synod, the Central Committee of the United Advance presented suggestions for future action. Having learned that

. . . a united approach appeals to leaders and laymen alike . . . Our suggestions for the future focus upon consideration of a united approach to the Church. We believe that the success of the United

Advance Fund warrants a careful study of a united approach on a permanent basis. We therefore suggest that the General Synod appoint a commission (to be called the Commission on United Approach) to make a thorough study in the areas of planning and promotion . . . In the area of planning, this commission should have the following responsibilities: 1. To study and review the activities and needs of the Boards and Institutions of the Church in relation to a balanced and properly coordinated program. 2. To study and evaluate the various phases in the history and past record of the Reformed Church in benevolent giving and to suggest the most effective methods and program of approach to the Church. In the field of promotion, this commission should suggest plans and methods to enlist interest and support of the local church and the individual church members . . . If this or a similar promotional program is carried on, we shall be pursuing the original aims set up for the United Advance Fund, which were: 1. A new sense of responsibility on the part of our people; 2. A more adequate understanding of the total program of the Church; 3. An endeavor to make all of our churches truly stewardship churches; and 4. Confrontal of every Reformed Church member with a thrilling Kingdom program. [13]

The General Synod adopted the recommendation, and a ten-member commission was appointed.

After a year filled with activity and study, the commission reported to the 1950 General Synod. Its study had included a review of previous efforts at stewardship in the Reformed Church, a survey of the programs being carried out by other denominations, and an analysis of the needs of the Reformed Church. The primary needs of the church were identified to be:

Our denominational program should be coordinated . . . In the area of planning we need (a) a clearly defined and coordinated denominational program conceived on a long-range basis, with the annual program carefully planned and projected with special emphasis . . . (b) a comprehensive benevolent budget representing the Church's needs on the denominational level . . . (c) an organization, based upon democratic representation drawn from the various areas of the Church, to study the needs and programs and make recommendations to the General Synod, functioning as General Synod's permanent committee. We suggest that this committee be called the Reformed Church Stewardship Council . . . In the field of promotion, we need: (a) adequate stewardship cultivation, coordinating and integrating existing facilities wherever possible, in presenting the benevolent needs . . . (b) detailed methods of presentation to every member of the local congregation through committees, called Stewardship Councils, in each Particular Synod, Classis and local church, and through effective promotional materials and tools. . . .[14]

The report concluded with recommendations for the formation of the Stewardship Council. Its responsibility was

To be the responsible agency for coordinating, stimulating, and promoting the general denominational program and for insuring effective communication of the total Church program to the local congregations and the individual church members . . . (Its) membership 1 minister and 1 layman from each Particular Synod, 2 women from the membership of the Church at large, the four presidents of the Boards of Foreign Missions, Domestic Missions, Education and Ministers' Fund, retiring President of General Synod, the Stated Clerk of General Synod and one executive from the four Boards as corresponding members.[15]

The report included an extensive organizational chart for the new council. "The necessary operating expenses shall be met from General Synod Funds by the Board of Direction, from assessment on Church membership. If the Council finds that it must employ part-time or full-time leadership, the expense involved and the nomination must be approved by General Synod."[16] After thorough debate, the General Synod found itself unable to adopt these "far-reaching" recommendations. It commended the commission for its work, and asked it to continue its studies in cooperation with the Staff Conference and report to the 1951 General Synod.

After the year's study and consultation, the commission presented a series of recommendations to the 1951 General Synod. The majority of the new recommendations were an expansion and detailing of those presented the previous year. The major new emphasis came in the recommendation to hire an executive officer, to be elected by the General Synod upon nomination by the commission. Once again it was recommended that the expenses of the commission and its staff be paid through the General Synod assessment budget. Even after an additional year of study and more information, the General Synod was not ready to take this major, pioneering step. The report was received and referred to the classes for study.

In 1952 the "Commission on a United Approach" was able to share the results of the classical studies. "The general conclusion is that the large majority favor a united approach to the denominational benevolence program and of this program to the churches as well as a much greater emphasis and urgency in Stewardship, but a number of Classes wish to limit the proposal as to centralization, additional personnel and more expense."[17]

Rather than present specific recommendations in 1952, as it had done extensively in 1950 and 1951, the commission suggested that the General Synod decide "what organization and provisions it wishes to authorize for the denominational benevolence and stewardship program."[18] The General Synod responded by appointing a special committee to review the reports of 1949, 1950, 1951, and 1952 and prepare recommendations for its adoption. With the exception of the appointment of an executive officer and the organization chart, the special committee recommended the adoption of the 1951 recommendations of the Commission on a United Approach. The Reformed Church Stewardship Council was established for a two-year period (to be evaluated by the 1954 General Synod) and the treasurer of General Synod was instructed to pay its expenses. The United Advance, which was begun by the 1946 General Synod, made its final, and possibly most significant, impact on the Reformed Church in 1952 with the creation of the Reformed Church Stewardship Council.

IV

The Reformed Church Stewardship Council—An Agency for Coordinating Budget Building and Fund Raising

After three years of study and discussion, the Reformed Church Stewardship Council was established by the General Synod of 1952. It began to function that fall and continued to serve the Reformed Church until 1968 when, with the Boards of World Mission, North American Mission, and Education, it was merged into the newly-established General Program Council.

PURPOSE

The General Synod established the Stewardship Council to

> present to the general synod a comprehensive program and to insure effective communication of the total Church program to the local congregations and individual church members . . . (including) (a) the proposals of the Boards as submitted through the Staff Conference, and the financial appeals of the Educational Institutions after approval by the Board of Education. The proposals of other Reformed Church agencies shall be included after approval by a related Board. (b) Any other proposals that may be presented . . . which aim to appeal to the whole Church for financial support . . . and recommend to the general synod a comprehensive benevolence program to be commended to the whole church.[1]

After the annual General Synod had adopted the "comprehensive benevolence" program, the council was to coordinate "the presentation to the church of the approved benevolence program . . . (and) review plans and methods for the promotion of interest and support of all the approved program. . . ."[2]

The creation of the Stewardship Council brought the Reformed Church in America's second major revision to the Church Order adopted at the great Synod of Dort. The first occurred with the formation of the mission boards of the General Synod in the early nineteenth century. More than a century later the Reformed Church created a council (the word was nowhere defined and some of the proposals used the word commission) to review and coordinate the budget-making and promotional activities of its boards. Neither of these major revisions arose from careful theological reflection on the nature of the church and its assemblies. Neither the delegates to the early-nineteenth-century General Synods nor the delegates to the mid-twentieth-century General Synods that debated these latter-day additions to the classical Reformed Church order presented rationale from theology or polity for their addition to the life of the church. In fact, both the boards of the nineteenth century and the Stewardship Council of the twentieth century were created by legislative action, and no amendments were initially proposed in the government of the Reformed Church to provide for them. The challenges of the times called for new instruments, and the General Synod, though hesitant and deliberate, was prepared to create them. Theological reflection, and revisions in the official polity of the church, would follow the practical implementation of the new structures.

ORGANIZATION

The first Reformed Church Stewardship Council was composed of sixteen members—somewhat smaller than initially proposed by the Commission on a United Approach. The membership consisted of: one member from each board of the church (Board of Foreign Missions, Board of Domestic Missions, Board of Education, Ministers' Fund, and *The Church Herald*), three members at large, appointed by the president of General Synod, the president and the stated clerk of General Synod, five lay persons appointed by the particular synods, and one representative from the educational institutions.

Two important shifts occurred with the establishment of the

membership of the Stewardship Council. First, staff members of the various boards of the church became full members of a General Synod agency. Prior to this time, staff members did not have the privilege of membership in official bodies of the General Synod. Second, the particular synods elected their own representatives to the council. An earlier report had called for "democratic representation" on the council through election by the various particular synods. The membership provisions for the new "council" sought to achieve a representative base throughout the church. The purpose was to insure an adequate hearing for the diverse mind of the church on the priority matter of reviewing budgets and establishing financial goals for its ongoing mission programs.

Two General Synods made changes in the membership of the Stewardship Council during its fifteen years of service to the Reformed Church. The 1961 General Synod shifted the executive secretaries of the boards from membership on the council to consultants to the council, added persons from the four program boards of the church, and increased the membership of the council to provide for six local pastors (with the division of the Particular Synod of Chicago into the Particular Synods of Chicago and Michigan, there were already six lay persons from the particular synods, and this revision added six pastors). When the responsibility for recommending the annual benevolent budget to General Synod was shifted to the General Synod Executive Committee, the membership of the Stewardship Council was reduced through the removal of those persons, mainly representatives of the four program boards, whose primary task had been the review of the annual budgets. With the exception of these changes, the Stewardship Council served the Reformed Church under its original membership and mandate until 1968.

FIRST REPORT

The newly-formed Stewardship Council held it first meeting in the fall of 1952 and presented its first report to the General Synod of 1953. The report focused on the council's two main areas of responsibility: the development of a comprehensive benevolent budget for the Reformed Church, and the promotion of the benevolent budget adopted by the annual General Synod.

The Stewardship Council had reviewed the 1954 budget requests of the national boards of the church. Because six of the sixteen members of the council represented boards which had presented budgets for review, the task of the council was made easier but more complex: easier because persons were present to explain all portions of the budgets under review; more complex because any revisions or adjustments in the submitted budgets needed to receive the concurrence—or at least acquiescence—of the representative of the particular program under review.

The council proposed, and the General Synod adopted, the following benevolent budget for 1954:

	Budget	% of Undesignated
Board of Foreign Missions	$ 790,000	37%
Board of Domestic Missions	640,000	30%
Church Building Fund	106,000	5%
Board of Education and educational institutions	433,000	16%
The Ministers' Fund	154,000	12%
TOTAL	$2,123,000	100%

The Stewardship Council also presented its plans for promoting the 1954 benevolent budget throughout the church. The council planned to send to all ministers a letter which would acquaint them with the work of the council and the benevolent goals of the church for 1954. Workshops were planned for all the classis and particular synod meetings, to stress the importance of stewardship programs in the local church and to personalize the mission/educational program requiring funding for 1954. Promotional materials were prepared to present the needs of the church to lay persons. "Our Father's Business," a professionally-prepared brochure, visually portrayed the financial needs of the boards and agencies within the General Synod benevolent budget.

As it implemented its new responsibilities for reviewing the budgets of the church's boards, the council had carefully prepared a budget-building process for the approval of the General Synod. The delegates approved the following process: "an operating budget shall be prepared by the boards and submitted to the Staff Conference for study and integration. The unified total askings of all the boards shall be submitted to the Stewardship Council for study and possible revision at a spring meeting of the council and shall then be submitted by the council to the General Synod for consideration and approval."[3] This new process significantly altered the relationship between the General Synod and its boards. Previously, each board had presented its budget and financial request directly to the General Synod. Now, requests had to be presented to an elected "council" of the church for review, and possible revision, before delegates to the General Synod would receive them. In addition, participants in General Synod would receive an integrated budget, not separate presentations by the various programs of the General Synod.

The 1952 General Synod had decided to evaluate the work and existence of the Stewardship Council after two years. Nonetheless, the newly-formed council reported in 1953 ". . . that while the present structure, in fact the very existence, of the Stewardship Council is subject to review and change, the continued existence of such a council for more than the present two year period has been clearly and emphatically asked by the church at large."[4] The members of the newly-created Stewardship Council believed, and history was to confirm their belief, that the Reformed Church in America had established a new, permanent pattern for the relationship between its mission/educational boards and the delegates to the annual General Synod. The new pattern was established through the experience gained in the successful United Advance fund-raising program, and for the purpose of reviewing the annual budgets of the boards and coordinating fund raising for the approved budgets. Gradually, as will be shown in the next chapter, the process of budget review led to a new, and more extensive, review of the relationships between the General Synod and its continuing boards.

STAFF

The Commission on a United Approach to the church strongly urged the employment of an "executive officer" for the newly-formed Stewardship Council, but the 1952 General Synod did not choose to implement this recommendation. The commission reported in 1951:

> In view of the important function and the large responsibility of the Commission on Stewardship and the necessity of executive leadership we recommend the employment of an Executive Officer to be elected by the general synod upon nomination by the commission . . . The responsibility of the Executive Officer will be to work under the direction of the Commission on Stewardship in formulating the annual denominational program for the entire church, and in developing promotional and educational procedures for bringing about understanding and acceptance of the program by the churches and the individual members . . . The Executive Officer should be a mature man in his prime; energetic, imaginative, and ingenious, who is well acquainted with the denomination, its program and problems . . . Whereas the Commission on Stewardship will function as general synod's permanent committee on denominational program, will operate under its direction and as a total service to the whole denomination, we recommend that the funds be raised by the general synod through assessment on church membership.[5]

The 1952 General Synod chose not to appoint a staff member. Maybe they did not do so because of the classical concerns for increased expenses. Maybe they did not do so because of the recommendation that the expenses for the executive officer be placed in the assessment budget, which, with the exception of some nineteenth-century inclusion of funds for theological professors, had been limited to the direct expenses of the General Synod. Because the assessment was a "tax" on the membership of the local churches, items were not easily or quickly added to it. With the exception of the stated clerk, all the other staff members of the church were supported by the budgets of the boards from funds voluntarily given by the churches. Since the special committee of 1952 did not give its reasons for not recommending an executive officer, we are left to speculation.

The Stewardship Council functioned for two years without a staff person. After this time, possibly because the two-year evaluation period had come to an end, the council recommended that "the Staff Conference give consideration to the cooperative employment of a part time minister of stewardship, the expense to be borne by the participating boards on a basis to be mutually agreed upon."[6] The General Synod adopted the recommendation, and referred it to the Staff Conference for implementation.

After a year of study, the Staff Conference concluded that a part-time secretary would not adequately meet the needs of the Stewardship Council. It had contacted the stewardship departments of other denominations and had held extensive conversations with Dr. Thomas K. Thompson, executive director of the joint department of stewardship and benevolence of the National Council of Churches. Through the information gained from these contacts, the Staff Conference recommended that a full-time secretary for stewardship be employed for a five-year period. Initially, all the boards agreed to the recommendation, and assured the funding necessary to employ someone for five years. Just before the 1955 meeting of General Synod, the Executive Committee of the Board of Domestic Missions asked synod to defer action on the recommendation until answers could be provided for three questions. How will the stewardship department be organized and what will its functions be? What is the exact task of the full-time secretary and to whom will he be responsible? What is the actual annual cost of establishing such a department and engaging a full-time secretary? The General Synod honored the request of the board and delayed action until 1956.

In its 1956 report to the General Synod the Stewardship Council presented a recommendation for the employment of a full-time secretary and proposed a budget for the office. It recommended that the secretary report to, and be subject to, the newly-created executive committee of the Stewardship Council. The report assumes that the expenses, which were detailed in an annual budget, would be met by each board paying a proportionate share. The General Synod adopted the recommendation and endorsed the employment of the Rev. Howard G. Teusink.

Howard G. Teusink served as the secretary of the Stewardship Council for twelve years. Immediately before accepting the position with the council, he served as a youth secretary for the Board of Education. During the 1960s, the position of associate director was established. A layman, Edward Unser, first filled the position. The Rev. John Hiemstra, who had served churches in Iowa and Michigan, succeeded Unser and continued in the position until shortly before the work of the Stewardship Council was integrated into the General Program Council.

PROGRAMS

During its sixteen-year period of service to the Reformed Church, the Stewardship Council carried out programs to provide funds for the regular, annual benevolent budget of the church and conducted two special campaigns for major, capital funds. While its programs seeking to communicate and raise funds for the annual budget were many, the major ones fell into five categories: promotional materials, proportionate giving, goals for local churches, every member visitation, and stewardship/ communication workshops.

Several years before the formation of the Stewardship Council the boards had begun the publication of "Our Father's Business," a brochure which was published annually and graphically portrayed the mission programs of the church for the coming year. The council continued this piece and made available additional promotional items, including filmstrips, other brochures, and personal presentations. Through the distribution of promotional information, the council sought to inform the members of the Reformed Church about the challenging programs which were dependent upon RCA members for support.

The United Advance had stressed the importance of proportionate giving in its stewardship materials and had set tithing as a goal for individuals. The Stewardship Council materials and annual reports to General Synod stressed the importance of this giving style for the Christian.

> There is no more effective means of enabling men to keep a proper perspective in the midst of lavish blessings than the Biblical principle of Systematic Proportionate Giving, beginning with the tithe. Such giving inescapably confronts the giver with God—*first!* It underscores the consciousness that God is the source of all one receives. It enables the believer to put the necessities and luxuries of life in their proper place. The Scriptures set the principle before us for our Blessing, not our bane. Our church needs to teach this truth far more resolutely than we have ever done before. Let us not be timid and hesitant where the Scriptures are bold and challenging.[7]

Several years later all churches were encouraged to form a "ten per center" club of those who had agreed to follow the biblical principle of tithing.

The most ambitious program of the Stewardship Council—a five-year plan called Stewardship Advance—was presented to the 1958 General Synod. It incorporated a precise organizational structure to carry out the plan at the particular synod, classis, and congregational levels. The minimum goal for each local church was to increase its benevolent contribution by forty percent in 1959—with those currently giving less than the denominational average being asked to increase more than forty percent. Although no specific goals were established for local churches, the General Synod did adopt benevolent budgets for the next five years (1959-1963). The 1959 budget for current program was $3,105,200, an increase of $413,000 over the 1957 giving. By 1963, the goal was a budget for current program of $4,577,000, a $1,472,000 increase in five years. In addition, a new, special capital budget was developed which began at $710,000 for 1959 and increased to $1,440,000 by 1963. The Stewardship Advance plan established the goal of increasing giving from the Reformed Church to its mission/educational programs from $2,692,504 in 1957 to $6,017,000 in 1963. In 1957, for the first time in its history, the Reformed Church had given more than its approved budget to the denominational benevolent budget. The plan sought to build on this momentum!

As the Stewardship Advance program reached its second and third years, it became clear that the goals would not be reached. Gradually the General Synod reduced the goal for the next year and approved revisions in the program. As the Stewardship Advance came to its end, the General Synod adopted the recommendation of the Stewardship Council that "responsible shares" be established for each classis in the denomination. The "responsible share" was to be fifty cents per week per member, or, where a classis had exceeded that amount, a fifteen-percent increase over its 1962 giving. Each classis was expected to develop a "responsible share" for its churches in order to reach the classical goal.

The "every member visitation program" was seen as a key to stewardship in the local church.

> Another practice which has powerfully assisted men in deepening their dedication to Christ is the Every Member Visitation. This program skillfully employs the scriptural practices of visitation and commitment. The heart of the practice is simply the visitation of each member in his own home to tell the story of the church and to seek his voluntary, grateful commitment to Christ through the church. United Stewardship Training Schools make it possible to train a group of leaders from each church within a given geographical area in such a way that they are then able to go back to their respective churches and train the local helpers who will conduct the visitation.[8]

Through the training of persons to carry out the every member visit, the commitment to stewardship was progressively spread through the local church. Through the actual visits, each member learned about the outreach programs of his church, locally and nationally, and was challenged to respond with his gifts.

A fifth major area of concentration for the Stewardship Council was workshops for training in stewardship techniques and sharing information regarding the programs of the Reformed Church. Thousands of persons throughout the country participated in training sessions for every member visitation, tithing, communicating mission programs, etc. Through these workshops people in the Reformed Church gained new understanding and skills in stewardship and a deeper awareness of the multiple mission and educational programs of their church.

The Stewardship Council participated in two major fund-raising campaigns during its time of service to the Reformed Church. As the campaigns to raise $750,000 for a new building at Western Seminary and $150,000 for campus maintenance at New Brunswick came to an end, the General Synod of 1953 was asked to approve a campaign for $500,000 for the three colleges. The delegates to the 1953 General Synod, faced with a desperate need for capital funds to build new churches, authorized "a campaign throughout the denomination for $750,000 . . . the Colleges would receive two shares of each dollar collected in the campaign, and the Board of Domestic Missions would receive one share."[9] When the Board of Foreign Missions asked to be included in the campaign, the goal was raised to $1,500,000. The monies to be divided forty percent for the three colleges, thirty percent for church buildings, and thirty percent for capital needs on the foreign fields. The Eendracht Campaign, "in unity there is strength," raised a total $1,079,881 toward its $1,500,000 goal.

After the conclusion of the Eendracht Campaign, Central and Hope colleges and New Brunswick Seminary conducted major fund-raising efforts for campus improvements. By 1963, stimulated no doubt by the inability of the Stewardship Advance to raise monies toward its large annual capital goals, conversations had begun regarding a new, denominational fund drive. The 1964 General Synod authorized the Stewardship Council to engage the firm of Ketchum, Inc., to conduct a new, capital funds campaign throughout the church. This was the first time professional fund-raising counsel was utilized by the church. The Reformed

Church Development Fund, conducted in the years 1965 through 1969, resulted from the design of Ketchum, Inc. The Development Fund raised $3,897,000[10] toward its goal of $6,000,000 (a goal which Ketchum, Inc., had cautioned was too high). The goals for the beneficiaries of the Development Fund were: Hope College, $2,000,000; Central College, $1,100,000; Northwestern College, $900,000; North American Missions and Church Extension, $1,200,000; World Missions, $400,000; New Brunswick Seminary, $350,000, and Christian Education, $50,000.

EQUALIZATION

The members of the Reformed Church in America had been giving undesignated monies for many years. Rather than identify a specific program or program board to be the recipient of the funds the donor, whether an individual or a church, would simply give the money to the Staff Conference. For many years these funds were divided according to a board's percentage of the total approved benevolent budget. Thus, when the Board of Foreign Missions had a total of thirty-seven percent allocated to it from the total budget, it received thirty-seven percent of the undesignated monies.

An overture from the Classis of California presented the first request that the procedure for distributing the undesignated monies be changed. The classis overtured the 1953 General Synod to change the procedure by paying all the salary supplements for ministers being supported by the Board of Domestic Missions, all salary, travel expenses, and parsonage rents for the five synodical missionaries, and the travel, salary, and other expenses of the office of the minister of evangelism before distributing the funds according to the percentages in the approved budget. The General Synod did not implement the change requested by the overture, but it did ask the Stewardship Council to study the matter carefully. The Stewardship Council recommended to the 1954 General Synod that no change be made in the procedure for distributing the undesignated monies.

By 1958, the Stewardship Council had revised its thinking and recommended a change in the procedure. The purpose of the change was to "equalize" the total receipts of the various participants in the General Synod benevolent budget. The proposed plan had been developed so that "the percentage table for the distribution of undesignated benevolence gifts, that is, those which do not name a specific board or institution as recipient, may be more sensitive to the mind of the church." The new plan developed by the Stewardship Council provided that "at the conclusion of the year all boards which have received more than their asking shall return to the Staff Conference such funds in excess of their askings as shall have come from undesignated funds. These returned undesignated funds, together with other undesignated funds, shall be used to assure all other boards of their full askings."[11] The General Synod adopted the recommendation of the Stewardship Council. This change in the procedure for distributing the undesignated monies gave the budget-building process authority. A board would now receive monies, through the use of the undesignated funds, according to its approved budget, not according to the designated giving by the church and its members. The new procedure, rather than carrying out the "mind" of the church shown by its designated giving, carried out the "mind" of the church gathered in the annual General Synod which established budgets based on the recommendation of the Stewardship Council.

Within less than a decade, the new equalization system altered the funds available for mission and program in the RCA. A comparison of the years 1955 and 1965 shows the impact:

Receipts from Reformed Church	1955	1965
Board for World Mission	$ 869,978 (38.4%)	1,576,174 (37%)
Board of Domestic Missions	$ 788,850 (34.8%)	1,376,925 (32%)
Church Building Fund	54,826 (2.4%)	155,367 (4%)
Board of Education and educational institutions	424,089 (18.7%)	927,374 (22%)
Board of Pensions	130,108 (5.7%)	218,987 (5%)
TOTAL	$2,276,851	$4,254,827

A more graphic portrayal of the impact of the new equalization system results from applying the old and the new procedures to the undesignated pool of monies for 1965.

	NEW	OLD	
Board for World Mission	103,358 (12.95%)	295,299 (37%)	−191,941
Board of Domestic Missions	255,788 (32.05%)	239,431 (30%)	+16,357
Church Building Fund	104,975 (13.15%)	39,905 (5%)	+65,070
Board of Education and educational institutions	214,991 (26.94%)	127,696 (16%)	+87,295
Board of Pensions	118,933 (14.91%)	95,774 (12%)	+23,219

The major beneficiaries of the new system were the Board of Education, Central College, Northwestern College, and the Board of Pensions. Some years before (around 1950) there had been discussion regarding placing the needs of the fund for retired ministers in the assessment budget, to be certain that an adequate income could be paid to all retired servants of the church. The new equalization system muted those conversations and provided pensions for retirees until it became necessary in 1971 to establish a special assessment to provide a minimum income for ministerial retirees. Central College, because it was not located in a geographical center of the Reformed Church, always had more difficulty raising monies for its needs. After the pool of undesignated monies had seriously declined and the General Synod decided to give them all to the new General Program Council, Central College conducted aggressive fund-raising programs within the church and began to look to foundations and alumni for increased annual giving.

Providing new financial resources to the Board of Education made the greatest program impact on the life of the Reformed Church. The additional funds came as the board was publishing the Covenant Life Curriculum with several other denominations and as American Protestant churches began to provide increasing staff services for the burgeoning educational programs in their local churches. The exceptionally large increase in undesignated funds for the Board of Education—$87,295 in 1965 alone—made it possible for the board to increase its staff and provide significant new services to the church. The executive staff of the board had been four in 1954.[12] It had grown to eight by 1964[13] and nine by 1965.[14] Without the new equalization policy this growth in staff providing educational services to local churches would not have been possible. By the mid 1970s, when the undesignated pool of monies had declined from a high of $1,200,000 to less than $150,000, the General Program Council had a difficult time financing the staff services to congregations it had inherited from the Board of Education.

Within two years after its initiation, the Board for Christian World Mission overtured the General Synod to return to the former procedure for distributing the undesignated monies. The Overtures Committee recommended no action on this overture because the new equalization system helped "those boards which annually have greater difficulty in meeting their budgets than does the Board for Christian World Mission."[15]

The Stewardship Council, though it conducted extensive stewardship and fund-raising programs, had not been able to alter the basic giving patterns of the Reformed Church. From the very beginning of the mission and educational programs of the General Synod, the work of "foreign" missions attracted the best giving from the church. Not only was this true in the normal giving each year, it also was consistently carried through in the special fund-raising programs. For example, the United Advance met 90.5% of its goal for world mission programs; 86% for domestic mission programs; and only 72% for the Board of Education, the colleges, and the seminaries.

UNUSUAL REFERRALS

With the creation of the Stewardship Council, the General Synod, for the first time in its history, had a continuing group to coordinate the program of the church. Because the Stewardship Council had a broad mandate, the General Synods of 1953 and 1954 referred some unusual matters to it for study and later report. The 1953 General Synod asked the council to study: "the relationship and policy of our denomination to the educational institutions;"[16] "the salaries of board secretaries and associates and to make recommendations to the boards in regard to general salary scales;"[17] and "to consider recognizing Temple Time, 'because it is heard in every Particular Synod of our church and around the world' as the radio voice of the Reformed Church in America."[18] The delegates to the 1954 General Synod asked the council to study the organization of the boards with special reference to the election of their members; to provide a list of the specific salaries of the executive secretaries of the boards; to prepare a list of special days for observance in the church; and to study the matter of a two-year term for delegates to General Synod in order to insure a continuing body.[19]

As it reflected on the two-year trend of these referrals, the Stewardship Council began questioning the wisdom of its becoming the general reference group for the annual General Synod. Based on its reflections, it reported to the 1955 General Synod

> from the nature of some of the matters referred to us by the 1954 General Synod it may appear that they lie outside the scope of the Stewardship Council. The members of the Council were among the first to sense this. Without wishing to appear overly sensitive on it, we do respectfully ask that before matters are referred to us, Synod will consider carefully the nature of those items. We are aware that some lie outside our jurisdiction; and while we grant that there must be certain flexibility about the work done by the council, we are anxious that it become an easy clearing house manifestly outside our charter.[20]

The mere existence of the Stewardship Council had called attention to the Reformed Church's need for a continuing group to supplement the life and work of the annual General Synod meeting. Our next chapter describes the process which met this need through the establishment of the General Synod Executive Committee by the 1961 General Synod.

CONTRIBUTIONS

The Reformed Church Stewardship Council brought many contributions to the denominational life of the Reformed Church. Our study will conclude by highlighting four of them: a major dollar increase in giving for benevolent programs of the General Synod; a new, deeper focus on Christian stewardship throughout the church; a utilization of secular fund-raising techniques for the benefit of the church's mission; and, perhaps most important, new possibilities for coordinating the varied mission/educational programs of the General Synod.

In 1952, the year the Stewardship Council was formed, the members of the Reformed Church in America gave $2,742,874 for the General Synod benevolent budget and $9,790,531 for congregational purposes. By 1968, the year the Stewardship Council was merged into the General Program Council, RCA members gave $5,022,536 to the General Synod benevolent budget—to which needs to be added $1,760,836 for particular synod and classical mission programs that were included in the 1952 total for a total of $6,783,372, and $25,818,314 for congregational purposes. In 1952 21.8% was given for benevolences and 78.1% used for local congregational purposes. By 1968, the percentage for benevolences had dropped slightly to 20.8%—though it dropped to 15.4% if the monies for particular synod and classical programs are not included.

The council was able to accomplish its best results in the years 1953 to 1959. In fact, in 1953 the General Synod benevolent budget received almost $100,000 more than its goal—the first and only time this had happened. Another first was accomplished in 1959. Through the change in distributing the undesignated monies it had been possible to meet all the 1959 approved budgets for the boards. Each of the boards and institutions received 100 percent of its approved budget. The council was not able to sustain the growth pattern of the fifties into the sixties. After several years of small growth, the 1963 increase amounted to only $1,220. In both 1967 and 1968 actual decreases from the previous year were experienced.

The Reformed Church had not had a consistent stewardship program prior to the formation of the Stewardship Council. Though the responsibility for stewardship had been lodged with various boards and departments, including for some years in the office of the stated clerk, it was no one's primary task. Because of the experience gained through the United Advance program, the church began to understand the need for, and benefits of, an ongoing program in Christian stewardship. The council provided significant printed resources for the church which stressed the stewardship responsibilities of the Christian. Probably its most significant impact came through engaging hundreds of lay persons in the task of sharing information on the biblical principles of stewardship and the mission/educational programs of the church.

As new techniques in fund raising and marketing were being developed in the United States, the Stewardship Council provided a channel for utilizing them in the life of the church. The most obvious utilization came through the employment of Ketchum, Inc., for the Reformed Church Development Fund, but the council benefited from these and other secular advances in many of its programs.

As the United Advance had prepared the way for the Stewardship Council, the council prepared the way for the next major shift in the General Synod structure of the Reformed Church. As the council coordinated the budgets of the boards of the General Synod, people began to look for a more coordinated program for the church. As annual General Synods debated issues and found it necessary to refer matters for more extensive study and later report, the delegates began to sense the need for an official body of the General Synod with a broader mandate than the Stewardship Council. The council had coordinated the results of the budget-building processes of the boards of the General Synod, but the church now looked for more than coordination of results. The

Stewardship Council, through its efforts in coordinated budget building and unified promotion of the General Synod benevolent program, prepared the way for the General Synod Executive Committee.

V

The General Synod Executive Committee—A Permanent Committee to Represent the General Synod in the Life and Work of the Reformed Church

The Reformed Church Stewardship Council was the first major change in the General Synod structure in over a century. The next change, the establishment of the General Synod executive committee, took only nine years. Among the factors influencing the church to establish the executive committee were the positive work being done by the Stewardship Council and the need for a group to carry out the "general" needs of the church between the annual sessions of General Synod. In the early years of the Stewardship Council the delegates to the General Synod had referred some unusual matters to it, but the council cautioned against its being used as the recipient of "broad" referrals from the General Synod.

BEGINNINGS

The "progress campaign" of the 1920s had produced the Progress Council, which sought to coordinate the work of the various boards of the church. When it became ineffective, a president's council was established. Several years of experimenting with it showed that it could not adequately cope with its mandate. Rather than continue the President's Council, the Staff Conference was created for the purpose of coordinating (at the staff level) the work of the General Synod boards. The Staff Conference was comprised of the executives of the boards (Foreign Missions, Woman's Foreign Missions, Domestic Missions, Women's Domestic Mis-

sions, Education, Ministers' Fund). Its purpose was to coordinate—at the staff level—the work of General Synod's boards.

The Rev. M. Stephen James, president of New Brunswick Seminary, served as the president of General Synod for the years
1944 and 1945. After a year of traveling throughout the church
and reflecting on its life, he recommended through his "State of
Religion" report:

> to secure greater continuity in plan and program through our gen-
> eral synod, to advise with the President of general synod, I would
> recommend the formation of a committee of five members rep-
> resentative of the church at large. This committee would not have
> membership in general synod, but would be advisory to the Pres-
> ident at his call and together with the Staff Conference of the
> Boards of benevolence would constitute a cabinet for correlating
> and promoting the program of general synod from year to year.[1]

After reviewing his report and recommendations, the review
committee of General Synod did not share President James's vision. They reported:

> It is the mind of the committee that, in the light of the gradual
> demise of the President's Cabinet during the past 10 years or so,
> and, in the light of the fact that the constitutional position of the
> President of General Synod is such that he is clothed with no other
> authority than to preside at the meetings of Synod and such other
> functions as may by the Synod be designated for him; and in the
> light of the fact that the guiding of the work of the church is by
> our constitution and practice delegated to the various boards of
> the church, such a committee would only have personal value for
> the President in what he deems to be the exercise of his office. As
> such it need not be appointed by Synod, nor officially recognized
> by the church . . . Each President shall be free . . . to consult
> with all and sundry, and to use the fruits of such counseling in the
> administration of his duties at his own discretion.[2]

Between 1945 and 1957 the Reformed Church did not discuss
the establishment of a president's cabinet or an executive committee for its General Synod. A great deal of discussion and at-

tention was devoted to coordinated budget building and fund raising from which resulted the United Advance and the Stewardship Council. Both of these vehicles showed the church the benefits of a coordinated program for the General Synod, but discussion on a "council" to coordinate more than promotion and fund raising did not take place during these years.

Shortly before the 1958 General Synod, *The Church Herald* carried two articles on "Unity in Program and Action." Author of the articles was Loring B. Andrews, a layman from the Particular Synod of New York, who served as a member of the Stewardship Council. The first article declared the challenges facing the Christan church to be

> (1) to fight any deterioration in the moral conviction and spiritual strength of our people in the face of the atheistic propaganda of communism; (2) to fight the loss of positive values in the face of materialistic influences and in the midst of a culture derived from technology; (3) to retain and strengthen the faith of every committed Christian; (4) to gain added strength by winning the uncommitted; and (5) to marshall and apply the combined moral force of our legions of Christ with the greatest strength and vigor on every front, both within and without our nation.[3]

Having articulated the challenges before the Christian church in the late fifties in his first article, Andrews proposed a structure for meeting these challenges in his second article.

> . . . a continuing year-round corporate denominational organization which would administer the unified denominational program . . . The Executive Council would comprise two ministers and two elders from each of the six Particular Synods, the President, the immediate Past President, and two elders chosen at large by general synod . . . Vice-presidents of the Corporation would be the Presidents of the several existing Boards . . . The Executive Council would be autonomous in its power to set policy for the denomination and its policies would be binding at all levels within the denomination . . . The report of the Executive Council would be the only report presented to general synod for its approval.[4]

The historic mission/education boards were viewed, by Andrews, as subsidiaries of the executive council. Through this new structure, each member of the RCA would be challenged to "strongly witness for Christ in every act of his daily life and influence the uncommitted to do likewise, and translate a part of that action into both financial and physical support of the program at every level—local, regional and national."[5]

Andrews's articles thoroughly applied the contemporary organizational model for secular corporations to the Reformed Church, and its implementation, according to Andrews's thesis, would make it possible for the church to meet the five major challenges of its day. Although not the first time the structure of American corporations had been recommended for the Reformed Church, the article was certainly the most extensive application of the corporate model to the mission and witness of the Reformed Church.

FIRST PROPOSAL

The Reformed Church in America had spent the year between the synods of 1957 and 1958 studying a major revision in its constitution. Along with incorporating a great many suggestions for revision in the proposal presented to the 1958 General Synod, the committee noted

> the most important change in this second revision is the provision
> for an executive council for the denomination. This new body
> stands between the General Synod and the several boards, insti-
> tutions and agencies and serves as the means by which General
> Synod may exercise its continuing control over the entire denom-
> inational program. It is elected by the General Synod, and is re-
> sponsible solely to the General Synod. It would assume some of
> the present functions of the Stewardship Council, but it differs
> from the latter in that there are no employed board secretaries in
> its membership . . . It will be noted that one of the functions of
> the executive council is to formulate policy for the denomination,
> subject to approval by the General Synod. This may raise some
> questions. Your committee is convinced, however, that this will be
> one of the important functions of the council. The area of denom-

inational policy is one of our greatest weaknesses at the present time. Determination of policy rests nominally in the General Synod, meeting only five days a year, and with different personnel at each annual session, the General Synod cannot adequately make policy, and, in fact, does not. In the absence of a central, continuing policy-formulating body, the denomination is being committed to policies in missionary work, education, church extension, and otherwise by individual boards, classes and unofficial bodies of individuals. In its short sessions the General Synod can do little more than rubber stamp what is brought to it for approval . . . To be of any value at all, this council must be so constituted that it can take a disinterested, objective view of all phases of the denominational program, and avoid bias in favor of any special interest. We believe this has been accomplished by providing that a majority of its members be elected by the General Synod from nominations by the several particular synods.[6]

The proposed membership for the new executive council was:

the president, vice-president, and immediate past-president of general synod; two ministers and two elders from each of the particular synods; the presidents of the Board of Direction, the Boards of Foreign Missions, Domestic Missions, Education and Pensions; and the chairman of the Editorial Committee of *The Church Herald*. Its powers and duties were to be: (a) to administer the affairs of the Reformed Church in America between the sessions of the General Synod; (b) to coordinate the work of the several boards, institutions and agencies into a unified denominational program; (c) to formulate policy for the denominational program, subject to review and approval by the General Synod; (d) to receive the reports of the several boards, institutions and agencies and to submit to the General Synod a single, comprehensive report based thereon; (e) through the office of the Treasurer of General Synod to receive, account for and disburse to the appropriate boards, institutions and agencies all contributions for the denominational program; (f) to exercise such budgetary controls over the several boards, institutions and agencies as may be directed by the General Synod; (g) to establish and administer an office of publicity and promotion, in cooperation with the several boards, institutions and agencies; and (h) to perform such other duties as may be delegated to it from time to time by General Synod.[7]

President Howard Schade, in his 1958 "Report on the State of Religion" presented to the delegates to General Synod, declared:

. . . a reappraisal of the duties of the officers and of the manner in which the agencies of the church are related to General Synod, although advised by many presidents in the past, has been consistently tabled. Can it be that the church prefers a stumbling and fumbling administration to one of order and defined procedure? The church lives in an age which requires continuing alertness to spiritual and moral needs . . . to meet the growing needs of a rapidly expanding church in a day when important decisions cannot always wait upon an annual meeting of the General Synod, it is strongly recommended that there be established an executive council to act as an ad interim agent between sessions, with its actions subject to review and confirmation by Synod.[8]

The delegates to the 1958 General Synod strongly agreed with their Committee on the Revision of the Constitution and with President Schade. The proposal to form an executive council was overwhelmingly approved. It was an amendment to the constitution of the church, so two more steps were required for its implementation. Two-thirds of the classes had to approve the amendment, and the 1959 General Synod had to ratify the action of the classes.

The Committee on the Revision of the Constitution reported to the 1959 General Synod that more than seventy-five percent of the classes had approved the proposed amendment to the constitution. Their report stated:

. . . the most important change which has been made in the structure of the denomination is the establishment of the Executive Council. We find that this idea has received general support, and several classes which failed to ratify the proposed amendment made it clear that they approved of the council but were withholding ratification pending the clarification and refinement of certain aspects of the plan. The committee will probably find itself in substantial agreement with most of the suggestions made, and others will doubtless arise when the new council goes into operation. Since it will require a year to get the council organized and another year to put it into operation, we have plenty of time to smooth out the details. In this connection we are recommending the appointment of a steering committee to direct the organization of this new executive arm of the denomination.[9]

Marion de Velder, who had served as director of the United Advance and chairman of the Commission on a United Approach to the church, was president of the 1959 General Synod. Unlike his predecessor, Howard Schade, he did not endorse the establishment of an executive council, even though it had been ratified by a large majority of the classes. In his "State of Religion" report he urged caution because the denomination faced a basic question regarding the relationship between the functioning of the successful Stewardship Council and the about-to-be-created executive council. Four of the eight functions which were to be assigned to the new executive council were being effectively implemented in the life of the church through the Stewardship Council. De Velder went on to describe studies toward ". . . more effective and efficient organizational structure and procedures . . ." being carried out by fourteen other American denominations. Based on the lack of clarity regarding the responsibilities of the Stewardship Council and the newly-proposed executive council and the extensive studies being carried out by other denominations, he recommended that the General Synod not ratify the establishment of the executive council and, instead, "consider the larger and imperative matter of extensive study of denominational structure, program and operation."[10]

The General Synod followed the advice of its president rather than its Committee on the Revision of the Constitution. Although it did not ratify the amendment establishing an executive council, it did establish a new study committee. The members of the committee were to be: two recent past presidents of General

Synod, a member of the Board of Direction, the chairman of the Stewardship Council, the chairman of the Committee on the Revision of the Constitution, a layman, and the stated clerk of General Synod. The committee was charged with the task of studying the position of the president of General Synod and the issues surrounding the proposal of an executive council for the General Synod.[11]

The special committee reported to the 1960 General Synod. After several recommendations regarding the office of General Synod president, it reported

> that further action on the proposed Executive Council at the present time would retard the progress of the stewardship program (which was in the second year of its major five year "Advance"). It is further recommended that the Committee on the Revision of the Constitution make further study of the Executive Council and consult with other denominations about their experience with bodies comparable to the Executive Council in their structure.[12]

In spite of the approval of seventy-five percent of its classes, the Reformed Church had apparently decided to delay for several years the implementation of the "corporate" model for her General Synod structure.

THE GENERAL SYNOD EXECUTIVE COMMITTEE

Henry Bast, professor of homiletics at Western Seminary and radio preacher for Temple Time, said in his 1961 presidential report to General Synod:

> . . . early in my tours through the church I encountered a number of questions about the program of the denomination . . . There were questions about the coordination of program. This problem is felt by pastors, laymen and the executives responsible for the administration of the program . . . This problem is not new and a number of men have worked diligently on it for several years. A year in this office working on the problem myself has led me to a profound, humble appreciation for the answers others have come up with.[13]

Rather than develop a personal solution to the problem, Bast invited past Presidents Marion de Velder and Howard G. Hageman, and Vice President Norman E. Thomas to join him in developing a recommendation for presentation to the 1961 General Synod. This four-man group proposed the establishment of a General Synod executive committee for a three-year experimental period. Its membership was to be: the president of General Synod, the vice president of General Synod, three immediate past presidents of General Synod, the stated clerk, and four pastors and six elders from the church at large. The responsibilities of the committee were to:

(a) implement decisions and policies of general synod through proper channels and agencies; (b) support, strengthen and coordinate the work of the several boards, institutions and agencies of the RCA; and (c) perform such other duties as may be delegated to it at this or succeeding sessions of general synod.[14]

The 1961 General Synod overwhelmingly adopted the recommendation of its president. The General Synod Executive Committee was created. The Reformed Church had begun to adopt the "corporate" model for its own structures. This was the third (or fourth if the creation of the Stewardship Council in 1952 is counted) major departure from the church order of the great Synod of Dort instituted by the American church. The first, necessitated by the constitutional situation in the United States, involved the separation of church and state. The second, in response to the great missionary movements of the early nineteenth century, established mission boards to carry out the biblical thrust to evangelize. The third established an "executive committee" to function on behalf of the General Synod between its annual sessions. All of the departures were stimulated—or necessitated—by the American experience of the church. Yet, none of them were preceded by careful theological reflection on the polity of the church. The times called for change, and the Reformed Church implemented the change.

The 1961 General Synod also elected the members to its newly-established executive committee. They were: president, Norman E. Thomas; vice president, Bernard Brunsting; three immediate past presidents, Henry Bast, Howard G. Hageman, and Marion de Velder; four pastors, Harvey B. Hoffman, Daniel Y. Brink, Raymond Van Heukelom, and Bert Van Soest; and six elders, Max De Pree, Ekdal Buys, Maurice Te Paske, Arad Riggs, Carl Cleaver, and Adrian Heerschap. Four of the six elders had held, or currently were holding, major positions of leadership on the boards of the church. De Pree had chaired the Board of Foreign Missions. Buys had chaired the Board of Domestic Missions. Te Paske had chaired the Stewardship Council. Riggs served as president of the Board of Direction, the corporate board for the General Synod. Thus, within itself, the General Synod Executive Committee included persons with intimate knowledge of the diverse mission/educational programs of the church.

As the three-year experiment drew to a close, the 1964 General Synod approved an addition to its Rules of Order which permanently established the executive committee. The membership (the nominations by the particular synods was the major change) was to be: president, vice president, three immediate past presidents, one minister and one elder nominated by each particular synod, three elders at large, and the stated clerk, ex officio. The three fairly broad and simply stated responsibilities set forth by the 1961 General Synod had become twelve:

(a) To administer the affairs of the Reformed Church in America between the sessions of General Synod; (b) To hold four stated meetings each year and special meetings when necessary; (c) To submit an annual report of its work to the General Synod; (d) To recommend the time and place of meeting of the General Synod; (e) To prepare the agenda and program for the General Synod meeting; (f) To recommend the budget for the General Synod; (g) To have supervision over the office of the Stated Clerk; (h) To make appointments to fill vacancies in offices, commissions, and committees of the Reformed Church in America or of the General Synod, unless otherwise provided. Appointees shall serve until the next regular meeting of the General Synod, when the General

Synod shall elect persons for such temporarily filled vacancies; (i) To be responsible for initiating studies and evaluations of policy, strategy, long range planning, effectiveness and efficiency within the denomination; (j) To submit to the General Synod any recommendations considered useful for the development of the effectiveness and the efficiency of the life, work and organization of the Reformed Church in America; (k) To implement Article 12, Section 10 of the constitution: "General Synod shall have power to maintain a friendly correspondence and cooperative relationship with the highest judicatory or assembly of other Christian denominations and with interdenominational agencies, in all matters relating to the extension of the Kingdom of God"; and (l) to perform such other duties as may be delegated and referred by the General Synod to the General Synod Executive Committee.[15]

STAFF

The 1961 General Synod, which established the experimental General Synod Executive Committee, also concluded the career of the Rev. James E. Hoffman as the stated clerk of the General Synod. He had begun his service in 1942, and had been elected to his position by the General Synod of 1943. Because Hoffman informed the 1960 General Synod that he intended to retire in 1961, the synod instructed its president, Howard G. Hageman, to appoint a special committee to "nominate a new Stated Clerk" to the General Synod of 1961.

The 1960 General Synod had also approved a recommendation which significantly altered the responsibilities of the stated clerk.

. . . that the office of the Stated Clerk of General Synod be so reconstructed that the Stated Clerk shall be the church's official representative at various ecumenical, public, Classical and Particular Synod occasions; that the Stated Clerk shall be the true liaison officer between the individual Churches and the General Synod . . . that added personnel be provided to handle bookkeeping and other requirements of the office of Stated Clerk so that the Stated Clerk not be bound to routine desk work.[16]

The special committee developed a job description which implemented these referrals, and the 1961 General Synod adopted it. Provision was also made for an assistant to the stated clerk who would supervise the administrative functions of the stated clerk's office and also administer the central services (printing, mailing, purchasing) required at the denomination's headquarters.

The special committee nominated the Rev. Marion de Velder, and the General Synod elected him to a five-year term as its stated clerk. De Velder, who had served the North and South Hampton Church, Churchville, Pennsylvania; the Hope Church, Holland, Michigan; and the First Church, Albany, New York, was serving as senior minister of the Central Reformed Church, Grand Rapids, Michigan. He had previously served the denomination as director of the United Advance, chairman of the Commission on a United Approach to the church, member of the Board of Education, and president of the 1959 General Synod. In addition to the responsibilities outlined by the special committee, de Velder served as an ex officio member and the secretary of the newly-created General Synod Executive Committee.

With the exception of an informal proposal developed by Donner B. Atwood, 1966 president of General Synod, the responsibilities and functions of the stated clerk's office were not reviewed from 1961 until the major reorganization implemented in 1968. In a February 16, 1966, letter to Dr. Norman E. Thomas, Atwood shared reflections on the office of stated clerk and a proposal for a new office, that of general secretary. He developed his proposal because of an increasing concern about the lack of liaison between the boards and agencies of the church and their staff members. He proposed that the Reformed Church engage a "General Secretary" to whom all the staff of the church's boards, including its colleges and seminaries, would report. He believed that a new office was required because

> . . . the Stated Clerk's office is so deeply involved in the mechanics of daily operation and the interrelationship between General Synod and local congregations, and also between General Synod and ecumenical groups and agencies, that the Stated Clerk's office is unable to function at what I would term the higher and broader level of responsibility of oversight of the total denominational program. As it now operates, it seems to me, the office of the Stated

Clerk is more of an information agency than it is an office for the overview of the work of all the boards . . . The lack of coordination between the boards and staff and the fact that the Stated Clerk has no authority . . . but an assumed responsibility . . . to give direction to the total program . . . is not only unfair but extremely unwise . . . A General Secretary of the RCA could be the person who had the direct week to week, month to month responsibility for a continuous evaluation oversight . . . Under his umbrella could come the responsibility for planning and research, something we desperately lack in the RCA . . . The Stated Clerk's office could continue to function within the scope it now has in that the Stated Clerk's and the General Secretary's areas of responsibility would be aimed into these other regions suggested above.[17]

President Atwood related his proposal for a general secretary to the structure of the Reformed Church (see page 220 for organizational chart). Initially, he had planned to recommend this new office to the 1966 General Synod, but he later decided to refer the matter to the Sub committee on Denominational Structure. Because of this referral, the responsibilities of the stated clerk remained unchanged until 1968.

STUDY OF ALL BOARDS AND AGENCIES

The General Synod Executive Committee (GSEC) began functioning after the 1961 General Synod and presented its first report to the synod of 1962. Its report highlighted the activities carried out during its organizational year and presented a number of recommendations for the consideration of the synod. The 1962 General Synod adopted two recommendations which significantly shaped the life and work of the church (and the GSEC) throughout the sixties.

The first of the two recommendations was presented by the GSEC. It authorized the appointment of a special committee of twelve RCA persons to serve as a joint committee with twelve persons from the Presbyterian Church in the United States, (PCUS). The responsibilities of the Joint Committee of Twenty-four were:

(1) to engage in joint conferences to study and explore areas of common concern; (2) to initiate correspondence and discussion between our boards and agencies having responsibility in these areas; (3) to report the results of these studies and explorations; and (4) to recommend further steps to the General Synod and to the General Assembly toward filling our common purpose as stated in this resolution.[18]

The committee actively pursued its assignments for six years and presented a plan of union to the General Synod and General Assembly (of the PCUS) meetings in 1968. The presbyteries of the PCUS and the classes of the RCA voted on the plan between the 1968 and 1969 meetings. More than the required seventy-five percent of the presbyteries approved the plan, but the classes of the RCA did not reach the two-thirds majority required for approval. Thus, after almost a decade of careful work by the Joint Committee of Twenty-four, the merger of the two churches was defeated.

The second recommendation had originated with the Board of World Missions (the new name adopted for the former Board of Foreign Missions in the fifties). The board had overtured the General Synod "to initiate a study of all boards and agencies under its direction that they may be organized and administered to express most effectively our obedience to Christ in these changing times."[19] The General Synod, without further comment, referred the overture to the General Synod Executive Committee. With this simple referral the process was set in motion that completed the adoption of the twentieth-century "corporate" model for the mission/educational structures of the church. After five years of studying the "boards and agencies" of the RCA, the 1967 General Synod authorized the merger of its historic mission/education boards.

The GSEC began its discussion of this referral immediately after General Synod and, at its September, 1962, meeting, appointed a special subcommittee to conduct the study. The members of the subcommittee were: Max De Pree, chairman, Ekdal Buys, Maurice Te Paske, and Arad Riggs. De Pree was an executive at the Herman Miller Company, a creative, growing office furniture design and manufacturing firm in Zeeland, Michigan. Buys was the head of an investment securities firm in Grand Rapids, Michigan. Te Paske conducted a private law practice in Sioux Center, Iowa. Riggs conducted a law practice in New York City. Interestingly, no pastor was appointed to the committee; thus, it did not include persons with formal theological training. As was noted earlier, De Pree had chaired the Board of Foreign Missions; Buys had chaired the Board of Domestic Missions; Te Paske had chaired the Stewardship Council; and Riggs continued to serve as president of the Board of Direction. It is also interesting to note that three of the four persons came from the Midwest.

Dr. Douglas Blocksma, a psychologist who specializes in organizational relationships within management and industry, served as a consultant to the committee. He had earlier served on the Board of Education and thus had some familiarity with the board structures and programs within the church. Marion de Velder, the stated clerk, served as an ex officio member of the committee.

The group was named the Subcommittee on the Study of Boards and Agencies. By 1966 it had acquired the new name of the Subcommittee on Denominational Structure. De Pree remained the chairman of the group until 1967, providing the major leadership for its work and writing all of its early reports.

The Staff Conference, the informal group of executives serving the boards of the RCA, also appointed a committee to "Study the Organization of the Boards and Agencies." Initially, the two committees kept in contact through correspondence, but by 1964 a series of meetings was held between the two committees. By 1965, the Staff Conference had discharged its committee and assigned the task of relating to the work of the special GSEC subcommittee on structure to the stated clerk; the director of the National Department of Women's Work, the executive secretary of the Stewardship Council, the executive secretary of the Board of Pensions, the executive secretary of the Board of World Missions, the executive secretary of the Board of Education, and the staff chairman of the Board of North American Missions the task of relating to the work of the special GSEC subcommittee on structure.

As the GSEC was carrying out its study on the boards and agencies of the RCA, the Boards of North American Missions and World Missions appointed a joint committee to consider the possible merger of the two boards. Rather than have multiple groups studying the program structure of the Reformed Church, the GSEC took the following action at its January 26, 1967, meeting:

> . . . to request the Boards of North American Missions, World Missions, and Education to join with the GSEC in a study of a new structure for the Boards of North American and World Missions, including consideration of the resulting interrelationship with other facets of program organizations; and further, to implement the study by establishing a committee composed of one board member and one staff member from the Board of North American Missions, Board of World Missions, Board of Education and the GSEC; and further, that a member of the Subcommittee on Denominational Structure, appointed by the subcommittee, and the coordinator serve as representatives of the GSEC on the study committee; and further, to instruct the coordinator to undertake the staff assignment to develop the design of the new structure for presentation to the study committee . . . (and) that the GSEC shall present the proposed new structure to the General Synod with the approval of the boards involved.[20]

The members of the new study committee were:

Board of Education	Frederick Olert, Christian Walvoord
Board of North American Missions	Ruth Peale, Beth Marcus
Board of Pensions	Edward Gately, Theodore Zandstra
Board of World Missions	Clarence Linder, Edwin Luidens
Stewardship Council	Donald McCabe, Howard Teusink
National Department of Women's Work	Celeste Van Zyl, Anita Welwood
General Synod Executive Committee	Max De Pree, Robert Harrison

When the 1967 General Synod merged the boards of New Brunswick and Western seminaries to form the Board of Theological Education, its new chairman, Arie R. Brouwer, was invited to join the study committee. The official name of the committee became the "Study Committee on New Structure for Program."

Throughout the early years of the study process, discussions were held regarding the advisability of engaging professional management consultants to help the church with the study. The 1964 General Synod encouraged the employment of consultants. After discussing this action of the General Synod, the GSEC voted for ". . . the Subcommittee on the Study of Boards and Agencies to pursue their studies with all possible speed and employ whatever consultants are needed as authorized by General Synod."[21] Two years later, rather than employ consultants, the subcommittee had decided to employ a new staff person with the title "Coordinator for Implementation of Changes in Denominational Structure." The GSEC deferred approving the employment of a new staff person until after the 1966 General Synod had approved the first implementing steps for the new structure. When the 1966 General Synod, without dissent, voted to establish the new Office of Administration and Finance, the GSEC approved the employment of a coordinator.

Mr. J. Robert Harrison was employed as the Coordinator for the Implementation of Changes in Denominational Structure. He had joined the staff of the Board of World Missions as an assistant treasurer in the early fifties and had become treasurer of the board in the early sixties. Prior to working for the RCA, he had been employed by a public accounting firm. Because of his financial and organizational background, Harrison was assigned the new responsibilities for establishing the new Office of Administration and Finance and for implementing the "one corporation" concept for the RCA. He began his work on September 1, 1966, and continued in the coordinator's role until the summer of 1970.

PROPOSALS FOR A NEW DENOMINATIONAL
STRUCTURE

The subcommittee spent the fall and winter of 1962 reviewing the present program structures of the Reformed Church and preparing an "outline" for carrying out its mandate. The outline was presented to the May, 1963, meeting of the GSEC. It proposed carrying out the study in the following sections:

> Forward; Statement of the Problem; Statement of Goals; Criteria and Principles to Guide Decision Making; Study of Where we Are—including organizational charts, lists of strengths and weaknesses of present structure; Relationships (who should be consulted interdenominationally, and interaction with the present boards and agencies); Review of Other Studies; Recommendations; Questions and Problems; Proposal of Alternative Solutions; Evaluation of Alternatives; Statements of Recommendations; Plan for Implementation; and Recommendations for General Synod.[22]

Having prepared this extensive outline for conducting its study and presenting its results to the Reformed Church, the subcommittee had also completed several major sections of its envisioned report.

After its review of the outline, the GSEC made several revisions and adopted it as the charter for the study on boards and agencies. The goals of the study were to

> . . . establish a climate and an organization that: (1) Enables the program of the denomination to receive the primary attention and thrust of the church in an atmosphere of urgency and efficiency; (2) Places responsibility for execution and support of the programs into the Particular Synods and Classes area of activity to enlist the broadest possible involvement of the membership; (3) Encourages each Christian to serve actively and meaningfully in the Lord's work to the utmost of his ability; (4) Assures efficient, effective handling of the administrative, financial, personnel and business affairs of the denomination on a sound, professional basis but al-

ways as a subordinate function to the program of the denomination.[23]

Thirteen criteria and principles were adopted to guide the study and test the alternatives resulting from it:

(1) Primary emphasis should be placed on formulating and executing the program of the church; (2) The mechanics and means of maintaining, publicizing and supporting the program of the denomination should be de-emphasized; (3) The climate should be encouraged which enables the participation and involvement of individuals throughout the denomination, as opposed to the concept of effective action only as the result of the commitment of a minority of the group; (4) Key measurements should be used in evaluating the kind of work we do as individuals, as well as boards, agencies, and the denomination as a whole; (5) Simplicity; (6) Must differentiate between the formulation of policy and strategy, and the execution of resulting programs; (7) Competence, resulting from a combination of talent, experience and preparation is an important qualification for individuals as well as boards and agencies; (8) Economy; (9) Sensitivity to the needs of the situation; (10) The climate should encourage change and maturation in individuals, as well as groups, so that we are at all times in touch with today's reality; (11) We must learn to be comfortable in the process of confronting as opposed to avoiding or brushing aside difficult or embarrassing matters; (12) Representation on boards and agencies must be handled both on a democratic basis and on a competence basis; and (13) There should not be redundant overlapping of membership on boards and agencies, thereby focusing responsibility into limited groups and limiting participation and involvement by a broad representation of the denomination.[24]

The 1963 and 1964 General Synod reports of the GSEC share segments of the study outline and report progress on accomplishing the study.

The first specific proposal for a new program structure for the Reformed Church in America was presented to the September, 1964, meeting of the GSEC. Since the Reformed Church had decided to make the GSEC a permanent addition to its structure, the study subcommittee could proceed to designing a new program structure which included a continuing role for the executive committee. The proposed structure had five boards for the program of the church. They were: Board of World Missions with departments for North, Central, and South America, the Middle East, the Far East, Church World Service, and personnel; Board of Stewardship and Evangelism, with departments for stewardship education and evangelism, church extension, inner-city and campus Christian life; Board of Family Life, with departments of social action, curriculum and church life, including adult (men's brotherhood, women's work), youth, and children; Board of Administration, with departments of office management (including personnel and purchasing) and financial management, including accounting, payroll, insurance, investment, auditing and financial, reporting; and a Board of Interpretation and Publication, with an office of interpretation including *The Church Herald* and an office of publication and sales.[25] The organizational chart listed the five boards under the GSEC, which was the only group directly reponsible to the General Synod.

The GSEC endorsed the five-board proposal for discussion in the life of the church. The proposed five-board structure made two basic changes in the program structure of the church. The first, and most important, separated the various professional services required by the program boards—accounting, interpretation, printing—from the various program boards and integrated them into one board serving the total program of the General Synod. The second basic change came through consolidating all the programs of the church into the three Boards for World Missions, Stewardship and Evangelism, and Family Life. In addition to expanding the work of the proposed Board of World Missions to incorporate the mission type programs of the Board of North American Missions, the proposal linked stewardship and evangelism. Stewardship and evangelism were linked because both arose from the disciplined Christian life.

Several refinements were suggested to the five-board proposals. All of them related to the three boards proposed to carry responsibility for the program aspects of the church's life. The major refinement suggested three different program boards: Board for Congregational Life, including children, youth, men, women, curriculum, evangelism, stewardship, and membership retention; Board for Christian Leadership, including colleges, seminaries, campus ministries, continuing education for ministers and staff, counseling ministers, and retirement service for church employees; and Board for Mission (and Service), including South and Central America, North America (including inner-city and extension), Africa, Asia, Church World Service, International Relations, and personnel. A second refinement renamed the Board of Family Life the Board of Christian Education and suggested that the work of *The Church Herald* be expanded to include promoting the work of all the boards and agencies. A third refinement called for the addition of a fourth program board, a Council on Church Planning, RCA. This group would become responsible for church extension and retention and work with churches in town and country.

After considering the proposed refinements and reflecting on its original proposal, the subcommittee developed a simplified structure for the RCA. Under the GSEC it proposed: Board of Mission; Board of Education; and an Office of Administration and Finance. (The simplified organizational chart is printed on page 221.)

NEXT STEPS

The GSEC reported to the 1965 General Synod that "an organizational concept was proposed by the Subcommittee on the Study of Boards and Agencies. This concept was examined carefully by the entire General Synod Executive Committee. After serious discussion of the concept and thinking that produced it, it was accepted in principle."[26] The GSEC's report went on to inform the delegates that it would be focusing on nominations and administration during the next year. Its report declared:

(1) Since organizational effectiveness and efficiency are directly related to the competence of the boards and agencies, the subcommittee—working closely with General Synod's Committee on Nominations—will seek to establish the principles and methods whereby the most representative and the most competent people available will be procurred for service on boards and agencies. (2) . . . Because of the importance of the "program" of the denomination and because of the enabling role that efficient and well focused administration can play in helping the denomination to carry out its program, the Executive Committee has asked that this area become the second phase of specific study.[27]

The Subcommittee on the Study of Boards and Agencies spent the summer of 1965 preparing its next major proposal, which it shared with the GSEC at its October meeting. The proposal returned to many of the features of the initial five-board organization discussed in the fall of 1963. Five major program units were recommended: Board of Missions; Board of Evangelism and Stewardship; Board of Family Life; *The Church Herald*; and Council on Higher Education. In addition, an Office of Administration and Finance and a Committee on Research and Development were proposed. The chart included the office of the stated clerk, and a committee of staff executives, to be chaired by the stated clerk. Although not specifically stated in the proposal, *The Church Herald* was apparently assigned the task of promotion and interpretation in this structure.

The committee had prefaced its chart with three comments:

(1) There seems to be a growing concensus concerning the overall concept that a separate administrative and financial unit is not only sensible but urgently needed . . . (2) The proposals concerning the office of Administration and Finance are seen by the subcommittee as specific proposals and very close to the point at which action can be taken. (3) The thinking on the role of the Particular Synod is presented by the subcommittee as an initital concept and not as a final proposal ready for action.[28]

The explanatory notes attached to the charts stated:

(1) Membership on the various boards to be representative from each particular synod. (2) The committee of staff executives to be composed of: Chairman, Stated Clerk; and membership—General Secretaries of Boards of Missions, Education, Family Life and Office of Administration and Finance. (3) Proposed organization is based on the assumption of a "single" RCA corporation. Many of the unified functions implied would not be feasible on a "cooperative" or participating basis if the separate entities each had a corporate responsibility. (4) The personnel functions would apply only to "headquarters personnel." The Board of Missions would have its own personnel office for selecting and training missionary candidates.[29]

(The organizational charts for this new program structure are found on pages 222 and 223.)

For the first time, the GSEC had before it a clear statement on the need for a single corporation. As early as 1958 the Committee on the Revision of the Constitution had recommended that the new executive council "Through the office of the Treasurer of General Synod . . . receive, account for and disburse to the appropriate boards, institutions and agencies all contributions for the denominational program."[30] Legal counsel had cautioned against implementing this proposal because each of the boards had been separately incorporated under New York State law, which provided for each of the corporations to conduct its own financial affairs, including the receipt of contributions from the church. In order to avoid any possible confusion with the laws of New York State under which the program corporations of the church operated, the subcommittee recommended the formation of one corporation for the various program boards. With one corporation, all the financial and administrative functions could be integrated without violating the corporate laws of New York.

Based on the organizational charts accepted by it in October, 1965, the GSEC prepared its recommendations for the 1966 General Synod. After thoroughly discussing the report of the GSEC, the synod voted to establish the proposed Office of Administration and Finance "with the understanding that progressive steps will be taken toward the single corporation concept."[31] Prior to the adoption of this recommendation, Max De Pree, who had chaired the restructuring process from its beginning in 1962, addressed the delegates. He cautioned:

> Organization is a "fluid" structure or vehicle, which enables individuals and groups to "perform" at or near their potential. Essentially, an organizational structure is a connecting agent; connecting individuals, groups, and functions . . . The "normal condition" for an organization is to be in a state of "change." This proposal . . . is a serious effort to improve our stewardship and effectiveness. It is a serious effort to free those who are responsible for the programs of the denomination . . . This proposal is "not final" . . . It will need to be kept up to date in coming years . . . Lastly, this proposal, if you decide to approve it, will be very demanding . . . It will demand understanding, cooperation, confidence, humility and terribly hard work. It will bring forth sweat and frustration. It will require much love and grace. We should approve it only if we are very serious about our stewardship.[32]

With the approval of the 1966 General Synod for the establishment of the Office of Administration and Finance and the adoption of the "one corporation" concept, the first specific implementing steps had been taken for the new structure. The Subcommittee on Denominational Structure, the Study Committee on New Structure, and the coordinator greatly increased their activity in the development of the new structure. After several meetings at which various organizational models were reviewed, the Study Committee approved a new (the third major proposal) structure for the program of General Synod. This proposal called for Commissions on Education and Mission, and Offices of Administration and Finance, and Promotion and Communication (the first time this office was proposed). The commissions were to have thirty-three members, two laymen/laywomen and one minister nominated by the particular synods, and twelve persons at large. The Council on Planning and Research was retained, linked to the office of the stated clerk. It was to have eighteen members, with each particular synod naming one minister, the General Synod six laymen or laywomen, and the GSEC six persons at large. Although the proposal had been approved by the Study Committee and the GSEC, two boards asked that professional consultants be engaged before adopting the details of the new structure. Therefore, the GSEC did not present a detailed organization to the 1967 General Synod, but rather a recommendation for the merger of the Boards of Education, North American and World Missions, and the Stewardship Council.

The delegates to the 1967 General Synod received a booklet describing the GSEC's recommendations on a new structure for program. The booklet included: "Definition of Organization," "Principles Involved in Considering Reorganization," "Steps Taken from the 1962 General Synod to the 1966 General Synod," and "Steps Taken From the 1966 General Synod to the 1967 General Synod." The booklet concluded with a listing of the actions of the three boards and the Stewardship Council endorsing the recommendations being proposed by the GSEC. The delegates to the 1967 General Synod extensively discussed the proposals— four of its standing committees debated them. All four of the standing committees recommended the adoption of the GSEC recommendations.

Based on the principles

(1) All important in the life of the Christian church is its mission; (2) The purpose of organization must be to enable living people and living groups to perform at or near their potential; (3) The responsibility for the execution and support of the church's program must be largely shared at the Particular Synod and Classis level so that the broadest possible involvement of the total church membership is possible; and (4) We must be concerned that representation be handled both on a democratic basis and on a competent basis.[33]

The General Synod took the following actions:

1. To approve the establishing of one corporation for the National Program of the RCA through merger of the Board of Education, the Board of North American Missions, the Board of World Missions and the Stewardship Council, together with any other organization that may vote to be included. (a) The General Synod is to have authorization over the corporation. (b) The corporation will have one or more representatively selected program units for determining program policies and implementing the same. Approximately one-half of the members of the program unit or units shall be nominated by the Particular Synods. All members shall be elected by the General Synod. (c) The corporation will have one or more professionally supervised administrative service units. The unit or units are to serve program and under no circumstances are they to determine program policy. (d) The corporation will have three categories of executive staff personnel. There shall be one chief executive of the corporation; each program unit and each administrative service unit shall have one chief executive; and each program unit and each service unit may have other executive staff personnel. (e) The basic reorganization is to be accomplished as rapidly as possible with minimum disruption of personnel and program. (f) The new organization is to be geared for flexibility and possibility of continuing change in order to meet the demands of the rapidly changing world situation; and further, 2. To instruct the General Synod Executive Committee to employ a professional consultant or consultants to study and advise on the specific design for the corporation in consultation with the involved organizations, including the procedure for implementing the merging of the existing organizations into the corporation; and further, 3. To authorize the General Synod Executive Committee to make the decision on the specific design of the corporation within the concepts approved by the General Synod after submission to the Boards of Education, North American and World Missions and the Stewardship Council, or other organization(s) that may request to be included; and further, 4. In the event that the new design requires formulation of units prior to the 1968 General Synod, to authorize the General Synod Permanent Committee on Nominations to nominate to the General Synod Executive Committee and the

General Synod Executive Committee to elect the members of the newly formed units. 5. That the General Synod authorize the study of its overall functioning and organization, including its Executive Committee and other Committees and Commissions, by the professional consultant or consultants employed by the General Synod Executive Committee for report and possible recommendation to a subsequent meeting of General Synod; and further, 6. Recognizing the need for national changes of structure to have relevance to the regional and local programs and organizations, to instruct the GSEC through its Sub-Committee on Denominational Structure to enter into discussions and to study for ways in which the local, regional and national programs may be related and integrated more effectively; and further, 7. To report to the 1968 General Synod the specific design of the corporation for the three Boards and the Stewardship Council and the progress of the discussions and study with the Consistories, Classes and Particular Synods.[34]

The 1962 General Synod had begun the process of reorganizing its boards for mission and education through the simple referral of an overture to the GSEC. The overture called for study, which was conducted for the next five years. After reviewing the various studies and reports, the 1967 General Synod empowered the GSEC to establish "one corporation" for the denominational program of the RCA.

A NEW PROGRAM STRUCTURE

Immediately after the 1967 General Synod, the coordinator began to interview professional consultants to "study and advise on the specific design for the corporation." After evaluating a number of firms, the firm of Edward N. Hay, Philadelphia, Pennsylvania, was retained to guide the RCA into the new "one-corporation" structure. The Hay firm provided a number of secular consulting skills to the corporate world (generally profit making) and specialized in professionally developed systems for remuneration. It did not have special expertise or experience in designing mission structures for a church. The firm began its work in August and carried it out in five phases: orientation; data gathering within the staff, the existing boards and agencies and throughout the denomination at large; analysis of data and the development of recommendations; implementation of the process of reorganization; and critique.

By December, 1967, Edward N. Hay had prepared a "proposal in progress" for presentation to the GSEC. It was entitled a "proposal in progress" to underscore its preliminary, tentative nature. The proposal contained two major, new ingredients: a General Program Board and an Office of Human Resources. Although one program board was proposed, it was divided into sections on mission and education, with each to have its own general secretary. Hay supported its recommendation for one program board by saying:

> The Reformed Church in America may be numerically small, but this fact has in no way limited the scope of its activities, although it has limited the effectiveness of some of them . . . as things are presently arranged, it is almost impossible for the denomination to consider, on the one hand, all its various human and financial resources, and on the other, to consider the needs of the world according to the priority of mission indicated by the denomination's values. As a result, there is the unedifying spectacle of well-meaning boards, agencies, staffs, churches, classes and synods all vigorously competing for communicants' contributions for their own programs and goals.[35]

Hay also recommended a new membership base for the General Program Board. Rather than base the membership in the particular synods, as had been advocated from the very beginning of the study process, Hay recommended a classis base for the membership. Each classis was to nominate one member, totaling forty-five, and the General Synod would nominate and elect fifteen members at large. Hay stated:

> The more a Council is composed of members elected from a relatively unsophisticated and widely dispersed electorate, the less

the chance it has of having a significant number of experienced, capable members. On the other hand, a purely nominated council, while it is more likely to have high quality membership, may be much less representative—or even if it is not—it may "appear" to be so, which can be equally harmful. What we recommend here is a practical compromise intended to offer maximum benefits with a minimum number of drawbacks.[36]

The GSEC approved the "proposal in progress" and authorized its presentation to the three boards and the Stewardship Council. On March 4, 1968, the GSEC received a report from Edward N. Hay which recommended a "new structure for the program of General Synod, RCA." The three boards and the Stewardship Council had approved the report, and the GSEC, acting under the authority granted to it by the 1967 General Synod, adopted the report and set in motion the implementation of the new structure. In adopting the new structure the GSEC once again affirmed that "the new organization is geared for flexibility and the possibility of continuing change in order to meet the demands of the rapidly changing world situation."[37]

The new structure provided for the retention of the GSEC and the creation of: a General Program Council; an Office of Human Resources; an Office of Promotion and Communications; an Office of Administration and Finance; and a Long Range Planning Committee. (A chart of the new structure is found on page 224.) In addition, the Reformed Church would retain its Board of Direction, Board of Pensions, Board of Theological Education, National Department of Women's Work, Editorial Council of *The Church Herald*, and the three boards of the colleges. After several years of discussion, the GSEC decided to drop the Long Range Planning Committee. During the 1970s the members of the GSEC also became the members of the Board of Direction and the Board of Pensions. Thus, one group of persons performed four specific "trustee" functions for the Reformed Church. With these exceptions, the program structure adopted in March of 1968 served the Reformed Church through the 1970s.

After Hay had recommended a General Program Council

(GPC), there were several proposals which would have changed the GSEC itself into the General Program Council. The advocates of this change called for a unicameral rather than a bicameral structure for the RCA. Because the bicameral structure was adopted, it became necessary to carefully delineate the responsibilities of the continuing GSEC and the newly-createdly GPC. The GSEC was responsible for:

(1) Effective overall budget planning, measurement and control; (2) Ecclesiastical planning and implementation to insure continuity of a viable church; (3) Continuity of competent, motivated staff personnel through the Stated Clerk and General Secretary; (4) Effective organization structure and policy implementation through the Stated Clerk and General Secretary; and (5) An informed General Synod body, aware at all times of the plans, programs, status and direction of the church. The General Program Council was to be responsible for: (1) Decisions of program and budget priorities and strategies on a short- and long-range basis within the framework of available funds and long term objectives; (2) Program plans for all ministries and their effective implementation through the Stated Clerk and General Secretary; (3) Budget projection for program within the framework of total available income; and (4) Measurement of ongoing program to insure effective implementation. The relationship was further spelled out to be: The General Synod Executive Committee is to relate to the new structure on behalf of General Synod in accordance with existing constitutional provisions . . . the GSEC shall recommend budget ceilings to the General Program Council for the GPC and other units, and may raise questions relating to program policies and priorities with the GPC. However, the General Synod itself must decide on major differences of judgment, if they exist, between the GSEC and the GPC. The GSEC cannot overrule the GPC on decisions relating to program policies and priorities within the approved budget ceilings.[38]

The General Program Council was to be "responsible for decisions on policies and priorities of all programs on behalf of General Synod, unless there is a specific assignment of some portion of program responsibility to some other unit."[39]

The Hay proposal also recommended, and the GSEC adopted, a new structure for the denominational staff of the RCA. The proposal called for a general secretary and stated clerk (the two staff positions suggested by Donner Atwood in 1966 had been joined into one by the Hay proposal), but the GSEC dropped the stated clerk from the position title. The General Secretary's staff was composed of: Secretary for General Synod Operations (the former administrative assistant to the stated clerk), Secretary for Program (the chief staff person for the GPC), Director of Administration and Finance, Director of Promotion and Communications, and Coordinator of Human Resources. The Coordinator for the Implementation of Changes in Denominational Structure continued to serve on the General Secretary's staff until the summer of 1970. One change, establishing the position of Executive Secretary to serve under the General Secretary and to carry the management responsibilities for him, was made in this structure in its early years. With this change, the position of Secretary for Program was abolished, and a new position of Secretary for Operations was established to carry out the internal administrative tasks for the General Program Council.

The persons appointed to these new staff positions brought a blend of continuity and newness. Marion de Velder, the former stated clerk, was appointed to the new position of General Secretary. Arie R. Brouwer, who had served parishes in Corinth, Michigan, and Passaic, New Jersey, was appointed Secretary for Program, and later Executive Secretary. He had previously served the denomination on the Board of World Missions, the New Brunswick Seminary board, and the Board of Theological Education. Beth E. Marcus, an executive secretary of the Board of North American Missions, was appointed Director of Promotion and Communications. Robert J. Kleinman, a lay businessman from Traverse City, Michigan, was appointed Director of Administration and Finance. Alvin J. Poppen, who had served a parish in Clover Hill, New Jersey, and as a missionary in Hong Kong and Taiwan, was appointed Coordinator of Human Resources. He had served previously on the Board of Theological Education. Marvin

D. Hoff was later appointed to the new position of Secretary for Operations. He had served parishes in Hawthorne, New Jersey, and Palos Heights, Illinois, and had most recently been the General Program Council's Secretary for Asian Ministries.

A MISSION BUDGET FOR THE GENERAL SYNOD

When an executive council was first proposed for the Reformed Church, it was not immediately established because too many of its functions were already being carried out effectively by the seven-year-old Stewardship Council. When the 1961 General Synod established the General Synod Executive Committee for a three-year experiment, the responsibilities of the GSEC purposely did not overlap with those of the Stewardship Council. All promotional and budget-building tasks (the ones which most conflicted with the Stewardship Council) were omitted from the responsibilities of the GSEC. As the draft permanently incorporating the GSEC into the Rules of Order of the General Synod was being prepared, it included the responsibility

> to have oversight through a financial reporting system of the entire denominational fiscal picture, at appropriate and periodic intervals, and to be responsible for submitting the denominational benevolence budget to the General Synod, and through the office of the Treasurer of General Synod, receive, account for, and disburse to the appropriate boards, institutions, agencies all contributions for the denominational program.[40]

After its review, legal counsel reported "these provisions usurp powers of the boards incorporated by special acts of the legislature of the State of New York. The General Synod by constitutional change, a by-law change or resolution, cannot change the law of New York."[41] Because of this legal opinion, all the financial responsibilities proposed for the GSEC were removed.

Almost immediately after the GSEC began to function on a permanent basis, the Boards of North American and World Missions requested it to assume the task of building the annual General Synod mission budget. The General Synod Mission budget included the: Board of World Mission, the Board of North American Mission, the Board of Education, the Board of Pensions, Kirkside, Central, Hope, and Northwestern colleges, and New Brunswick and Western seminaries. The Stewardship Council had been responsible for reviewing the budget requests of these participants and recommending a General Synod mission budget to the annual General Synod since 1952. With the permanent establishment of the GSEC, the boards felt it should more properly carry out this task for the church. After several meetings between representatives of the Stewardship Council and the GSEC, it was mutually agreed to transfer the budget task to the GSEC.

The GSEC conducted its first review in 1966 as it prepared a 1967 General Synod mission budget for recommendation to the General Synod. A very extensive process was developed and carried out for the first two years. Two factors, the merger of the largest participants in the General Synod mission budget into the GPC and the radical decline in undesignated giving, significantly altered the importance of the General Synod mission budget and reduced the impact of the GSEC's role in the process. When there was a large pool of undesignated funds, the annual budget decision influenced a participant's share of the money contributed for Reformed Church mission. As the undesignated funds declined from a high of $1,200,000 to $150,000 in the early 1970s, there was not enough money to "equalize" the income of the various programs of the church. Without money to "equalize," the General Synod mission budget decisions lacked authority and meaning.

As the undesignated funds declined, the importance of the donor designation grew. More and more donors (in the majority of instances the donors were local Reformed churches and the designations were made by their deacons) limited the programs to which their funds could be given through specific designations. Because of these designations, the budget-building process became less important, and the decisions of the donors became more important. Without undesignated money to support budget decisions, a budget-building process was not able to function adequately.

Although the GSEC's role in building the annual General Synod mission budget has lost a great deal of significance, it is still looked to for leadership in meeting the "funding" needs of the mission/educational programs of the church. In his President's Report to the 1972 General Synod, Christian Walvoord observed: "the supply of money has dwindled from $4,241,000 in 1969 to $4,200,000 in 1970 to $4,070,000 in 1971 . . . The attitude of those responsible has changed from concern to anxiety, from anxiety to alarm, and from alarm to crisis. Panic has not yet set in."[42] Based on the recommendation of President Walvoord, the GSEC was charged with the responsibility of calling a "Consultation on Funding" of "national and regional people, those who spend and those who pay, with three purposes: (1) to assure financial support for national programs, (2) to preserve the traditional balance between assessment and benevolence, (3) to provide channels so that national as well as regional programs gain an equal hearing in the congregations and consistories of the church."[43]

The GSEC called the consultation for January 25 and 26, 1973. The participants included: one from each of the particular synods (6); one from each of the colleges (3); two from the Board of Theological Education; and thirteen from the General Program Council (including two representatives of Reformed Church Women). The consultation produced a series of recommendations on askings and assessments, procedures for judicatory approval of fund-raising efforts, and renewed programs in stewardship education. Its recommendation to form the Staff Consulting Group has probably had the most significant and continuing impact on the RCA. In order to improve communication between those administratively responsible for budgets dependent upon the giving of the members of the Reformed Church, the Staff Consulting Group was to include: senior staff of each particular synod; presidents of the colleges and seminaries; the director of Reformed Church Women; the editor of *The Church Herald*; the Executive Secretary and three to five national staff members; and the General Secretary, who was assigned the leadership role for the group. One of the early designs for the new program structure of the Reformed Church had included a "staff cabinet" (Donner Atwood's 1966 proposal had suggested that the General Secretary supervise the total denominational staff, including the presidents of the colleges and seminaries), but this had not been implemented in the 1968 reorganization. With the establishment of the Staff Consulting Group in 1972, an informal grouping of leadership staff had been established for the church.

CONTRIBUTIONS OF THE GENERAL SYNOD EXECUTIVE COMMITTEE

The establishment of the General Synod Executive Committee was the Reformed Church's first step in adopting the twentieth-century corporate model for the life of the church. After more than fifteen years of discussion and the review of various proposals for a continuing body to carry on the work of the General Synod between its annual sessions, the 1961 General Synod voted to experiment with an executive committee for a period of two years. The experimental executive committee, which was made a permanent part of the "Bylaws and Rules of Order of the General Synod" in 1964, convinced the Reformed Church that the time had come to make a major addition to its General Synod structure. The General Synod Executive Committee has served the church well. The 1967 General Synod empowered it to carry out the most important change in program structure the church had made since 1832. As Edward N. Hay interviewed members of the Reformed Church in the fall and winter of 1967, the firm learned that the GSEC was the most respected and trusted leadership group in the RCA.[44] Although a new part of the Reformed Church's structure for mission, the GSEC quickly brought continuity, representation, and competence to the life of the church.

Prior to the establishment of the GSEC, only the program boards of the church functioned on a continuing basis. The General Synod met annually, and there was a new group of delegates each year. If important matters in the life of the church needed immediate attention, only the three officers of the General Synod (president, vice president, and stated clerk) could function for the church. In 1959 the appropriate number of ministers and elders called for a special meeting of the General Synod to rule on an ordination controversy in the Classis of Passaic.[45] The three officers decided that, even though the constitutional provisions for calling a special session of the General Synod had been met, the costs of calling the delegates together made it unwise. With the formation of the GSEC this type of decision could be made by a broader group of church leaders.

The Reformed Church benefited from a second type of continuity from the service of the GSEC. In addition to having a leadership group continuing between the annual sessions of the General Synod, the membership of the GSEC brought continuity to its leadership. The majority of persons served on the committee for six years (two three-year terms) and thus had time to gain experience in wrestling with the issues facing the RCA. Until the formation of the GSEC, only the program boards had a continuing membership. This often meant that the members of the program boards were more able and qualified to make decisions in the life of the church than the delegates to the annual General Synod. When the GSEC was established to serve for the General Synod between its annual sessions, the General Synod itself had a continuing role in decision making in the life of the church and a group of persons with the background and experience to make the decisions.

The new GSEC also strengthened a broader representation in the life of the RCA. The Stewardship Council had been the first group to be formed, in part, by persons elected by the particular synods. All other committees and boards of the General Synod had members elected by the General Synod, although geographical balance became increasingly important. The majority of the members of the GSEC represented their own particular synods and could be expected to articulate the stance of their synod on the issues before the GSEC. In addition, the presence of the vice president, president, and three former presidents of the General Synod strengthened the representative nature of the committee. Since the election of the vice president and president is open to all the delegates to an annual General Synod (although the offices traditionally alternate between East and West), the persons holding the offices broadly represent the life of the RCA. Being a representative group, the GSEC has generally had within its membership the diversities present in the RCA, and has been able to forge these diversities into forward-moving decisions.

The GSEC has also been a competent group. During its early years it included the former presidents of the Board of North American Mission, the Board of World Mission, and other boards and agencies of the church. The elders elected to the GSEC by the particular synods were almost always persons who had served with distinction in some aspect of the church's life. This competence has brought quality and strength to the work of the GSEC.

The GSEC, even though it brought a great many new strengths to the life of the Reformed Church, did not (or chose not to) provide leadership for the mission and educational program of the church. Because of the mandate from the 1962 General Synod, it moved rather quickly to developing a new mission structure for the RCA, rather than providing leadership to the existing program boards. Thus, the most important contribution the GSEC made to the life of the Reformed Church in the sixties was the formation of the General Program Council.

VI

The General Program Council—One Council for the Reformed Church's Mission and Educational Program

The General Program Council (GPC) held its first meeting on June 17, 1968, at Warwick Estates, Warwick, New York. The council's unique and awesome responsibility was "for all program not specifically assigned to someone else." Unlike the Stewardship Council and the General Synod Executive Committee, the GPC did not begin its task afresh. Because it arose from a merger, the GPC inherited the diverse programs and policies of the Board of World Missions, the Board of North American Missions, the Board of Education, and the Stewardship Council. In addition, unlike its predecessors in the nineteenth century, the GPC stood in a significant stream of "tradition" in the world missionary movement.

The General Program Council began its work as religion entered into a period of decline in the United States. Membership in churches had plateaued in the mid-fifties, but the continued growth of the population had continued to provide some growth for religious institutions in the U. S. By the mid-sixties almost all religious institutions had moved into a period of membership decline—not just a time of "no growth." The Reformed Church experienced this decline and dropped from a 1966 high of 233,000 adult members to a 1978 low of 215,000 adult members. In addition to the decline in value American society placed on membership in religious institutions, the Reformed Church was negatively impacted by the migration of people from the cities and rural areas of the nation to the suburbs, and from the Northeast to the Southwest.

The General Program Council was faced with an immediate financial crisis. Because giving to the national programs of the Reformed Church had plateaued by 1962 and inflationary pressure had produced rising budgets, the GPC inherited a budget with a built-in deficit of $200,000. As we saw in our section on American philanthropy, American giving as a percent of the gross national product had peaked in 1971 and then had begun a steady decline. At the same time, the ravages of inflation radically increased the costs for local churches and made it more difficult for them to contribute to denominational mission programs.

The General Program Council began its leadership role as the life of the Reformed Church was being confronted with some of the radical differences within her life. When the proposed merger with the Presbyterian Church in the United States was defeated, the 1969 General Synod was brought face to face with these deep differences. As the General Synod debated these basic differences, a delegate presented the following resolution:

Whereas: 1. Discussion in the Reformed Church in America at many levels and at General Synod is revealing that division among us appears to be non-negotiable; 2. A separation of our denomination in anger is certainly not to the glory of God; 3. The continued existence of a particular denomination, especially one which is as fractured and fragmented as ours, is not necessarily to the glory of God; and 4. The orderly dissolution of a denomination such as ours *may be* to the glory of God; Therefore be it resolved that the General Synod of 1969 at this session direct the president of General Synod to appoint a joint committee of 24 with 12 representatives of the divergent views within the RCA to be assigned the task of drafting a plan for the orderly dissolution of the RCA to be reported to the General Synod of 1971.[1]

The General Synod referred the resolution to its Committee of Reference (the GSEC), which thoroughly discussed it and reported a "Plan for Understanding." The plan called for the appointment of a committee of eighteen to "explore every possibility for understanding and reconciliation within the RCA. . . ."[2]

> If this committee finds the differences and the basic concepts of mission and ecumenical relations to be irreconcilable and non-negotiable in the RCA, be it resolved that this committee report its findings to the Synod of 1970 and that then another Committee of 18 may be appointed and instructed at the Synod of 1970 to draft a plan for the orderly dissolution of the RCA and report that plan to the Synod of 1971.[3]

The Committee of Eighteen worked throughout the year and reported to the 1970 General Synod in two areas: a listing of the tensions in the Reformed Church; proposed solutions for relieving the tensions. The committee presented ten recommendations, and the 1970 General Synod adopted all of them. The major ones were:

> The General Program Council's "Goals for Mission" be adopted as a blueprint for the entire Church as a basis for mission in the world today. A loyal endeavor to implement these goals and priorities will spearhead the process of reconciliation and may require further theological definitions to augment those now defined in the Standards of Unity . . . General Synod affirm an open position on interchurch cooperation, working with all groups in the attainment of our mission goals and that ecumenical involvements be subjected to a continuous evaluation of their potential contribution to those goals . . . General Synod instruct the General Program Council to initiate a crash program of instruction for laity (men, women, youth) in the areas of personal witnessing and responsible leadership.[4]

In this milieu, and with a very broad and diverse heritage, the General Program Council began its work. After reviewing the new mission/education structure of the Reformed Church and surveying the many programs contained in its inheritance, the

GPC appointed two ad hoc committees to begin working on its future. They were the Ad Hoc Committee on Goals for Mission and the Ad Hoc Committee on Organization. The work of these two groups carried the GPC into its new task.

GOALS FOR MISSION

The Ad Hoc Committee on Goals for Mission worked for more than a year. During this time it shared interim reports with the GPC and sought guidance from the church at large on its task. The committee presented its final report to the November, 1969, meeting of the GPC. It recommended nine areas for program goals in the Reformed Church and provided a priority rationale for each of the nine areas. The goal areas, in priority order, recommended by the committee were: (1) evangelism; (2) human welfare; (3) education; (4) family; (5) church renewal; (6) social relationships; (7) communication; (8) unity of the church; and (9) worship. The GPC adopted the report and its priority listing of goal areas "as a foundation paper toward formulation of General Program Council policies."[5] Staff was instructed "to work on objectives in (the) light of aforementioned goals."[6] The GPC's early determination to develop "Goals for Mission" provided a goal foundation for all of its future work. The initial goals, as we will see, provided a theology of mission for the GPC. From this mission-based foundation, the GPC developed all of its programs for the RCA.

The staff eventually reduced the nine goal areas to five: evangelism and church growth; Christian community; human welfare; personal growth; and relationships and social issues. The General Program Council carried out its work in these five goal categories for the decade of the seventies. Several revisions were made in the preambles to the categories and in the specific goals of each category. By 1980 the category preambles and goals were:

PROLOGUE

The Constitution of the General Program Council states: "The General Program Council shall be the program agent of the General Synod of the Reformed Church in America to participate in God's mission to the world in Jesus Christ and to enable and equip the Church to be a sign of the Kingdom." In selecting themes and concerns for our goals, we must seek to do justice to the total perspective of the Gospel of the Kingdom. There are a great variety of ministries and programs; all of them find their central focus in Christ and His Kingdom.

The fundamental premise in all Christian ministry is the Gospel itself. When it is faithfully proclaimed, fellowships of believers form and develop. This we stress in our first statement of concern, "Evangelism and Church Growth." But what is the nature of Christian community life—how is it nurtured for the strengthening of the Church's mission? This concern is raised in our second statement, "Christian Community." The third statement on "Human Welfare" affirms the historic Christian concern for the well being of the total person, his/her physical as well as spiritual needs. "Personal Growth and Relationships" focuses on the Christian concern that people everywhere be encouraged to develop fully their God-given potentials. In an era when the aspirations of millions of people for self-development run high, the Church must not neglect this area of concern. The final statement on "Social Issues" refers to the Church's responsibility to apply the Gospel to all spheres of life.

EVANGELISM AND CHURCH GROWTH

The Church of Jesus Christ has been called by her Lord to proclaim the Gospel to men and women in every situation and to make disciples of all nations. Many signs in contemporary society point to a deep spiritual searching. A hunger for meaning gnaws at hearts and souls. Nevertheless, millions of people do not yet confess Jesus Christ as Lord and Savior, and consequently do not know the joy and peace which are found in Him.

In modern society, structures and systems increasingly affect the lives of people. Some of the "principalities and powers" of this world hold millions of women, men and children captive in the bonds of poverty, oppression and exploitation. We confess that Jesus Christ has overcome these powers. He is King of kings and Lord of lords!

Some do not believe because they have not heard the Gospel. Others have heard, but have rejected the way of Christ. Some— we must acknowledge in humility—have found it difficult to accept the Gospel of the Kingdom of God, because Christ's followers have failed to demonstrate the fruit of the Spirit.

We must proclaim to all people and powers that Jesus Christ is indeed Savior and Lord, using every feasible means of communication. Through the power of the Holy Spirit, we must share the new life in Christ in a world in need.

Goals:

A. Existing congregations experiencing renewal and growth.

B. New Reformed Church congregations and ministries reaching people in our increasingly secular society.

C. The use of modern communications media to share the Gospel of salvation in Christ in a way understandable to modern people.

D. An active Christian witness on college and university campuses.

E. Pioneer evangelism among the unreached peoples of the world.

F. Interfaith dialogue in which the church manifests a willingness to listen to other faiths, and to share its own belief in the Gospel of Christ.

CHRISTIAN COMMUNITY

The Church is to be a fellowship of forgiven people, a community of those who have found reconciliation with God, and who live out this new reality in their daily relationships with others. In a world of alienation, loneliness, and tragic estrangement, we are challenged to demonstrate that Christ is the answer. We must admit, however, that often members of our congregations have themselves not experienced the supportive fellowship of love and concern which we acclaim so emphatically. Throughout the centuries the world has had occasion to witness a spirit of conflict and competition among Christians which is contrary to the Spirit of

Christ. We proclaim a glorious Gospel of reconciliation while at times we continue practices of segregation and division.

Radical renewal in the Christian Church is possible when we rediscover the basic elements of the community which are ours in Christ. This also is one of the greatest contributions the Church can make to the strengthening of family life and the building of a deeper sense of community in our society at large. In the minds of millions of people, the credibility of the Church during the coming years will be intimately tied to the quality of our life together. Many young people are urgently asking that we match words of love and talk about forgiveness with a demonstration of these gifts in our common life in Christ.

Among some of our people—both young and old—there seems to be a longing for worship which incorporates the elements of order and spontaneity, commemoration and celebration, and which leaves room for meaningful lay participation.

In too many instances those with deep problems (e.g. alcoholism, broken marriages) have felt compelled to join an anonymous fellowship at the fringe of the institutional Church in order to find help in a healing community. There is an urgent need for the Church to reclaim an area that belongs to the heart of her very being: a community life that helps to make people whole.

Goals:

A. Congregations where Christian fellowship and mutual caring are experienced.

B. Christian communities knowing biblical truth in relation to the contemporary world.

C. Corporate worship related to the daily life experiences and vocations of the worshipper which encourages lay participation, spontaneity, and diverse forms of communication.

D. Support, through finance and personnel, of church structures that facilitate Christian community life.

HUMAN WELFARE

The Gospel of Jesus Christ is the Gospel of the abundant life. In response to that Gospel and out of the riches of His grace, the church concerns itself with any form of human misery in any place. It seeks to be obedient to Christ, who said, "Love your neighbor . . . feed the hungry. . ."

Conditions in the world require that we increase our response to Christ's gifts and our neighbor's need. Hunger and malnutrition are widespread in the United States and in other countries of the world. Unless dramatic action is taken, the outlook for the next decade is predictable: over-population, war, famine, and pollution everywhere. The Church has consistently called its members to ministries of compassion. These programs must be expanded and planned jointly with those whom we seek to serve in order that all people may live with dignity and self-determination.

Goals:

A. Programs in developing societies which deal with root causes of hunger and under-development.

B. Ministries of healing which deal with the person's whole being (spiritual, mental and physical).

C. Relief of acute human need due to natural disasters and our inhumanity to one another.

D. A church concerned with the life and welfare of its own personnel, both active and retired.

PERSONAL GROWTH AND RELATIONSHIPS

The Christian faith affirms that life's fulfillment takes place in communion with God and other persons. The Scriptures make it abundantly clear that in God's design for creation, people were not intended to live as isolated individuals, but in relationship with others.

Personal growth must be a priority of the Church because of the promise of a new humanity which is revealed in Christ. The Church must be ever mindful that the purpose of its programs is to serve the genuine needs of the people.

Christians are called to be deeply sensitive to the aspirations of people everywhere who are being crushed by cultural forces or social systems, whether political, economic, educational or ecclesiastical. The way of love provides for all people to develop themselves and their societies to the fullest of their God-given potential.

Goals:

A. Persons growing in self-awareness, interpersonal relationships and involvement in Christian ministry.

B. Church leadership enabled to develop their maximum potential for service.

C. Indigenous educational programs in developing societies which make possible personal growth and leadership development.

SOCIAL ISSUES

As Christians we are concerned with social issues because the Gospel calls us to bear witness to Christ and His Kingdom in every sphere of life. The Church has been established to serve that kingdom.

Social problems are moral ailments that afflict an entire society. There are times when the Church is part of the problem and shares in the captivity and the moral ambiguity which hold so many people in our world in bondage. A word from outside must break into our closed systems, a word from the Lord—a word of liberation and justice. The Church is called to respond to this Word by bearing a prophetic witness.

Racism and a way of life which has violence built into it are clearly social issues with which we ought to be concerned. Current cultural developments are putting increasing pressures on the modern family and on interpersonal relationships in general. We must seek to reach the hearts of those who hold others captive, but we must also work for the transformation of the systems, in all spheres of life, that enslave people.

As Christians we are part of the social order. Non-involvement is therefore not really an option. The question is "How and to what end?" Take, for example, the rapid social changes through which our world is moving. We can ignore them. We can resist them. Or, we can seek to have the goals of Christ's kingdom become the direction in which society is moving.

Goals:

A. Church members with an awareness, understanding, and concern for conditions facing the human family in the economic, political, cultural and technological arenas.

B. Honest self-appraisal on the part of the church in order to face its own implication in oppression, hunger, suffering and dehumanization.

C. Congregations which stimulate and support group and individual involvement in social concerns.

D. Church members bearing a prophetic witness against systems, structures and powers which oppress human beings, and supporting oppressed peoples in the struggle for a more just society. [7]

ORGANIZING FOR MISSION—THE COUNCIL

The Ad Hoc Committee on Organization developed a constitution and bylaws for the new General Program Council. As the committee carried out its work, it sought to find integrating principles for organizing the broad mission/educational tasks of the GPC and providing it with a committee structure. After exploring several models, the committee recommended four committees with their assigned responsibilities. They were: Planning, surveying needs to which the General Program Council should respond, recommending long-range program goals and priorities, and recommending new programs or their development by ad hoc committees; Evaluation, regular, general review and evaluation of General Program Council policy and program and recommending selected programs for intensive review by ad hoc committees; Policy Administration, review of administration primarily as reported in "Administrative Reviews," and recommending action on major administrative matters referred to it by staff; and Communication, relating the concerns of the classes to the General Program Council, assisting General Program Council members to communicate with their classes, and offering counsel regarding effective interpretation of GPC program and policy to the church membership.[8] The General Program Council functioned in these committees for the years 1970 and 1971.

After two years of experience with the functional committees, the GPC discovered that they did not adequately integrate its various programs and staff services, did not proportionately distribute the budget decision-making role of the GPC, and did not facilitate in-depth involvement by members of the GPC. Because of the difficulties experienced with the functional committees, it was recommended that the five goal categories be used as the committee structure for the council.

> The content of each committee responsibility will be defined by subject, rather than function, and presumably be easier for committee members to integrate . . . Primary responsibility for goals would be assigned to specific committees . . . Ad hoc Committees on budget review could be integrated into standing committees . . . The committee structure would not parallel the staff administrative organization or the old board organization . . . The committee structure would change as the goals change.[9]

The GPC experimented with goal category committees for two meetings and then approved them as the permanent committee structure of the council. The GPC continued to carry out its committee tasks in the goal category structure (evangelism and church growth, Christian community, human welfare, personal growth, and relationships and social issues) until the major reorganization of the council into three divisions in the fall of 1980.

ORGANIZING FOR MISSION—THE STAFF

When the General Synod Executive Committee created the General Program Council in 1968, it also approved a staff organization for the new council. The staff structure was the Associate General Secretary-Program (almost immediately changed to Secretary for Program), who provided leadership for a program staff of executive secretaries World Ministries (3), Church Renewal and Evangelism, Church Planning and Development, Leadership Development, and Resource Development and Program Interpretation. As Arie R. Brouwer, who had been appointed Secretary for Program in April, began his responsibilities, he recommended a new structure for the program staff. It called for three divisions—World Ministries, Church Planning and Development, and Church Life and Mission. The Secretary for Resource Development and Program Interpretation was also continued in the new structure. The GSEC approved the new staff structure, and it served the GPC until the creation of "centers" in 1973.

The members of this new staff were: Secretary for World Ministries, John E. Buteyn, a former member of the staff of the Board of World Missions; Secretary for Church Planning and Development, Russell J. Redeker, a former member of the staff of the Board of North American Missions; Secretary for Church Life and Mission, Arthur O. Van Eck, a former member of the staff of the Board of Education; and Secretary for Resource Development and Program Interpretation, Issac C. Rottenberg, who had served parishes in New Shrewsbury and High Bridge, New Jersey. The divisions of Church Life and Mission and World Ministries had a number of staff people with specific program and administrative responsibilities.

As the Reformed Church explored its diversities following the 1969 General Synod's appointment of the Committee of Eighteen, it initiated a study on the location of its national offices. The national offices had been in New York City from their beginning. Periodically, committees evaluated the feasibility of moving the offices to a more geographically central location. As a part of this exploration on the desirability of retaining the national offices in New York City, the General Program Council developed its "centers" proposal which assumed that the re-

sources of the Reformed Church could be more thoroughly released for mission through several decentralized locations rather
than through one central office.

As the church discussed the centers proposal, Arie R. Brouwer,
executive secretary, prepared a brief brochure entitled "Classes
Question Centers!"

> Mission Festival '71 . . . demonstrated that world mission cannot
> be carried out in separation from local mission. The dispersal of
> world mission staff, missionaries and Christians from other coun-
> tries across the Reformed Church is an essential part of the center
> style. I believe it is fundamental to a renewal of our participation
> in world mission. The Reformed Church must be brought into
> more direct contact with the rest of the world church.[10]

The guidelines for the establishment of the individual centers
were:

> (1) In the population centers of the Reformed Church; (2) Near the
> clients to be served; (3) At the same site as synodical offices wher-
> ever feasible; (4) Close enough to other major RCA service agencies
> in the region to expedite relationships; (5) Relationship to other
> service agencies is to be given consideration; (6) Access to available
> office space; and (7) Initial number limited by present available
> resources.[11]

Individual centers throughout the church were to be linked in
"regional groups." The guidelines for regional groups were:

> (1) Centers serving churches in the same cultural or social eco-
> nomic situations or with essentially the same interests or problems
> should constitute a regional grouping; (2) Centers geographically
> near each other should have a regional administrative linkage which
> facilitates transfer of resources from one center to another—this
> could be done through a common administrator; (3) Regional groups
> should be complementary to synodical structures. This will make
> possible flexibility as social, economic regions undergo change. It
> will also encourage the cooperation of two or more judicatorial

structures who must work together in ministries which cross their boundaries; (4) Regional groups should ordinarily be designed so that staff of any one synod need relate to only one regional group; (5) The number of regional groups should be sufficiently limited so as to make it possible for regional secretaries to have easy communication with each other and staff in the denominational office in order to foster denomination wide communication and resource sharing.[12]

The General Program Council established four regional groups: Northeast (Particular Synod of Albany); Eastern Metropolitan (Particular Synods of New Jersey and New York); Midwestern (Particular Synods of Chicago and Michigan); and Western (Particular Synod of the West). The individual centers were located in Schenectady, New York; New York, New York; Grandville, Michigan; Lansing, Illinois; Orange City, Iowa; Pella, Iowa; and Anaheim, California.

The guidelines for assigning program staff to the various centers were:

(a) Each center should have enabling staff skilled in the process of planning and evaluation, development of resident skills, and correlation of resources and needs; (b) Each center or region should single out a major program focus for special attention; (c) Each center may have additional staff with specialized skills who will provide direct services to congregations. Particular skills will be determined by study and in consultation with the region. Care will be taken not to duplicate services of other agencies; and (d) Each regional group will have staff in the following areas: service to congregations, world missions, services to retired personnel and stewardship development.[13]

With the establishment of the centers, the General Program Council staff was reorganized. The new structure for the GPC staff was based on the regional centers, rather than the functional divisions adopted in 1968. Under the supervision of executive secretary Arie R. Brouwer served four secretaries for regional services (Douglas Walrath for the Northeast, Arthur O. Van Eck for the Eastern Metropolitan, Gordon Timmerman for the Midwestern, and Delbert Vander Haar for the Western); Secretary for Promotion and Communication, Issac C. Rottenberg; Coordinator of Human Resources, Alvin J. Poppen; and Secretary for Operations and Finance, Marvin D. Hoff. (A chart of this staff design is found on page 225.)

Through the creation of the centers, the General Program Council sought to "center" the services of the program staff, especially those related to the world mission program, in the life of the local churches across the denomination. The primary purpose was to more effectively relate the members of the local churches to the world missionary movement, both for their personal growth through understanding and participating in the mission of the church and for their financial contributions.

PEOPLE IN MISSION

As the staff of the newly-formed GPC began their work, they wrestled with the challenges facing them in the life and work of the Reformed Church. Immediately, they faced a major financial challenge. Their first budget had a $200,000 deficit, and inflation increased the projected deficit for their second budget. Before the GPC had completed its first year, the 1969 General Synod had brought to the fore the currents of division and suspicion in the RCA. As they began their work for the GPC, the staff began exploring the possibilities of holding a national RCA conference on mission. It was hoped that a national conference on mission, focusing on the ministries being conducted by local churches, would provide new understandings across the lines of division within the church.

The Congress on Evangelism held in Minneapolis, Minnesota, from September 8-13, 1969, provided the model for an RCA conference on mission. The congress, which was attended by 130 persons from the RCA, demonstrated that a mass gathering could be a very meaningful and moving experience. Because the designers of the congress had carefully provided a balance between large gatherings with platform presentations and small groups working on a wide variety of subjects, persons were deeply moved by their experiences in Minneapolis. The RCA participants in the congress, especially the members of the GPC staff who had already begun discussing the benefits of planning an RCA conference on mission, left Minneapolis with a vision of new beginnings in the life of the RCA.

At its fall meeting (1969), the General Program Council approved the preliminary plans for hosting a conference on mission. It was to be called the "Festival of Evangelism."

The word "evangelism" speaks of an almost 2,000 year tradition during which the disciples of Christ have sought to share the message and the reality of the new life which he came to bring to the world. The word "festival" indicates that, in the midst of all the agonies through which both church and world are passing in our day, we stand ready to affirm, experience and rejoice in the reality of the risen Christ which comes to God's people through the Holy Spirit.[14]

The festival was scheduled for April 1-4, 1970, in Cobo Hall, Detroit, Michigan. The Classis of Lake Erie agreed to be the host classis for the festival.

As the festival task force began its work, members wrote a statement of expectation, declaring:

In obedience, we intend to listen to what God is saying to the world through Scripture, the witness of the Holy Spirit and the urgency of human need; and to discover the ministry in the world to which Christ the Lord is calling his church. In faith, we expect: -to discover together what the message of the Bible is concerning the mission of God's people in his world; -to enter into the brokenness of the world which God has loved so much that he sent his Son; -to gain a deeper insight into the wide variety of ways in which Christians share the good news of Christ; -to encounter fellow Christians in frank and open recognition of both our unity and diversity in Christ, and to find the glorious freedom which is offered in him. By "being all together in one place" we shall joyfully expect the Lord to "do a new thing among us."[15]

The "listening" was to take place in small groups designed for personal sharing and exploration at key moments throughout the festival, church-at-work groups which presented more than twenty-five training experiences for the church to reach out into its world, and platform presentations by resource persons. The three platform presentations were: "A Call to Evangelism," by John Anderson, Jr.; "When the Saints Go Marching Out," by Leighton Ford; and "Evangelism: The Response of the Church," by Tom Skinner. Dr. Howard Hageman presented the meditation, "So Send I You," at the closing communion service.

God did a new thing. Maybe it would be more appropriate to state that he did new things in the lives of the persons who gathered at Cobo Hall. The festival was the largest national assembly of the Reformed Church, with more than 1,500 full-time and 500 part-time registrants. The platform presentations, the various small group meetings, and the midnight conversations in the corridors all added up to a unique experience for God's people in a church struggling to find its identity for serving Christ in the seventies.

Tom Skinner brought a powerful message to the festival participants. A black evangelist who grew up in Harlem and participated in the life of its street gangs before his conversion to Christ, Skinner spoke of:

> The three main issues that the church must address itself to if it is indeed going to be the church. First of all there is the issue of identity. In our society people are trying to discover who in the world they are . . . The second issue is that of community. Once I find out who I am and what my bag is, I have to know who the cat sitting next to me is and what he is all about . . . The third issue is the issue of power . . . The issue in American society is where do we get the power to do what is right?[16]

As he brought his message to a close, Skinner challenged the festival audience to do something.

You want to do something? Instead of challenging your kids to go to Africa or Asia or South America, start instituting some movement to Harlem, Bedford-Stuyvesant, Watts, Los Angeles. Start putting your financial resources into black Christians who are working in the black community trying to reach their people. Get your college presidents to start providing scholarships to black kids who want a good Christian liberal arts education and change your curriculum to meet them. Start instituting in your schools studies in black history and tell your own kids what is happening in the black community. Let the real estate men in your churches know that you are disgusted with their block-busting policies and their refusal to sell to blacks. Get the employers and executives in your church to create jobs for hard-core blacks and to create opportunities for black executives in their companies. If you are a pastor, go back to your church and start preaching against racism. Have the nerve to stand up and tell your church boards that you are no longer interested in your salary at the expense of truth . . . But let me close by saying, you can't do it without life. You can't do it until there has been a radical change from within. Christ must be living in you, and he must lead you out to face and meet the needs of society and to heal its brokenness because, as I said before, Jesus Christ is the answer, if we only know what that really means.[17]

After Skinner had finished preaching, the hushed awe of the audience became focused on several young blacks from a Detroit Reformed Church carrying a cross down the center aisle. Upon reaching the platform, they, one by one, expressed their protest against the sins in the world and declared: "I crucify race prejudice," "I crucify hatred towards others;" "I crucify indifference." They then invited persons desiring to crucify their old lives to join them in a symbolic march around the auditorium and out into the streets of Detroit. Hundreds joined them. They spilled out into the main streets of downtown Detroit following a cross and singing the hymns of the faith (such as "The Battle Hymn of the Republic"). Cars stopped to allow them the right away of the streets. Pedestrians watched from the sidewalks. Young and old from the Reformed Church marched for Jesus at midnight in the streets of Detroit.

The next morning, less than twelve hours after marching in the streets of Detroit, the festival participants heard an impromptu speech from the Rev. William Mason, a black RCA minister. He declared:

> It is a solemn responsibility that I take up this morning. Like Jacob, I have wrestled with the angel all night long, but unlike Jacob, I have been unable to let him go because he has not yet blessed me . . . The excitement of this convention must not obscure the fact that in an age of revolution for the black man this festival is not adequately speaking to the liberation of the black man. Lest I be abstract, I will cite some concrete problems: 1. The R. C. A. has not actively sought the black man . . . 2. There are about half a dozen black ministers in the R. C. A. . . . 3. There are a handful of black students in R. C. A. colleges, and most are unhappy . . . 4. Black congregations in the R. C. A. are considered mission fields rather than full, participatory, and contributory equal bodies . . . 5. *The Church Herald*, which could be a liberating journal, speaks mainly for and to a certain section of the church . . . 6. The decision-making bodies of the church do not guarantee black representation . . . 7. Opportunities for blacks in key administrative positions are almost nil . . . 8. The Black Council was formed out of crisis paternalism and it is not a vital black voice in the denomination. . . .[18]

After some hushed, and not so hushed, dialogue, regarding the statement of Bill Mason, festival participants agreed to break into small groups and personally search their hearts on the challenges laid before them by the Revs. Skinner and Mason.

As festival participants gathered at the closing communion service, a teen-ager rose to declare that it would be sinful to partake of the Lord's body because of the unresolved issues set before the Lord and the assembly by the Revs. Skinner and Mason. In a moving declaration, he invited people to abstain from the elements as a sign of the brokenness and sin in the life of the assembly and the church. Mr. Mason then responded by calling persons to receive the grace of Christ in the Supper, and commit themselves to serve Him in the future. Gathered in the more than seventy small groups, the assembly prayed, sang, wept, laughed, and received the gifts of Christ's body and blood. A "new thing" had truly happened in the life of the Reformed Church. God had invaded the closed lives of many people, who now stood open to his leading and new fellowship with their brothers and sisters in the church. Throughout the life of the RCA, but especially at the 1970 General Synod, people sensed a new spirit moving through an old, almost broken, church.

MISSION FESTIVAL '71

Within days after the moving close of the Festival of Evangelism in Detroit, the members of the General Program Council and their staff had begun to plan for a second festival. Was this merely an attempt to capitalize on a technique that had worked, or was it a serious attempt to wrestle with mission in the life of the RCA? Had the GPC learned a new trick for healing some of the wounds of the RCA, or did it seek to lead the church into new understandings of, and commitments to, the mission of Jesus Christ in the 1970s? In reponse to the question, "Why Mission Festival '71?," GPC Executive Secretary Arie R. Brouwer wrote:

> Because we need help! . . . Is there anyone these days who does not have more questions than answers? The questions are felt everywhere . . . Today's temptation—and many have yielded—is to use the old slogans and the familiar language at home while the mission away from home undergoes change . . . Mission Festival '71 provides an opportunity for the people of God gathered in the Reformed Church in America to hear the "open truth" from people engaged in mission all over the world. A large cross-section of Reformed Church and overseas church leaders will be there to speak and hear the truth. Together we will hear the call for renewal and change.[19]

Between October 6 and 9, 1971, more than 1,200 persons concerned about the world mission of the church of Jesus Christ gathered in Milwaukee, Wisconsin. Immediately before the festival the GPC had sponsored a Consultation on World Mission at Green Lake, Wisconsin. The consultation brought together more than 100 persons from across the Reformed Church who were engaged in world mission. The consultation was a more intellectual exploration of the issues in world mission.

Under the theme "a new commitment to an old task," the participants in the festival heard addresses in plenary sessions, participated in "church-in-dialogue" groups, and gained new insights from the more than twenty-five practical workshops on mission. The plenary addresses were: "Our Mission: to Introduce Men to Jesus Christ," by Eugene Nida; "Jesus Christ and the Church's Mission," by Paul E. Little; "Missionary, Go Home," by John Gatu; and "The Present Crisis in Mission," by Jose Miguez-Bonino. Gatu and Miguez-Bonino, the two speakers from the Third World, provided the greatest challenges to the festival participants.

Dr. John Gatu was serving as general secretary of the Presbyterian Church of East Africa at the time. He had earlier, at a private meeting of the Africa committee of the Department of Overseas Missions of the National Council of Churches in New York, called for the withdrawal of foreign missionaries for a period of five years. Unaware of this earlier statement, mission festival participants were stunned to hear Gatu declare:

> In this address I am going to argue that the time has come for the withdrawal of foreign missionaries from many parts of the Third World, that the churches of the Third World must be allowed to find their own identity, and that the continuaton of the present missionary movement is a hindrance to the selfhood of the church . . . Ivan Illich has put it very clearly: "Men and money sent with missionary motivation carry a foreign Christian image, a foreign pastoral input, and a foreign political image." . . . We cannot build the church in Africa on alms given by overseas churches, nor are we serving the cause of the Kingdom by turning all bishops, gen-

eral secretaries, moderators, presidents, superintendents, into good, enthusiastic beggars, by always singing the tune of poverty in the church of the Third World . . . But I am also saying that we in the Third World must liberate ourselves from the bondage of Western dependency by refusing anything that renders impotent the development of our spiritual resources, which in turn makes it impossible for the church in the Third World to engage in the mission of God in their own areas . . . I started by saying that the missionaries should be withdrawn from the Third World for a period of at least five years. I will go further and say that missionaries should be withdrawn, period. The reason is that we must allow God the Holy Spirit to direct our next move without giving him a timetable. Who knows what we shall need after that period?"[20]

People filed out of the auditorium for their church-in-dialogue groups in stunned silence or hushed conversation. Some broke into tears in their groups, feeling rejected in their deep call to serve God in mission. Some wrestled genuinely with this thunderbolt challenge from a servant of Christ. A special workshop was quickly organized to provide for discussion of this unexpected challenge to a new commitment in mission.

Jose Miguez-Bonino, while sensitive to the impact made by Gatu's call for a moratorium, declared:

The basic fact, though, to which all the other factors are related, is this—and the crisis we face hinges on it—we have discovered that the missionary enterprise of the last one hundred and fifty years is closely related to, and interwoven with, the expansion of the economic, political, and cultural influence of the Anglo-Saxon world . . . certain things are clear. First, this is the process through which the world has been, and increasingly is being, divided into the affluent, northern world, and the impoverished, so-called Third World. Second, this constantly deteriorating situation is no longer accepted by the Third World . . . Third, consciously or unconsciously, and mostly unconsciously, the missionary enteprise has been related to the routes of expansion, the channels of penetration, the slogans, the cultural patterns of this process of expansion and domination. Fourth, Christians in both the sending and the receiving countries are increasingly aware of, and concerned with, this fact, which results in remorse, uncertainty, loss of confidence, and crises in identity for many missionaries and national church leaders, both here and overseas . . . The real problem is that the alliance of missions and Western capitalistic expansion has distorted the Gospel beyond recognition, and that evangelism, prayer, worship, and personal devotions have been held captive to an individualistic, other-worldly, success-crazy, legalistic destruction of the Gospel . . . Your church, your money, your people will either reinforce the pattern of domination and exploitation, or participate in this struggle for liberation . . . I wish I could spare myself and you the harshness of what I am going to say, but I don't think I can. The struggle which we are called to join, which I am calling you to join, pitches us against the policies and interests of this country, at least against the policies and interests that dominate this country.[21]

A new challenge was placed before the festival. Rather than soften the challenge brought by Gatu, Miguez-Bonino deepened it.

Throughout the festival people wrestled with the challenges presented to them by Gatu and Miguez-Bonino. In small groups, at the dinner table, in hotel rooms, festival participants struggled with twentieth-century mission themes and issues. As with the Festival of Evangelism, Mission Festival '71 concluded at the Lord's Table. People received strength for their spiritual pilgrimage, a pilgrimage of mission, through the broken body and shed blood of Jesus Christ. But, the questions were not answered, the issues not wrapped up and settled. Edwin Mulder, then pastor of the Second Reformed Church of Hackensack, New Jersey, wrote:

Mission Festival '71 confronted us with some very real issues. What is the future of missions? What shape will the missionary endeavor of the church take? I tried to listen carefully, especially to those speakers who were making a "strange" sound. The Festival convinced me that I need to do my homework in the area of the missionary endeavor of the church. Personally I would like to have had someone help us make our re-entry on Friday night. I can anticipate that someone will say, "But that is just the point, we need to agonize and wrestle with the implications of change." I only hope that there will not be those who throw up their hands and say that we need no longer concern ourselves with the rest of the world.[22]

Through mini-festivals in the major geographical centers of the Reformed Church, the agonizing and wrestling continued. Mission Festival '71 brought home to many persons throughout the Reformed Church the need for a new commitment and understanding of the mission of Jesus in the world.

FAMILY FESTIVAL

As persons filed into the large auditorium in Milwaukee for Mission Festival '71, a large billboard invited them to attend the Family Festival of the RCA in the summer of 1972. The festival spirit had captured the Reformed Church. Some debated the wisdom of planning two festivals in successive years (the Family Festival was already in the planning stages when discussion on the Mission Festival began), but both went forward. Families of the RCA were invited to the beautiful YMCA camp in Estes Park, Colorado, for the third festival. Located in the majestic Colorado Rockies, the YMCA camp provided an inspiring site for the Family Festival.

Three thousand children, youth, and adults gathered at Estes Park. Between July 21 and 24 festival participants explored many themes related to family living in the latter part of the twentieth century. Under the theme of "New Life in Family Living," the participants listened to addresses by Dr. Roy Rodgers, shared in covenant clusters on the subjects "Forces that Affect the Family—Conflict," "Ways to Strengthen the Family—Covenant," and "Equipping the Family for Mission—Commitment," participated in rap sessions on family conflicts, sex education, family Bible study, the effects of radio and television, abortion, how to build marriages, and many others, and were entertained by popular figures, including Pat Boone, the Murk Family and ten students from the drama department of Hope College who presented a drama entitled, *You're a Good Man, Charlie Brown*.

As Dr. Louis H. Benes, the editor of *The Church Herald*, reported:

> The Family Festival had to be a different kind of Festival from the Evangelism and Mission festivals. It needed a program fashioned to meet the needs and desires of little children as well as grand-parents. The program was well-rounded to meet these needs, pro-viding both a core of biblical study and discussion and also a rejoicing in the blessings of love within the family that made it a real "Festival."[23]

Both the Festival of Evangelism and Mission Festival '71 had brought deep challenges and confrontation into the public life of the Reformed Church, but in an atmosphere of acceptance and understanding. The Family Festival was more confirming than confronting, and through it the GPC engaged the people of the Reformed Church with one another and with current issues in their lives.

JUBILEE/76

The festivals created a new spirit and mood in the life of the Reformed Church. As persons from across the nation gathered at the three festivals, they had opportunities to be challenged in their Christian faith and to share with one another. Because of the times of personal sharing, as in the church-in-dialogue groups at Mission Festival '71 and the covenant clusters at the Family Festival, new ties and links were established throughout the Re-formed Church. As people from the RCA gathered at other meet-ings, especially the annual General Synods, these new ties and links deeply affected the spirit of the debates and discussions in the life of the church.

As the United States began preparations for celebrating its

bicentennial, the General Program Council established a task force to make plans for a time of celebration within the Reformed Church. Gradually, the task force adopted the Jubilee theme and the festival model for the RCA's celebration of the bicentennial.

Jubilee/76 was held at Slippery Rock College, Slippery Rock, Pennsylvania, August 13-16, 1976. Carol Wagner, chairwoman of the task force, described Jubilee/76 as

> an opportunity for us as a Reformed Church family to get together and reflect on what it means to be a Christian in our day . . . There are many "surface" bicentennial events, tempting us to treat our citizenship in shallow ways. We need to look deeper than this . . . The biblical concept of Jubilee will help us to handle such issues as freedom and justice . . . In our society, there's unequal application of justice. There are concentrations of wealth. There's worldwide hunger. There are false values in family life. We need better stewardship in our life-styles on all of these.[24]

The theme for Jubilee/76 was the twenty-fifth chapter of Leviticus. This theme was developed by the major speakers and workshops in four areas: land and goods: the economic order; freedom and justice: the political order; community and covenant: the social order; and God and country: the religious order. John Perkins, president of Voice of Calvary, a Christian community development ministry in Mendenhall and Jackson, Mississippi, gave the keynote addresses, exploring the economic implications of Luke 4 and providing practical suggestions for action in the economic order by individual Christians and local congregations. Through workshops, films, and dramatic presentations, the four themes from Leviticus were explored.

Jubilee/76 did not attract the number of participants attending the other festivals. A variety of reasons were given for the registration barely reaching 1,152 (the Festival of Evangelism had drawn 2,000; Mission Festival '71, 1,200; and Family Festival, 3,000). Some felt that the geographic setting was not good (Slippery Rock is at least a day's drive from any center of Reformed churches); others felt that the festival movement had ended in the Reformed Church; still others that the Jubilee theme was too political for members of the RCA. Even though John Stapert, who became editor of *The Church Herald* in 1975, wrote in reporting Jubilee/76: "the mood was a happy one, affirming the place of Festival/Jubilee events as an essential element in the life of the Reformed Church in America,"[25] Jubilee/76 was the last festival sponsored by the General Program Council. Some suggested a national festival event to celebrate the 350th anniversary of the RCA, but the birthday was celebrated at parties in the major geographical areas of the church. Through the four festivals the GPC had led the members of the RCA into new and deeper explorations of their faith and had provided an atmosphere for persons in the church to arrive at a new sensitivity to one another and to the working of the Holy Spirit.

MISSION PRIORITIES IN THE SEVENTIES

As the members of the General Program Council wrestled with their diverse inheritance of mission/education policies and programs, they began to establish priorities for implementing their responsibilities on behalf of the Reformed Church. A review of the GPC's decade of service to the church shows its major priorities to have been: shifting the mission resources of the Reformed Church from the personal growth and relationships goal category to the goal categories evangelism and church growth and social issues; reducing the resources of the Reformed Church being used in medical and educational institutions; linking with other denominations in developing and providing educational resources for local churches; maintaining mature, partnership relationships with churches throughout the world; and lodging responsibility for mission supervision and funding as close as possible to the program itself.

As the General Program Council organized its various programs into the new goal categories, the broad shape of its program became visible for the first time. Previously, the programs had been summarized on a geographical basis, so the members of the council merely saw the relationship of the resources being contributed to various areas of the world. With the division into the new goal categories, it was evident that the major mission resources of the Reformed Church were being allocated to personal growth and relationships—the goal category that included programs at educational institutions around the world. After seeing this allocation of its resources, the GPC decided to reduce the proportion in personal growth and relationships and increase the proportion in evangelism and church growth and in social issues. The GPC was successful in reducing personal growth and relationships and increasing evangelism and church growth; but it was not able to increase social issues; in fact its proportion of the annual program budget dropped. Between 1973 and 1980 the results were:

	1973	1980
Evangelism	560,659 (20%)	1,079,484 (26.5%)
Personal Growth	1,045,955 (38%)	1,013,849 (25%)
Social Issues	162,760 (6%)	189,396 (4.6%)

In addition to significantly increasing its support for evangelism programs outside the Reformed Church, the GPC, in the early seventies, added a second Secretary for Evangelism, whose purpose was to assist local churches in increasing evangelistic programs in their communities.

As the General Program Council reviewed the programs in the personal growth and relationships goal category, it became clear to members of the council that most of the funds were being used in educational institutions. In addition, significant funds were being contributed to medical institutions in the human welfare goal category. In order to wrestle with the problem of its relationships to institutions, the GPC appointed an ad hoc committee to develop guidelines for these relationships. In 1973 institutions were receiving more than one-third of its denominational mission contributions.

After almost two years of reviewing the institutional programs to which the GPC was related, the ad hoc committee presented two sets of guidelines to the November, 1971, meeting of the GPC. The GPC adopted the guidelines and spent the next years judiciously implementing them. The new guidelines for relationships to institutions were:

> The General Program Council should: Enable the establishment of institutions but not maintain permanent support. Permanent support hinders the self-sustaining function of institutions, prevents them from becoming truly indigenous and prevents the essential accountability of institutions to local boards. It also hinders the appropriate accountability of missionaries to institutional administration; Review institutional relationships carefully and regularly. Institutional ministries tend to proliferate and expand presenting a quantitative problem. They require increased resources and supervision from the General Program Council; Avoid competition with suitable community and government services when these become available; Surrender decision-making to institutional boards and administrators; Encourage a direct relationship between institutions and constituency. A means of facilitating this would be establishing voluntary agencies (societies) and withdrawing supervision and financial commitment when these agencies are established; Participate in drawing up mutually agreed upon action plans for aiding institutional autonomy; Assist in establishing local managing boards for all institutions; and Place all financial and personnel commitments on a cost/time frame basis. The General Program Council, in placing its missionaries within institutions, should: Assure that missionaries are accountable to the administrator and board of the institution. Missionary relationships to the General Program Council should not supercede this local accountability; Establish the financial support of missionaries by institutions at the level of the local salary scale; Promote an appropriate balance of indigenous and missionary personnel in institutional staffs, as long as personnel assistance is required, and assist in ar-

ranging a time schedule for reduction of missionary personnel in institutional staffs; Assist in formulating policies so that institutional staff members are paid for services rendered without regard to nationality. The implementation of such equity in remuneration may require increasing the salaries of national staff and/or withholding a portion of the missionary salary for expenses in the United States; Welcome flexible procedures so that financial commitment is not limited to support of missionary personnel but to provide the needed staff skills and expertise in the institution; Endorse missionary presence in government and community institutional programs as an appropriate form of Christian witness; and Participate in mutual review of missionary appointments with the institution and the missionary, reserving the final decision on appointment and re-appointment to the General Program Council.[26]

The GPC implemented these new guidelines in a variety of ways. In Japan, it received a salary grant from the schools to which GPC missionaries were assigned. In Oman, the hospital programs of the Reformed Church were integrated into the health care system of the government, and missionaries were assigned to work in government hospitals. In Brewton, Alabama, a local board composed of people from the community, from the Reformed Church at large, and from the GPC was established to supervise the high school program at Southern Normal. The application of the guidelines in two institutions, the Bahrain Hospital and the Annville Institute, will be presented in more detail.

The Bahrain Hospital (in the Middle East) had established a local Board of Managers in the 1960s. As the board became more and more active in supervising the hospital, it asked for the GPC's support in establishing an autonomous, private, Christian medical program in Bahrain. The GPC endorsed the request, and transferred the assets of its hospital to the new board and agreed to provide personnel for the new program. The local Board of Managers has successfully operated the hospital for almost a decade.

The GPC's experience with the application of the guidelines

to Annville Institute was less successful. An ad hoc committee reported to the November, 1972, meeting of the GPC:

> seeking to avoid duplication, (we) believe that substantially im-
> proved educational opportunities in the region's public schools no
> longer justify our involvement in that type of program . . . (we)
> propose that Annville Institute become a boarding facility for young
> people primarily from multi-problem homes and potential drop-
> outs. The students would do their regular classroom work in the
> local schools, but would be provided with a dynamic Christian
> "home environment". . . .[27]

Because the local steering committee and the staff of the institute did not concur in the proposal of the ad hoc committee,
the GPC did not implement this new direction for the institute.
A local board was established, and several years later it concluded
that the high school academic program should be dropped. The
board presently uses the facilities of the former institute for rec-
reational and spiritual programs for the youth and adults of the
surrounding area.

The General Program Council, through its application of the
guidelines and the careful work of a number of ad hoc committees, has been able to significantly reduce the Reformed Church's
involvement in medical and educational institutions. A decade,
which is actually a short time because most of these institutions
are at least fifty years old, has been required to accomplish this
shift.

As a successor to the Board of Education, the General Program
Council inherited responsibility for supporting local church educational programs for children, youth, and adults. The GPC chose
to carry out the nurture aspect of its mission task through establishing cooperative relationships with other denominations. The
Board of Education had also carried out its responsibilities in this
manner, especially in the preparation of the Covenant Life Curriculum, a joint endeavor of five American denominations.
Through its membership in Joint Educational Development and

a cooperative arrangement with the Christian Reformed Church, this aspect of the GPC's program was carried forward.

Joint Educational Development (JED) was a consortium of six denominations: the United Presbyterian Church in the USA, the Presbyterian Church in the U.S., the Episcopal Church, the United Church of Christ, the Christian Church, and the Reformed Church in America. JED sought to provide resources for local churches to utilize in carrying out their nurture responsibilities. By the end of the seventies, curricular materials had been prepared for church school programs. Utilizing a four-track approach to curriculum development, JED was able to provide great diversity from which local churches were able to choose those materials most suitable for their particular needs.

On behalf of the Reformed Church, cooperative relationships were also established with the Christian Reformed Church. The Bible Way curriculum of the Christian Reformed Church was used by many Reformed churches, and the staff of the GPC served as consultants for its editing and evaluation. Through its relationships with JED and the Bible Way curriculum of the Christian Reformed Church, the GPC was able to offer the educational programs of local Reformed churches a broad range of nurture materials.

The Reformed Church in America, through its Board for World Mission and its Board for North American Mission, had "church-to-church" relationships with the Presbyterian Church of Mexico, the Presbyterian Church of Taiwan, the Presbyterian Church of Singapore and Malaysia, the United Church of Christ in Japan, the Church of South India, the Church of Christ in China (Hong Kong), the United Church of Christ in the Philippines, and Middle Eastern churches in Bahrain, Oman, and Kuwait. The General Program Council became the Reformed Church's link to these diverse churches. During the first years of maintaining these links, the GPC functioned on a situation-to-situation basis. By 1976 it had developed enough experience to prepare a policy statement for guiding the relationships.

Several drafts of the proposed statement had been shared with the overseas churches. When the final draft was discussed by the council, representatives of the partner churches in India, Taiwan, Japan, Kuwait, and Mexico met with the council. The visiting churchmen shared the history and mission philosophies of their own churches with the members of the council. In meetings with the goal category committees, the churchmen and the members of the GPC discussed the calls for a missionary moratorium, the problems created by unilateral mission and action, the positive and negative roles of money in mission, and the benefits and strengths of long-term and short-term mission programs. Based on these extensive consultations with partner churches, the General Program Council adopted its policy statement on "World Mission Relationships."

> Goal: In obedience to Jesus Christ and in the spirit of mutual responsibility, the GPC commits itself to the development of sending and receiving relationships throughout the whole Christian church which strengthen the mission and enrich the life of all partners. Strategies: The General Program Council will use several strategies to achieve the above goal, and consequently, the term, function and form of the relationship will depend on the situation.

> "Joint Action"—Coordinated or cooperative action between two or more churches or mission agencies. Situation—GPC mission shall ordinarily be initiated through joint action. Term—Joint action relationships shall be continued for the duration of the action agreed upon or in accordance with denominational policy where applicable (e.g., NCC and WCC units). All such relationships shall be regularly examined in the budget process. Function—Joint action shall be undertaken for purposes of communication and coordination of separate programs and for purposes of cooperative action. Form—Joint action may be undertaken through consortia or co-operative agencies. The former serves as a center for communication and coordination. The latter is an agency created to act on behalf of its member units. The GPC shall employ both means in its effort to develop world mission relationships throughout the whole Christian church.

> "United Mission"—A mutual relationship between two or more churches for the purpose of common mission. Situation—United

mission shall be the usual form of GPC mission. Term—United mission shall continue as long as the GPC is related to other bodies in mission. Function—United mission shall be undertaken for the purpose of strengthening the mission and enriching the life of all partners. Form—United mission requires a mutual relationship which includes a shared life as well as a common task. Whenever possible, such a relationship shall include more than two churches of different ecclesiastical traditions and different racial, ethnic or national backgrounds. Responsible Christian witness may sometimes require a temporary discontinuance of some forms of united mission in order to permit independent action.

"Individual Action"—Action by a single church or mission agency. Situation—Individual action shall be undertaken by the GPC only for programs which the Council believes it must undertake even though it can secure no partners. Term—An individual action undertaken by the GPC shall be continued in that form for the shortest possible period. The Council shall make an intensive effort to secure other denominations, agencies, or judicatories as partners in that program. Function—An individual action shall be undertaken to bear a particular witness only when we are compelled by conscience. We shall seek to hear that witness as well as bear it. Form—An individual action shall be undertaken by the GPC only after thorough consultation with our traditional partners in mission and other church bodies directly affected by our action.[28]

Through this policy statement, which arose out of its mission practice as well as its mission reflections, the GPC committed itself to strive to be a mature partner in Christian mission. The days for unilateral action, except in exceptional situations, had passed.

Two church-to-church relationships will illustrate this crucial aspect of the council's life and work. The Reformed Church in America was one of the last to establish a church-to-church relationship with the Presbyterian Church of Mexico, as it carried on its missionary program in the State of Chiapas, the southernmost state in Mexico. Because most of its work had been with native Indians, it had not been as closely related to the programs and policies of the Presbyterian Church. Nonetheless, the GPC sought to be a responsible partner of the Mexican church. When there was a difference of opinion between the Presbyterian Church of Mexico and its mission partners on cooperation with the Roman Catholic Church, the GPC approved "the concept which recognizes the autonomy of the National (N.P.C.M.) Presbyterian Church in Mexico and acknowledges the right of that Church to formulate the conditions under which missionaries come to Mexico to serve under her direction."[29] The following statement communicates the GPC's spirit to the Mexican church:

> Although we may hold differing views concerning cooperative acts with personnel of the Roman Catholic Church, we do respect the autonomy of the N.P.C.M. Accordingly, therefore, we affirm the right of the N.P.C.M. to formulate the conditions under which missionaries shall labor. We will encourage our missionaries to work in your midst in a spirit of harmony, being sensitive to the N.P.C.M. and the ministries to which they are called . . . We continue to rejoice in the opportunities that God has given us to join in a ministry with you in Mexico and we look forward to the leading of the Holy Spirit as we join our endeavors in the days ahead.[30]

Several years later the NPCM adopted a statement accepting full responsibility for the mission programs conducted in its country. With the exception of missionaries working with the indigenous peoples, missionaries serving within Mexico were asked to leave. Although the missionaries of the GPC were expected to continue for a period of transition, the GPC voted to "request the National Presbyterian Church of Mexico and the Reformed Church in America to form a team to establish goals for the RCA-related work in Mexico that will emphasize the development of National Church leadership enabling that church to take primary responsibility for all mission programs now carried on in her judicatories. . . . "[31] Although the missionaries of the GPC have remained in Mexico, the supervision of their work has been more and more transferred to the General Assembly of the National Presbyterian Church of Mexico. The mission involvement of the

GPC in Mexico has become less and less "individual action" and more and more "united mission."

The GPC's church-to-church relationship with the Presbyterian Church of Taiwan has shown a different dimension of partnership in mission. When the Chinese from the mainland of China established the Republic of China on the island of Taiwan in 1949, they subjected the Taiwanese population to their authority and rule. Although the Taiwanese comprise more than eighty-five percent of the people on the island, they have had almost no voice in their national government. Because the Chinese government has been able to control all of the Taiwanese organizations on the island except the Presbyterian Church, that church has become the bearer of the hopes and aspirations of the Taiwanese people. Several times in the 1970s the Taiwanese church has issued calls for more representative and democratic government on the island, and each time the GPC has expressed its solidarity with the Taiwanese church.

In response to a 1972 statement by the Presbyterian Church on "Our National Fate," the General Program Council expressed its "admiration of, and support, for their statement . . . (and expressed) to the President of the United States and the Secretary of State our support for . . . the right of self-determination by the people now living in Taiwan. . . ."[32] The GPC called upon the members of the Reformed Church to write their representatives and senators expressing their support for self-determination for the Taiwanese people.

By 1974 the pressure of its government on the Presbyterian Church in Taiwan had increased, and the GPC called upon

> the President of the United States and the Secretary of State, as they presently negotiate new policies and relationships in Asia, especially with the People's Republic of China, to listen carefully to the voice of the silenced people in Taiwan who are faced with the threat of once again becoming the victims of world power politics. Our policy should seek an opportunity for the fifteen million people of Taiwan to participate in determining their own political future.[33]

A 1979 action declared:

> in affirmation of its partnership with the Presbyterian Church in
> Taiwan: the GPC (1) Reaffirms its sense of unity in Christ with the
> Presbyterian Church in Taiwan; (2) Reaffirms its support of the
> Presbyterian Church in Taiwan's concern for human rights and
> justice; (3) Affirms support for Taiwanese Christians in their desire
> to participate in decisions determining their future corporate life;
> and (4) Requests all congregations of the Reformed Church in
> America to remember in prayer the people and leaders of the
> Presbyterian Church in Taiwan.[34]

The government intensified and personalized the pressure on
the Presbyterian Church through the arrest and imprisonment of
its general secretary, the Rev. C. M. Kao, in the spring of 1980.
The GPC responded to the arrest of Mr. Kao by sending a lawyer
to inquire into the circumstances of his arrest and pending trial.
Mr. Harry De Bruyn, a former president of the General Synod,
represented the RCA to the Presbyterian Church of Taiwan during this time of intense pressure upon it from the government of
the island.

Through its church-to-church relationships the GPC sought to
honor the mission plans and strategies of its partners, and also
support them in their search for justice and peace. Increasingly
the Reformed Church lived as a "partner" in church-to-church
relationships, rather than the senior partner.

REGIONALIZATION

As the General Program Council began its responsibilities for
the diverse mission programs of the RCA, it appointed an Ad
Hoc Committee on Classis/Council Relationships of Pastors and
Congregations in North American Programs. Through the work
of this committee the GPC sought to lodge responsibility and
accountability for funding and supervision of mission programs as
near to the program as possible. The GPC did not want to supervise nor fund from afar. Based on the work of this committee
the GPC approved

the concept of dividing responsibility for program ministries along regional and national lines with Classes and Particular Synods having responsibility in their respective Missional Zones and GPC having responsibility outside those Missional Zones . . . the GPC shall assume accountability for a program within a Missional Zone of a judicatory only upon the request of or in consultation with that judicatory. . . .[35]

The American Indian churches were one of the mission programs affected by this commitment of the GPC. Although all of them had been transferred to classes within their geographical area (initially all of them had been members of the Classis of New York), the funding and supervision of these churches had remained in New York. Gradually accountability for these churches was assumed by their classes, and the GPC provided financial and staff services as requested.

The church extension and urban ministries programs of the particular synods also came under this policy of the GPC. During the early 1970s the GPC made "block grants" to the particular synods so that they could progressively assume financial, along with program, accountability for these mission efforts within their "zone." Although the GPC continued to make grants to the various particular synods for these programs, the commitment to "missional zones" did transfer a great deal of responsibility to the classes and particular synods.

ADVANCE IN MISSION

The General Program Council developed two special programs for leading an "advance" in mission within the Reformed Church. The first, focused on advancing within the regular program of the council, took place in 1972 and 1973 and was called "Advance in Mission." The second, implemented through a special five-million-dollar-fund drive, was the "Reformed Church Growth Program."

After the General Program Council had been serving the church for several years and had been able to accept responsibility for the diverse programs and policies passed on to it by the former boards, the membership of the Reformed Church became restless for new programs in mission. Two ad hoc committees were appointed to develop programs for advancing in mission. One was charged with responsibility for "Advance in Overseas Mission" and the other for "Advance in National Urban Mission." After a year of reflection, study, and program development, the committees presented their reports in the fall of 1973.

The Committee on Advance in Overseas Mission had explored the possibilities for establishing an overseas mission program in a geographical area of the world where the RCA had not served previously. After reviewing the needs for mission advance in its present relationships and the possibilities for a new geographical area, the committee recommended a series of new projects for advancing in the present areas of mission related to the GPC. The National Urban Mission Committee had arrived at much the same conclusion—urban advance should be carried out through the present sites for ministry in urban areas served by the Reformed Church.

After its review of the two "advance" reports, the General Program Council adopted the following programs for advancing in mission: the development of black and Hispanic ministerial leadership for the RCA, $20,000; evangelistic programs, including the appointment of a missionary couple in Ethiopia, $50,000; a leadership training program for the Presbytery of Chiapas, $15,000; seed funding to assist urban churches in beginning new programs in ministry, $25,000; relief and rehabilitation for Vietnam, $25,000; funds to provide training for lay people to acquire skills for urban ministry, $7,000; and a planning program to strengthen the World Mission Program of the GPC, $10,000. The programs were incorporated into the annual budget of the GPC, and provided a focus for "new" steps in mission.

As the Reformed Church continued to experience a decline in its membership through the impact of the social trends which were portrayed in chapter 2, discussion developed around the theme of "church growth." The president of the 1975 General

Synod, the Rev. Raymond Rewerts, focused his president's report
and the synod's worship experiences on church growth. The General Program Council devoted its November, 1975, meeting to
the theme. Gradually, a perspective on, and a program for, church
growth within the RCA developed. Through its "Reformed Church
Growth, Perspectives and Proposals," the GPC issued an invi-
tation to the members of the RCA to converse about church
growth and commit themselves to it for their church. The central
tasks for a growing church were described as: "cultivate the Christian community gathered in the Reformed Church; commit ourselves to God's mission; and celebrate life before God."[36] The
three central commitments

> will bear fruit only in the obedience of Reformed Church congre-
> gations and members. We will grow only if we have: a confident
> awareness of our identity in Christ and the significance of the
> Reformed Church in the Christian church; an urgent sense of
> meaningful life in Christ and the importance of that meaning for
> others; and an intense experience of Christian worship which en-
> hances life in the world.[37]

The Reformed Church Growth proposal, through its program
and its funds, sought:

> to provide leadership, sites and facilities for three to five new con-
> gregations in an area of rapidly growing population presently with-
> out Reformed churches which will result in at least one thousand
> new members for the Reformed Church by 1980; to provide lead-
> ership for five new ministries in the mainstream of American so-
> ciety in selected areas of Reformed church life and work which
> will result in at least three hundred new members for the Re-
> formed Church in America by 1980; to provide leadership for five
> new ministries among American minorities in selected areas of
> Reformed Church life and work which will result in at least three
> hundred new members for the Reformed Church in America by
> 1980; to work with at least 35 existing Reformed Church congre-
> gations which declare their intention to grow by at least fifty per-

cent in the next five years and which require outside resources to
achieve this objective; and to provide five missionaries in a frontier
area of mission who will seek to achieve objectives negotiated with
the indigenous church.[38]

The original goal for the fund drive was $3.5 million, which
was later raised to $5 million. With the conclusion of the com-
mitment phase of the drive, a total of $6 million had been re-
ceived in cash and pledges. By the middle of 1981, $5.5 had been
received in cash. From the perspective of meeting its financial
goal, the Reformed Church Growth Fund was the most successful
special denominational fund drive in the church's history.

The program impact of the Reformed Church Growth program
on the ongoing life of the Reformed Church has just begun, and
its results will not be clear for several years. Three new congregations were established in Dallas, Texas, a completely new area
for the Reformed Church. Many churches were established by
the particular synods, in areas new to the RCA, incuding North
Carolina, Missouri, and Kansas. Initially, new world mission relationships were established with the Pentecostal Union of Venezuela and the Council of Churches in Indonesia. The Rev. and
Mrs. Samuel Solovan have spent three years doing missionary
work in Venezuela, but other programs have not been implemented with the Pentecostal Union. Several factors made it necessary to shift the funds designated for Indonesia to various new
programs in Africa. The world mission goal of the growth fund
has probably been the least implemented.

FUNDS FOR MISSION

Our story about the thirty-five years in the history of the Reformed Church in America began in 1945 and ends in 1980. As
the Reformed Church rejoiced at the conclusion of World War
II, it faced major financial needs in its mission and educational
programs. The twenty years from 1925 to 1945 had been lean
years because of the Great Depression and World War II. As the
church assessed the great financial needs of its various programs,

the United Advance program was designed to seek new financial resources for rebuilding the programs of the church. Although the United Advance did not reach its goal of $2.5 million, the United Approach to the Church seemed to be the best vehicle for providing the funds needed to carry on the mission/educational programs of the church. To carry out this united approach, the Stewardship Council was formed and given responsibility for coordinating budget building and conducting a unified promotional program for the mission/educational programs of the RCA. As the Stewardship Council carried on its work, coordinated budget building did not seem adequate, and a General Synod Executive Committee was formed to represent the synod throughout the course of the year. As a part of the "corporate" milieu of the time, the GSEC provided leadership to the church. After six years of serious study, the GSEC recommended that the mission/educational programs of the church be merged into one "corporation" for program.

Although it was never explicitly stated that "one corporation" for program would provide additional financial resources for mission, this assumption seems to have formed part of the rationale for creating the GPC. The studies discuss "efficiency" and "effectiveness" and present the benefits arising from the presentation of one program to the church.

A comparison of the financial experiences of the GPC with the boards that preceded it is interesting. The last year for the boards was 1967; the GPC held its first meeting in June of 1968. The boards reported their financial results to the 1968 General Synod. Their income had been:

	TOTAL	RCA GIVING
Board of World Missions	1,804,872	1,599,601
Board of North American Missions	1,598,586	1,313,460
Board of Education	407,400	352,810
TOTALS	3,858,810	3,265,871

The comparable figures for the General Program Council in 1979 were: Total Income, $5,413,902; RCA Giving, $4,395,993. Thus, RCA giving for its denominational mission/educational programs had increased $1,130,122 in these eleven years for an increase of 34.6%. During the same period the funds spent on "congregational purposes" in the RCA increased from $24,867,268 to $64,308,641, for an increase of 158%. Two factors make the comparison between the giving to the boards in 1967 and to the GPC in 1979 less than direct. First, some of the programs of the former boards were being carried on by the particular synods and givings to them would not have come to the GPC. Second, the Reformed Church Growth Fund had income of $1,723,846 in 1979. This special fund was not included in the regular giving from the RCA—just as giving to the Reformed Church Development Fund was not included in the 1967 figures for the boards. Thus, the comparison is not mathematically precise, but it does show that the merger of three distinct programs of the church into one program corporation did not make a positive impact on giving for the denominational program in the RCA.

As the RCA giving to the GPC is analyzed more specifically, it shows the same pattern that historically had been experienced by the church. The programs for overseas mission receive the highest percentage of money from the church. When the General Program Council was able to significantly increase the giving of the church to its programs, the highest percentage of the new funds came for partnership in mission shares in missionaries, most of whom served overseas. Between 1971 and 1973, new secretaries for development concentrated on enlisting local church support for partnerships in mission, and the GPC experienced giving increases of more than ten percent per year. Without these increases in the early 1970s, the GPC would have received a very small increase in income from the RCA during its first eleven years of service to the denomination.

CONTRIBUTIONS OF THE GENERAL PROGRAM COUNCIL TO THE LIFE AND WORK OF THE REFORMED CHURCH IN AMERICA

The General Program Council began its work during a time of tension and turmoil in the Reformed Church. As the members of the RCA considered the possibilities of merger with the Presbyterian Church in the United States (Southern) some of the basic, radical differences within the church were brought to the surface. Less than twelve months after the GPC held its first meeting, these differences boiled over at the 1969 General Synod and led to the establishment of the Committee of Eighteen to seriously consider the dissolution of the RCA. During this chaotic time the GPC began its leadership role in the church, and provided its major impact. With its leadership in calling and designing the Festival of Evangelism, the GPC provided a new rallying point for the RCA at a time when its diversities could have led to its dissolution. A new unity was found in the multiple diversities of the RCA at Cobo Hall, and this unity carried the church forward from the almost dissolution proposed at the 1969 General Synod to a new basis for unity in ministry.

Through the Festival of Evangelism, the GPC created a new context for the members of the RCA to explore their differences, and points of unity. Prior to the festival, all of the conversations, and discussions (on a national level) took place at the annual General Synod. This decision-making atmosphere was not conducive to reaching personal understanding, but rather tended to accentuate the differences. The festival model helped people to meet each other, and learn about the points of unity which bound them together in Christ. As laity and ministers from across the Reformed Church began to explore their commitments to Christ and the gospel, they sensed a new oneness, and were led by the Spirit to a new unity in the midst of diversity.

The GPC not only created a new context for the members of the RCA, but also focused the discussion into a new arena. During the 1960s the discussions in the RCA had been on questions of biblical interpretation and ecumenicity. Through its "Goals for Mission," the GPC led the RCA into an intensive exploration of its mission for Christ in the contemporary world. The Festival of Evangelism and Mission Festival '71 brought this new focus to discussion and debate into the life of the church. As people wrestled with their personal goals for mission, they discovered a new commonality with fellow members from across the RCA. As they shared their frustrations and difficulties in living out their mission for Jesus in their local churches and communities, they were drawn together into the bond of fellowship in Christ. Mission, focusing the life of the church on the work of Christ in the world, became a new center for the RCA as its entered the 1970s. This center brought together the diverse elements of the church, and refreshed their ministry for Christ through the RCA.

The "Goals for Mission" of the GPC placed a major focus on evangelism. The report of the original ad hoc committee placed evangelism as the first priority, and this remained the top-priority mission goal of the GPC throughout the 1970s. Through its budget allocations, the GPC was able to increase the money allocated to evangelistic work within the United States and around the world. Through its program development, like "The Good News People," and the festivals, it led the members of the church into new understandings of evangelism and new commitments to the evangelistic task of the church.

Prior to the establishment of the GPC, the mission tasks of the Reformed Church were divided geographically and programmatically. The Board of World Mission cared for the programs outside the North American continent, and the Board of North American Mission cared for programs on the continent. The Board of Education provided training for adults in evangelism, and the Board of North American Mission led the evangelism program of the church. The structure of the GPC broke down these walls of geographical and programmatic division. Early in its history the GPC struggled to avoid returning, within its own structure, to these former divisions. Through organizing its life and work around the "Goals for Mission," the GPC avoided the former separations.

Geography became unimportant. Evangelism, whether in Sioux Center, Iowa, or Madras, India, or Tainan, Taiwan, became the tie that bound program decision making and leadership together. While very sensitive to the local context in which the evangelistic task was being carried out, the GPC functioned comprehensively in its program leadership.

The GPC also increased the relationship between the RCA and its partner churches overseas. With a new sensitivity to the importance of listening to persons from other cultures and churches, the GPC brought into the life of the RCA many persons from countries such as Mexico, Taiwan, India, Japan, Oman, and Bahrain. New understandings of the mission of the church in the twentieth century were forged through exposure to brothers and sisters from other countries.

When the mission programs of the RCA were merged under the responsibility of the new GPC, it became obvious that the RCA had drifted to heavy responsibility for institutional ministries. Having participated in the establishment of school, hospitals, and seminaries in several parts of the world, the RCA had continued to provide significant resources for these institutions. With the rapid rise of costs through inflation, and the failure of contributions to the church to keep pace with that rise, the percentage of mission dollars being spent to maintain institutions was high. The GPC was able to significantly reduce the percentage spent for institutional maintenance, and also stimulate autonomy on the part of a number of institutions.

One last observation regarding the contributions of the GPC. Prior to its establishment, the membership of the program boards of the RCA had been chosen by the annual General Synods. Although the membership increasingly had been spread throughout the church, they were still elected by the General Synod. With the majority of GPC members being elected by the classes, it became a representative body in the life of the church. Each classis, and later each particular synod, had *its* member on the council. Members could speak for the council at the meetings of their judicatories, and speak to the council for their judicatories at GPC meetings. Although this did not automatically remove the feeling of distance between the membership of the church and its mission board, it did shorten the distance.

Although it made major contributions to the life of the RCA in the 1970s, the General Program Council was unable to: continue the people involvement begun through the festivals in the early part of the decade; impact the mission-giving patterns of the RCA; establish an adequate identity for itself in the life of the church; and maintain the positive momentum of its first three to five years.

The four festivals creatively engaged people throughout the church in sharing and learning about the Christian pilgrimage. For reasons which are not clear, the GPC was unable to maintain this creative thrust. Some of it continued to take place in the regions, but Jubilee/76 was the last people event sponsored by the GPC.

Our story began with the call for a united approach to the church to meet the vast financial needs of the mission programs of the RCA. Rather than dilute the needs or the program through every board approaching the church, the 1946 General Synod approved the United Advance Program. It was hoped that this united program would lead members of the RCA to support the priority needs of the church's programs. They did not. Following their historic pattern, the members of the RCA gave most to the overseas mission programs. Throughout the years of the Stewardship Council, this continued to be true. The Stewardship Council finally proposed that the undesignated funds be used to equalize the receipts for the mission programs of the church. This equalization made it possible to fund programs which did not attract gifts from the church. Even though the GPC had responsibility for all the mission programs of the RCA, it could not impact the giving patterns of the church. The vast majority of the programs in overseas mission were supported by the RCA, and the others had to be funded in other ways. This was especially true for the services of program staff to the local church. The Board of Education had been able to expand its staff to serve local churches because of its radical increase in undesignated funds, but the GPC was not able to improve the giving within the RCA for staff services. Although the establishment of the centers throughout the church received excellent support, and the services of the staff were widely utilized, congregations did not support these services with their gifts. As the GPC entered the 1980s its inability to gain financial support for the program staff moved from the point of concern to crisis.

Being a "general" program council, the GPC had a difficult time establishing a clear identity for itself in the life of the church. Being responsible for everything except the educational work of the colleges and the seminaries, made it hard to place a focus on the tasks and programs of the GPC. Members of the GPC also felt this difficulty as they carried on their work within the goal structure. Because they were working with projects and program around the world, they felt a sense of dislocation. People tended to think in historic, geographic categories, and could not adequately shift to the more general goal categories.

A final critique—the GPC was not able to maintain its early momentum of impacting the life of the RCA. Obviously, as a church in crisis and turmoil, the RCA cried out for leadership and direction in the late 1960s and early 1970s. The GPC provided formative leadership at that time, but gradually became a common element in the life of the church. The Reformed Church Growth Fund, which met and exceeded its financial and program goals (a first for the RCA), became the vehicle for leadership at the close of the decade. Maybe shifting the attention of the RCA from the mission issues raised at the festivals, such as racism, missionary go home, and need for a new missionary movement, to the growth of the RCA itself blunted the forward thrusts of the church.

CONCLUDING OBSERVATIONS

Our story of the Reformed Church's mission structures from 1945 through 1980 began with the United Advance. Although that was not technically a new structure for mission, it did set in motion the events which culminated in the formation of the General Program Council. Rather than have the boards of the church seek their financial support separately, the delegates to the 1946 General Synod adopted the recommendation of the Staff Conference for a United Advance.

We also took into account that if the boards did not appeal to the church in unity, they would appeal separately. It would then be a free-for-all. Whichever board could tell the biggest "sob-story" or whichever presented the best "salesmen" would garner in the lion's share of the gifts.[39]

With the inauguration of the United Advance, the delegates to the 1946 General Synod set in motion the process which produced the Stewardship Council, the General Synod Executive Committee, and, finally, the General Program Council. How should one measure the effectiveness of these changes in the historic board structures of the RCA? Did they, especially in their culminating structure, the GPC, bring new mission vitality and witness to the life of the church? Or, were they merely structural changes which had no impact on the life and witness of the RCA for Jesus Christ?

First, and most importantly, the GPC engaged the people of the RCA in its newly formulated goals for mission. The RCA had struggled for a number of decades with its theological diversity, and rarely was able to break through to new understanding in the framework of its theological discussions. The goals for mission of the GPC, with their focus on the theology of the kingdom, brought new breath and life to these discussions within the life of the RCA. Because of the initial work on the goals for mission, the Committee of Eighteen could recommend in 1970 that the RCA remain together as a denomination and focus its energy and vision on the developing goals for mission of the GPC. Through organizing all of its life and work around the goals for mission, the GPC was able to refocus theological discussion and debate in the life of the RCA. With this refocus, and because of the kingdom breadth of the goals, the RCA found a new avenue for sharing its life and mission.

The GPC also succeeded in engaging the people of the RCA in its mission task. One of the early, clear goals of the new structure was to have a broader participation in the selection of the membership of the boards or board. Through the election of GPC members by each classis in the RCA, responsibility for the mission/education work of the denomination was moved much closer to the local congregations. During its first decade of service to the RCA, the GPC also engaged the people of the RCA in its mission through the festivals and the regional staff centers.

Until the four festivals—including Jubilee/76—the members of the RCA had not been in such direct interaction with one another around the responsibilities for the mission of the church of Jesus Christ. In the short space of six years, the GPC directly impacted the personal lives of many RCA members through its programs. People were engaged in mission reflection and discussion. The GPC succeeded in impacting the lives of thousands of people throughout the RCA. Unfortunately, the GPC did not sustain this momentum following Jubilee/76. The festival model had probably run it course, but the GPC did not develop ways to meaningfully engage people in mission reflection through the creation of new experiences through new models.

With the establishment of the regional centers, the GPC made another direct impact on the life of the local churches throughout the denomination. Prior to the establishment of the GPC, the Board of Education and the Board of North American Missions had placed staff persons in offices in Michigan and Illinois, but New York City remained the staff center. The GPC establishment of regional centers for its staff brought the resources of the staff into a more regular and direct contact with the life and ministry of local churches. Staff members had more opportunity to walk with the members of the RCA on their pilgrimages.

If the GPC had not been responsible "for all program not specifically assigned to someone else," it probably could not have developed its kingdom-based goals for mission, nor effectively engaged the people of the RCA in new mission experiences. If the old board structures had continued, then too much coordination and cooperation would have been required to bring about the adoption of a biblically based set of goals for mission, and utilizing them for relating the people of the RCA to their mission.

Without its total responsibility for the denominational mission program, the GPC certainly could not have implemented its most significant mission shifts. Being responsible for the total mission/ education program of the denomination, made it possible for the GPC to shift more resources to evangelism, and to social issue programs. It also was possible for the GPC to shift the RCA away from institutional mission programs, both within the USA and beyond, because it had responsibility for the total program of the denomination. Without this unified responsibility, it is doubtful that the GPC would have been able to make these mission shifts for the RCA.

While uniting the mission/education programs of its three former boards into the GPC produced some very positive results, there were at least three issues that the GPC was not able to creatively solve for the denomination. The GPC, even though it did creatively engage the people of the RCA in mission reflection through the festivals, could not reverse the decline in the percentage of local church contributions being given for denominational mission. During the early seventies there were several significant increases in annual giving to the GPC, but never in the same percentages as the increases in financial contributions to the local congregation, nor the programs of the classes and synods. The highly successful Reformed Church Growth Fund, which became the first fund to oversubscribe its goal in the life of the RCA, could not be duplicated by the GPC as it sought to raise funds for its annual, ongoing budget. The fears of success for the board telling the biggest "sob-story" or having the best "salesmen" did not materialize, but, neither did the next structure generate new funds for carrying on the mission of the church of Jesus Christ. In fact, the GPC's portion of money contributed through the local congregations of the RCA declined during its first decade of existence.

Not only was the GPC unsuccessful in maintaining its percentage of RCA giving, it also failed to broaden the designation of the contributions received from the RCA. Whenever the GPC increased its income from the RCA, the increase came for traditional overseas mission projects, such as the support of missionaries. The unified structure of the GPC made it no easier for it to generate financial support for the program staff of the denomination. Even though many of the program staff persons provided direct mission support to local congregations, the GPC was unable to generate financial support for these ministries.

Without adequate financial support for nurture ministries to the RCA, including evangelism, the GPC found it necessary to regularly retrench in this area of its program. Some had hoped that a unified structure, with a common ministry on behalf of the RCA, would make it easier to increase the financial support of the congregation for nurturing ministries to the RCA. The GPC could not realize this goal. In general, the members of the RCA provided financial support for the traditional "world mission" programs, and the other programs of the GPC had to be supported through declining undesignated contributions and general income. Whether the programs were spread through two or three boards, or united in one, the members of the RCA had not grown in their willingness to provide financial support for nurture/educational ministries within the denomination.

EPILOGUE

Our story has charted the Reformed Church's major changes in its mission structures from 1945 through 1980. We chose this period because it included four major changes in structuring for mission in the RCA, and because understanding these changes will help the members of the RCA participate in their mission structures for the last years of the twentieth century. In November of 1980 the General Program Council approved major changes in its internal structure, which, though they do not technically qualify for inclusion in this story, require a brief description and comment.

Three factors set in motion the studies which led the General Program Council to approve this major revision in its committee and staff structure. They were: the retirement of Marion de Velder as General Secretary and the subsequent changes in staff structure and personnel; the continuing concerns of the Social Issues Committee of the GPC regarding its small amount of program and budget; and the continuing concerns of the RCA, especially several of its General Synod presidents, that world mission was not sufficiently central and prominent in the work of the GPC.

Dr. Marion de Velder retired from the position of General Secretary at the 1977 General Synod. He had held the position from its inception in 1968. Arie R. Brouwer, who had served as Executive Secretary since 1969, was elected by the 1977 General Synod as the new General Secretary. By November of 1977 he had led the General Synod Executive Committee and the General Program Council into the approval of a new senior staff structure and the appointment of a person to a moderately new position, Executive Secretary for Program. The new staff structure had the Secretary for Promotion and Communication, the Coordinator for Human Resources, the Secretary for Operations and Finance, and the new Executive Secretary for Program reporting to the General Secretary. Previously, only the Executive Secretary had reported to the General Secretary and the other staff positions, including the four Secretaries for Regional Services, had reported to the Executive Secretary. Dr. John Walchenbach, most recently the senior minister of the Second Reformed Church of Pella, Iowa, was appointed Executive Secretary for Program and began his new reponsibilities in January of 1978. With the retirement of de Velder and the new staff relationships that were forged through these changes, an era of staff leadership came to an end, and new relationships and patterns were initiated. By summer of 1979, Walchenbach wrote the members of the General Program Council and told them that he did not anticipate continuing to use his gifts in an administrative ministry.

The second factor came from within the life of the General Program Council itself. From the beginning of the Goal Category Committees, the Social Issues Committee had the smallest budget and the smallest program. Some had recommended the new Goal Category structure precisely because it made this smallness very visible, and, they hoped, would lead the GPC to take remedial action. Although the GPC had known its very low program and budget in Social Issues for a number of years, the increases in program and dollars were not adequate to offset the inherited inequity. At the March 1979 meeting of the GPC, the Social Issues Committee reported that it reviewed a mere 4⅔% of the GPC program budget. To make a bad situation even worse, several of the programs it reviewed had also been reviewed by other committees. They asked for, and the GPC endorsed, a thorough review of the Goal Category Committee structure and the geographical staff structure.

The third factor came from a rising concern that the GPC, both in its committee and staff structures, did not adequately reflect the primary importance of the world mission task and responsibility of the Reformed Church. Several voices raised this concern, but two presidents of the General Synod stated it mostly clearly.

Dr. Louis H. Benes, former editor of *The Church Herald*, under the heading "More Overseas Mission" declared to the 1977 General Synod:

> I would also like to call our Reformed Church to a renewed and enlarged commitment to our overseas Christian witness . . . Our missionary personnel overseas and in Mexico has been reduced from 160 in 1952 to 87 today. Thirteen positions are presently vacant. . . . How has this all happened? One reason for this, I believe, is that we have lost the specific structures that gave priority to overseas mission. Most missionary organizations were initiated, not by denominational decisions, but by the stimulation of a core of committed people convinced of the need for great obedience to the Great Commission of our Lord. . . . In time, budgets were unified, and through restructuring the Foreign Mission Board was restructured out of existence. It lost its separate identity, its opportunity to make any special appeal, and became just one small part of the whole denominational program.[1]

Based on this section of Dr. Benes's report, the 1977 General Synod took the following action:

> to encourage the General Program Council to begin a transcultural evangelistic witness, in addition to the proposed new fields in the Growth Fund Drive, in at least two other unevangelized or inadequately evangelized areas overseas or in Mexico.[2]

The General Program Council responded to this referral with the appointment of an Ad Hoc Committee on Power in World Mission. The committee began its work in the spring of 1978, and presented its final report to the November, 1980, meeting of the GPC. The extensive and wide-ranging report presented goals and strategy for mission, guidelines for humanitarian aid and relationships with a great variety of political and economic situations, called for more adequate education programs in local churches and the RCA seminaries on the contemporary issues in mission, provided suggestions for the roles of RCA area secretaries and missionaries, and addressed a number of additional significant issues in the world mission task of the RCA.[3] Ironically, this report was adopted at the same meeting at which the GPC approved its new structure.

In his president's report to the 1979 General Synod, Harvey Hoekstra, who had served as a missionary in Africa for almost thirty years, "rejoiced" in the appointment of the Ad Hoc Committee on Power in World Mission. As a consultant to this committee, he worked with them on their report. Nonetheless, he went on to declare:

> Substantial changes will, however, need to be made if our commitment to world evangelization is to live up to God's intent. World Mission has not done well in the RCA with the disappearance of our Board of World Missions. . . . The GPC has lost some of the values built into the former Board of World Missions. While achieving some significant gains, the GPC also has its weaknesses. The GPC needs to be reorganized in such a way that world mission is again clearly defined, visible and specific, bringing to the task people with special skills and expertise. Without such reorganization of the GPC, the renewal and commitment I have called for is not likely to occur. It appears that the GPC as presently organized diffuses the work to such a degree that GPC members themselves as well as local congregations find it confusing and difficult to recognize definable programs.[4]

Having received the recommendation of its president, the 1979 General Synod adopted the following recommendation:

> To ask the GPC in consultation with the GSEC to review its present structure of program goal areas and explore the possibility of reorganizing in terms of a few major denominational tasks to report back to the Synod of 1980. Further, that this reorganization provide for a structure within GPC which would keep before the RCA the challenge of the unfinished worldwide mission task with special focus on cross cultural evangelism.[5]

The General Synod had spoken. The GPC, working with the GSEC, was given the task of restructuring itself. The Executive Committee of the GPC began the task at its July, 1979, meeting. They set up the following process:

initial discussions by the Executive Committee of the GPC, July, 1979;

planning meeting of the Administrative Council, August, 1979;

discussion meetings with the staffs of the four regional centers, September, 1979;

planning meeting of the General Program Council Executive Meeting including two previous chairpersons of the GPC, the president of General Synod, and several past members of the GPC, October, 1979;

report to the GSEC, October, 1979;

discussion meeting of the full staff, October, 1979;

discussion and action by the full General Program Council, November, 1979;

report to the GSEC, January, 1980;

discussion and action by the General Program Council on structure, budget and funding, March, 1980;

action by the GSEC, April, 1980;

discussion and action by the General Synod, June, 1980;

recruitment and employment of staff persons for new positions, May through November, 1980;

final General Program Council decisions on structure and staffing, November, 1980.[6]

Basically, the process was followed, and the final decisions on its new structure, and the staff to implement the structure, were made by the General Program Council at its November, 1980, meeting.

As the General Program Council Executive Committee was beginning its work on the 1979 General Synod referral on structure, John Stapert, in an editorial in *The Church Herald*, urged them to:

. . . be aware that there are some very real limits on what can be accomplished through restructuring and organization. At best, a restructure can respond constructively to the third of three primary questions. The first question is "Why are we here?" The second question is "What should we be doing?" And the third question (to which structural configurations and structural revision can respond) is, "What's the best way to do it?". . . . This recognition leaves the the GPC with a choice. It can either set aside the first two questions and go about its restructure in terms of the traditional criteria. . . . Or the GPC can begin rather with the much more difficult first and second questions. Doing so will initially be much more difficult, but it will make the third question about structure fairly easy to answer. In fact, answering the first and second questions will give the GPC its only opportunity to provide a worthwhile answer to that third question.[7]

The members of the GPC Executive Committee reviewed this editorial at their October, 1979, meeting. While affirming a number of the insights in the editorial, the Executive Committee concluded in a "letter to the editor" that

We are keenly aware that the "restructure cannot possibly tell us what the Reformed Church in America's mission is in the world." From its initial meeting to the present, the General Program Council has wrestled with goals for the mission program of the Reformed Church in America. These carefully developed goals have been regularly reviewed and updated. From the beginning, the mission goals of the General Program Council have been organized around the biblical concept of the Kingdom of God. This was endorsed by the General Synod of 1975 in its adoption of "An Evangelism Manifesto." "As Christians in the Reformed tradition, holding to the Scriptures as the Word of God, we joyfully confess our faith in Jesus Christ as Saviour and Lord and our unity with all Christians in the world mission of His Church." ". . . in the light of the Bible's pervasive theme—the Kingdom of God. . . . We affirm, therefore, our responsibility to proclaim, to manifest and to serve the Kingdom of God. We confess our dependence on the Holy Spirit for power to fulfill our calling until Christ comes

in glory. In gratitude for the grace given us, and in confidence that
our labor is not in vain, we commit ourselves to this mission,
praying as we go, 'Thy Kingdom Come!'" Our present task is to
develop a program structure which will strengthen these affirma-
tions in the life of the Reformed Church in America.[8]

At its November, 1979, meeting the General Program Council
received a report on the emerging new structure from its Executive Committee. John Walchenbach, the Executive Secretary
for Program, presented the report. He observed that the proposed new structure, in broad outline, called for a Council on
Church Planning and Development, a Council on Christian Discipleship, and a Council on World Mission serving within the
General Program Council. Each of the councils would be served
by its own program staff. The GPC approved the broad outline for
the new structure, and instructed its Executive Committee to
develop a detailed proposal and plan for implementation for presentation to the March, 1980, meeting of the GPC. In addition,
the GPC voted to instruct the Executive Committee to present
to the March, 1980, meeting of the General Program Council a
proposal for an assessment to cover staff services and program
grants, based on an across-the-board percentage of the receipts
for congregational purposes (excluding major capital funds received for local church use), which would take into consideration
the financial burden of the small church.[9]

The Reformed Church had not, with the exception of a few
times for professors of theology at its seminaries, assessed local
churches for staff services. Over the years "askings" had been
utilized, but never assessments—obligatory taxes on the local
congregation. This proposal stimulated the most discussion.

With the GPC's approval of the general directions for the new
structure, the general secretary (Arie R. Brouwer) conducted
"pastor's forums" throughout the denomination. The purpose was
to present the emerging directions for the structure and staffing
of the GPC, and receive the critique of local church leadership.

Having heard the "voice" of the church, the Executive Committee continued to work on the directions presented in November.

When the GPC met in March, 1980, the Executive Committee presented a detailed plan for the implementation of the new structure and its staff. Included in the plan were the purposes for the three new divisions (the Councils had become Divisions).

The Division of Christian Discipleship shall be the program agent of the General Synod of the Reformed Church in America responsible for assisting in enabling and equipping the people of God in the Reformed Church to participate in God's mission in Jesus Christ.

The Division of Church Planning and Development shall be the program agent of the General Synod of the Reformed Church in America responsible for coordinating the planning and development and assisting in the funding of new Reformed Church congregations and of established congregations requiring additional funding.

The Division of World Mission shall be the program agent of the General Synod of the Reformed Church in America responsible for carrying out or cooperating with other churches in God's mission in Jesus Christ through ministries not directly related to Reformed Church congregations or assemblies.[10]

The council also approved the tasks for the new divisions, the establishment of a new coordinating committee with its specific tasks, the membership for the newly constituted GPC, and a preliminary design for staffing the new structure. Its most important action, in hindsight, was

To report to the General Synod the General Program Council's intention to continue the study and development of a proposal to be presented to the Genral Synod of 1981 that, effective January 1, 1982, the work of the Division of Church Planning and Development and the Division of Christian Discipleship be funded through an assessment upon the classes computed on the basis of receipts for congregational purposes reported for the previous year exclusive of capital funds with the following understandings:

(1) The assessment for the work of the Division of Christian Discipleship would be 2% of the receipts for congregational purposes reported for the previous year exclusive of capital funds.

(2) The assessment for the work of the Division of Church Planning and Development would be 1% of the receipts for congregational purposes reported for the previous year exclusive of capital funds.

(3) The assessment would be computed to allow a deduction of .001% of the denominational total receipts defined in paragraphs one and two above with the understanding that each congregation would pay not less than .0001% and not more than .01% of the denominational total of the receipts defined above.

(4) The Divisions of Church Planning and Development and Christian Discipleship will be prohibited from soliciting funds for their operating budgets, and that any unsolicited funds received will be placed in the general reserves of the Trustees of the GPC.

(5) No money received through these assessments will be channelled to or through the NCC or the WCC.

(6) That the GPC will hold open hearings not later than March 1981, at or near the site of each regional office in order to discuss the needs of the region and the services which would be offered through the Divisions of Church Planning and Development and Christian Discipleship for report to the General Program Council and to the General Synod of 1981.[11]

Since the general secretary had shared the developing plans for the new structure, including the plan to "assess" for the Divisions of Church Planning and Development and Discipleship, through the "pastor's forums," the 1980 General Synod received a number of overtures regarding the plans of the GPC. All of them related to the assessment question. All of them urged the General Synod to direct the GPC to "cease and desist" from its assessment explorations. The General Synod voted to deny all of the overtures.

Having made its decision on the overtures, the General Synod turned almost immediately to a report from its Standing Committee on Financial Support. This committee had received the report of the GPC's plans for initiating assessments for the two new divisions. After a very thorough, and sometimes heated, debate, the committee presented the following recommendation to the synod

> To urge the General Program Council, in its continued study of funding for its programs, to explore every possibility of funding in addition to assessments, and further, to urge the General Program Council to take into consideration in its study the pain that both the Classis of Chicago and the Particular Synod of Chicago (and possibly other areas of the RCA) have expressed concerning assessment for program.[12]

Both the Committee on Financial Support and the delegates to the 1980 General Synod endorsed "study" of the assessment proposal, but neither were prepared to endorse the concept. After the 1980 General Synod, it was possible for the GPC to continue discussing assessing for the two new divisions, but the possibility of an assessment proposal passing was very remote.

During the summer of 1980 the General Program Council Executive Committee continued to develop the plans for implementing and staffing the new structure. *The Church Herald* contained advertisements for seven new staff positions. The Executive Committee interviewed applicants and prepared its staffing recommendations for presentation to the November meeting of the GPC. It also refined the proposals on division responsibilities, membership, the coordinating committee and its tasks. Once again the GPC reviewed the assessment question, and decided to pursue it in hearings throughout the denomination.

Having adopted the purposes for the three divisions and begun to function in them, the GPC approved the recommendations of its Executive Committee for seven new staff positions. They were:

Executive Coordinator, the Rev. Everett L. Zabriskie III
Secretary for Christian Discipleship, the Rev. Dr. Bert E.
  Van Soest
Secretary for World Mission, the Rev. Dr. Eugene
  Heideman

Secretary for Church Planning and Development, the Rev.
  Dr. Russell Redeker
Secretary for Africa and the Middle East, the Rev.
  Warren J. Henseler
Secretary for Social Issues, the Rev. Robert White
Secretary for the Americas, the Rev. Richard Vander Voet

The December 12 issue of *The Church Herald* announced the new appointments in a two-page pictorial spread. Several issues later, *The Church Herald* reported the appointment of a new treasurer for the national organizations of the RCA, Mr. Everett K. Hicks. The new structure, with its staff, began to serve the Reformed Church.

The new staff and councils began to implement the various programs they inherited from the Goal Category structure of the GPC. Since the funding issue loomed so large in the planning for the new structure, and became its Achilles' heel, our story will briefly follow its development. In response to the action of the 1980 General Synod, the GPC decided to conduct "conversations" throughout the church during February of 1981. Based on the results of the "conversations," the GPC decided "not to pursue assessments as a means of funding any of its programs at this time."[13] After a review of recent RCA giving for its national mission/educational programs, the GPC drew the attention of the 1981 General Synod to two significant conclusions.

> The first is that Reformed Church folk give best when asked to give on a personal basis. . . . The second conclusion from our history is that Reformed churches wish to be asked regularly to give.[14]

The GPC failed to identify the most important conclusion, the members of the RCA preferred to give their money for "world mission" causes and always had been hesitant—some would say negligent—in giving for educational and nurture ministries within the denomination. Because of this hesitancy, or negligence, the program developed by the GPC did not prosper.

Having abandoned the "assessment" possibility because of the outcry within the church, the GPC approved a "support share" program for the Divisions of Christian Discipleship and Church Planning and Development. In reality, the "support share" program was almost identical to the suggested assessment program, with the crucial exception that it was voluntary. A congregation was asked to contribute two percent of its income for congregational purposes to Christian Discipleship and one percent to Church Planning and Development. Several additional guidelines were developed for large and small congregations. The GPC began to implement the "support share" program in the fall of 1981.

As the members of the GPC and their staff began the first steps of implementing the "support share" program, a crisis developed which required immediate surgery. Having been alerted at its November meeting that 1981 expenses were beyond the budget, and that income had been falling below the budget projections, the GPC expected a deficit result for the year 1981 (the first major deficit since 1971). The final results were larger than the worst fears—$830,807. With total expenses of $7,006,241, the deficit was almost twelve percent. The expenses for 1981 had increased by $1,102,895 over those for 1980. They were also more than $400,000 over the budget that had been approved by the GPC.

The General Program Council Coordinating Committee immediately began to plan its proposed response to the fiscal crisis. Although non-staff suggestions were developed, like merging the Divisions of Christian Discipleship and Church Planning and Development, the major response was the termination of staff positions and persons. Between the end of January and the full meeting of the GPC in April, the Coordinating Committee held several meetings and prepared its recommendations. They asked Arie R. Brouwer, the general secretary, to share their proposals through meetings in major geographical sections of the church.

After the GPC had made its decisions, a total of seven executive staff positions (identical to the number of new appointments announced in *The Church Herald* fourteen months earlier) had been terminated. They were:

Director of Promotion and Communication
Coordinator for Northeastern Regional Services
Coordinator for Western Regional Services
Coordinator for Midwestern Regional Services
Coordinator for Eastern Metropolitan Regional Services
Executive Coordinator
Secretary for Development, Western Region[15]

Several additional persons left the staff. Some of the persons who had held the above positions continued to carry responsibilities for the GPC under contract. In addition, the GPC terminated eleven secretarial and office staff positions.

The GPC's report to the 1982 General Synod provided its rationale for the staff reductions.

> The GPC made these reductions *in the context of the total denominational program. Viewed in the light of services performed by the seminaries, colleges, and especially by the six particular synods, it seems clear that the unique ministry of the GPC is* World Mission. *The large amount of designated income received for World Mission program (about 90 percent of World Mission budget) indicates that this opinion is widely held in the church. It followed that necessary reductions in program should be made first in those programs* not unique *to the GPC and* not underwritten *by contributions from the congregations—namely, the service to Reformed Church congregations provided by the Division of Christian Discipleship and the Division of Church Planning and Development.* The proposed reductions therefore require that most of the services performed by the Regional Centers during the past decade will be continued in the future only to the extent that they are funded by the particular synods.[16]

How can one evaluate this fourteen-month experience in the life of the GPC? Several areas suggest themselves. First, the GPC entered into the new structure without an assured base of funding for the Divisions of Christian Discipleship and of Church Planning and Development. Second, the GPC employed new staff persons without an adequate understanding of the budget implications for these new persons and positions. Third, and most important from the perspective of this study, the GPC interrupted the progression of the previous restructures reported in this story. Each of them integrated the strengths of the old structure into the new, and moved forward. With its move to the three councils, the GPC reached back to past structures—both staff and board.

The General Program Council implemented the three-division structure without an assured base of financial support. From the very beginning of the proposals to implement a three-council structure, the documents declare the urgency of providing a funding base for the Divisions of Christian Discipleship and of Church Planning and Development. When the Reformed Church, both through the hearings conducted by the general secretary and the discussions at the 1980 General Synod, sent clear signals that it would not accept an "assessment" program for the two divisions serving the internal life of the denomination, the GPC did not reconsider its direction toward three separate divisions under the umbrella of the GPC nor did it develop alternatives for underwriting the programs of the two divisions. The Reformed Church's giving patterns had made very clear that funds would (could) not be generated for programs and staff serving the RCA itself, but the GPC did not have alternate program for funding the two divisions.

Second, the GPC had not adequately projected the financial costs for staffing the three divisions. Under staff needs and responsibilities, the document entitled "RCA Structure for Program" declares

In reviewing staff needs and responsibilities, the Expanded Committee agreed that the GPC would require a full time coordinator in addition to an executive for each of the three divisions. Division executives would be accountable to the coordinator in terms of administration and accountable to their respective divisions in terms of program and policy. The Coordinator would be accountable to the General Secretary. The Division of World Mission appears to require three area secretaries (America, Asia/Africa, Middle East/Reformed Church World Service) in addition to the division executive; the Division of Church Planning and Development appears to require only a division executive; the Division of Christian Discipleship would begin with the current number of staff positions and staff budget and would include program staff as well as the division executive.[16]

None of the planning documents for the new structure projected the costs for employing the staff to implement the structure. As the GSEC led the RCA in the process that produced the 1968 GPC, it prepared very detailed budgets for the staff positions projected within the new structure. Both the old positions and the new were submitted to minute analysis to determine the impact on the budget of employing the new staff. Because the GPC failed to do this, the major financial crisis of 1981 took place.

Since the GPC stopped its decade-long practice of printing a schedule of staff costs in the 1983 Program Planning Budget, it is not possible to precisely compare the 1980 staff costs with those for 1981. Nonetheless, the schedules in the budget do make clear that the major cause of the deficit was the huge increase in staff costs required by the new structure. Program expenses exceeded the budget by $52,197, but the World Mission areas of the budget had been underspent by almost $200,000. Thus, the portions of the program budget most directly related to the Divisions of Christian Discipleship and Church Planning and Development—the sections where staff costs were the major portion of the budget—were overspent by almost $250,000. In addition, the Promotion expenses increased by $117,472 and Administration expenses by $94,918—a total increase of $212,390. The GPC, in the first year of functioning in its new structure, had probably increased its staff costs by over $400,000. In addition, it spent $316,892 on transition expenses from the old structure to the new. If the GPC had demanded a careful projection of the costs for staffing the new structure, and learned before employing seven new executives that it was increasing its costs by almost $400,000 without a new method for funding its staff, the financial crisis of 1981 might have been avoided.

Third, the new structure adopted by the GPC in November of 1980 was not very new. Basically, it was a step into the past! The Reformed Church had functioned with three program boards for almost 200 years. The Boards of Education, Domestic Missions, and Foreign Missions—with differing names—were almost identical to the Divisions for World Mission, Church Planning and Development, and Christian Discipleship. With the exception of transferring North American mission programs to the Division of World Mission, and Evangelism and Social Issues to Christian Discipleship, the "new" divisions carried on the responsibilities of the "old" boards that had served the RCA. The GPC itself had functioned with a very similar staff structure, but abandoned it in a very short time. So, the "new" staff structure was the "old" staff structure that the GPC had utilized for the first eighteen months of its service to the RCA.

Our story has shared the major changes in its mission structures implemented by the RCA since 1945. We have seen each of them attempt to incorporate the strengths of the old structure and move beyond the weaknesses of the old structure. The GPC was not able to continue this momentum in its 1980 decision on structure. Instead of building on the strengths of its existing structure, and reducing its weaknesses, it reached into the past for its board and staff models. Almost immediately the "old" models brought a financial crisis which forced radical surgery and makes evaluating their service to the RCA very difficult. Having implemented the necessary reductions in staff and program demanded by the financial crisis, the GPC has continued to function in the three-divisional model. The strengths and weaknesses of the divisional model will have to be assessed at a later date.

Charts for Structuring for Mission: The Reformed Church in America

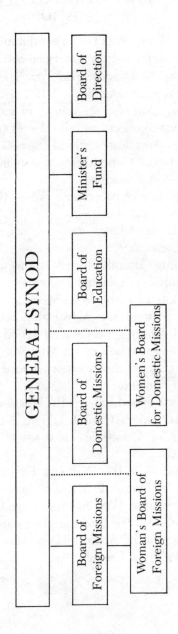

Boards of RCA, 1945

GENERAL SYNOD

Board of Foreign Missions

Woman's Board of Foreign Missions

Board of Domestic Missions

Women's Board for Domestic Missions

Board of Education

Minister's Fund

Board of Direction

FORMATION OF THE BOARD OF DOMESTIC
MISSIONS

1784   General meeting of elders and ministers considers sending missionaries to new American settlement

1786   General Body adds article on "Extension of the Church" to its regular agenda

1788   Commission of three ministers and two elders appointed to receive collections from classes and appoint missionaries to new American settlements

1791   Deputati of General Synod appointed to employ and supervise missionaries

1794   Committee of two ministers and two elders appointed to supervise missionaries

1800   Classis of Albany directed to assume supervision of missionaries

1806   Standing Committee on Missions, to be located in Albany, appointed by General Synod

1819   Standing Committee on Missions transferred to New York

1822   Formation of the Missionary Society of the Reformed Dutch Church and General Synod designation of it as new Standing Committee on Missions

1828   Formation of the Northern Board of the New York Missionary Society

1831   General Synod merges the Missionary Society of the Reformed Dutch Church and its Northern Board into the Board of Domestic Missions of the Reformed Dutch Church

1882   Formation of the Women's Executive Committee of the Board of Domestic Missions

1951   Merger of the Women's Executive Committee of the Board of Domestic Missions into the Board of Domestic Missions

1967   Merger of the Board of Domestic Missions into the General Program Council

FORMATION OF THE BOARD OF FOREIGN MISSIONS

1817   Formation of the United Foreign Missionary Society for work among the American Indian tribes

1826   Merger of the United Foreign Missionary Society with the American Board of Commissioners for Foreign Missions

1832   General Synod forms Board of Foreign Missions to work in cooperation with the American Board

1857   Separation of the Board of Foreign Missions from the American Board of Commissioners for Foreign Missions

1875   Formation of the Woman's Board of Foreign Missions

1946   Merger of the Woman's Board of Foreign Missions into the Board of Foreign Missions

1967   Merger of the Board of Foreign Mission (then called the Board of World Missions) into the General Program Council

Proposal for Offices of Stated Clerk and General Secretary

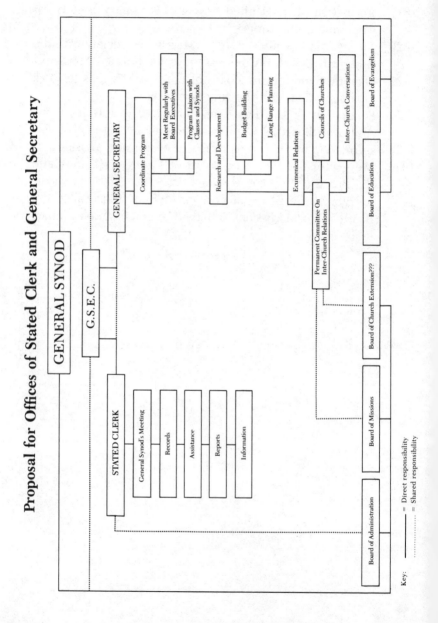

Key: = Direct responsibility
         = Shared responsibility

RCA Organizational Concept

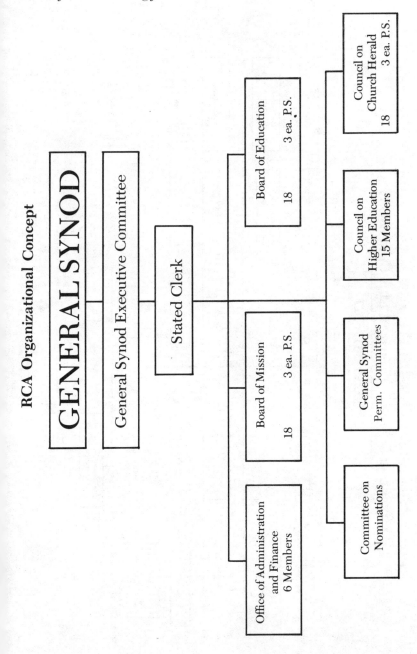

Organization Study, Reformed Church in America

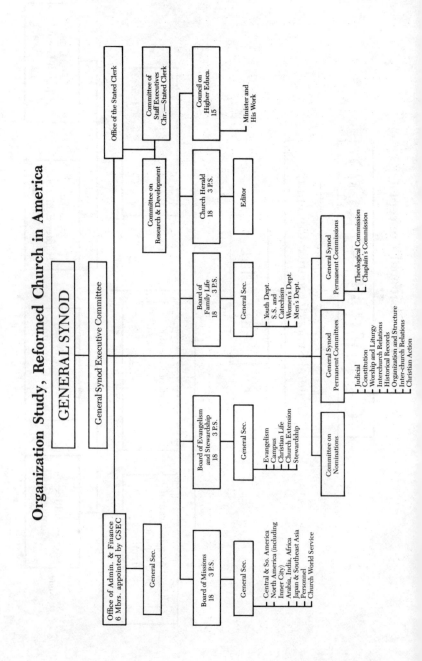

GENERAL SYNOD

General Synod Executive Committee

Office of the Stated Clerk

Committee of Staff Executives Chr.—Stated Clerk

Committee on Research & Development

Council on Higher Educa. 15
— Minister and His Work

Church Herald 18   3 P.S.
— Editor

Board of Family Life 18   3 P.S.
General Sec.
— Youth Dept.
— S.S. and Catechism
— Women's Dept.
— Men's Dept.

General Synod Permanent Commissions
— Theological Commission
— Chaplain's Commission

General Synod Permanent Committees
— Judicial
— Constitution
— Worship and Liturgy
— Interchurch Relations
— Historical Records
— Organization and Structure
— Inter-church Relations
— Christian Action

Board of Evangelism and Stewardship 18   3 P.S.
General Sec.
— Evangelism
— Campus
— Christian Life
— Church Extension
— Stewardship

Committee on Nominations

Office of Admin. & Finance 6 Mbrs. appointed by GSEC
General Sec.

Board of Missions 18   3 P.S.
General Sec.
— Central & So. America
— North America (including Inner City)
— Arabia, India, Africa
— Japan & Southeast Asia
— Personnel
— Church World Service

Organization Study, Office of Administration and Finance

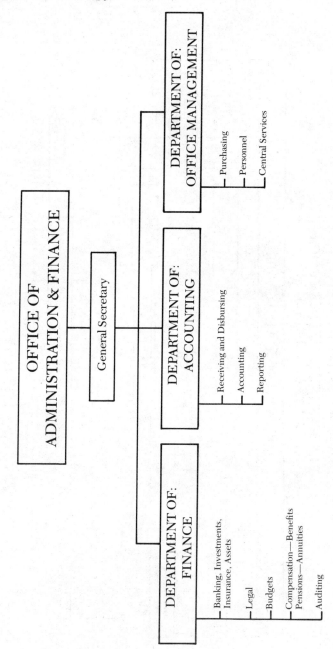

STRUCTURE FOR THE PROGRAM OF GENERAL SYNOD, R.C.A.

REFORMED CHURCH IN AMERICA
The General Synod

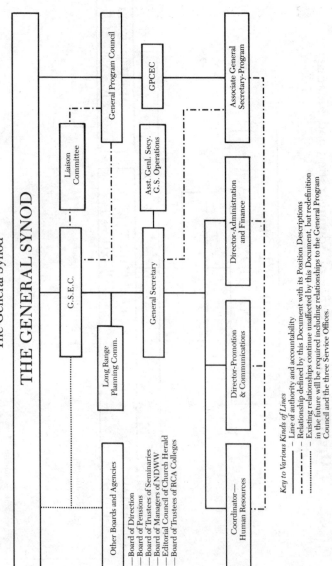

Key to Various Kinds of Lines

—— = Line of authority and accountability

—·—·— = Relationship defined by this Document with its Position Descriptions

······· = Existing relationships continue unaffected by this Document, but redefinition in the future will be required including relationships to the General Program Council and the three Service Offices.

CHART OF GENERAL SYNOD/GENERAL PROGRAM COUNCIL STAFF RELATIONSHIPS

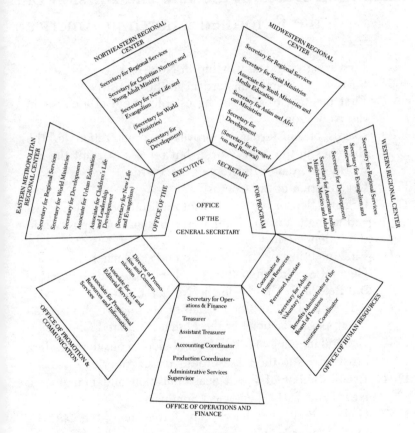

NORTHEASTERN REGIONAL CENTER
Secretary for Regional Services
Secretary for Christian Nurture and Young Adult Ministry
Secretary for New Life and Evangelism
(Secretary for World Ministries)
(Secretary for Development)

MIDWESTERN REGIONAL CENTER
Secretary for Regional Services
Secretary for Social Ministries
Associate for Youth Ministries and Media Education
Secretary for Asian and African Ministries
Secretary for Development
(Secretary for Evangelism and Renewal)

EASTERN METROPOLITAN REGIONAL CENTER
Secretary for Regional Services
Secretary for World Ministries
Secretary for Development
Associate for Urban Education
Associate for Children's Life and Leadership Development
(Secretary for New Life and Evangelism)

OFFICE OF THE EXECUTIVE SECRETARY FOR PROGRAM

OFFICE OF THE GENERAL SECRETARY

WESTERN REGIONAL CENTER
Secretary for Regional Services
Secretary for Evangelism and Renewal
Secretary for Development
Secretary for American Indian Ministries, Mexico and Adult Life

OFFICE OF PROMOTION & COMMUNICATION
Director of Promotion and Communication
Associate for Art and Editorial Services
Associate for Promotional Resources and Information Services

OFFICE OF OPERATIONS AND FINANCE
Secretary for Operations & Finance
Treasurer
Assistant Treasurer
Accounting Coordinator
Production Coordinator
Administrative Services Supervisor

OFFICE OF HUMAN RESOURCES
Coordinator of Human Resources
Personnel Associate
Secretary for Adult Voluntary Services
Benefits Administrator of the Board of Pensions
Insurance Coordinator

Several staff positions appear twice, since those persons carry out their responsibilities in two center regions. The position title appears without parentheses in the center region in which his/her office is located.

Significant Dates in the Life and Mission of the Reformed Church in America

1628 First congregational worship in New York

1664 Surrender of New Amsterdam to the British

1737 First meeting to discuss the establishment of a classis in the New World

1739 Classis of Amsterdam approves an organization for the churches in the New World, but refuses to grant the authority to ordain Ministers of the Word

1747 Organization of the Coetus

1755 Organization of the Coetus into an independent Classis, and formation of the Conferentie because of opposition to the independent Classis

1771 First meeting of the General Body, which became the General Synod when the church became independent of the Reformed Church in the Netherlands

1772 Adoption of Livingston's "Plan of Union" which reunited the opposing factions in the Dutch Reformed Church

1784 General meeting of ministers and elders considers sending missionaries to the new settlements of America

1784 Establishment of theological education and founding of New Brunswick Theological Seminary

1786 General Body adds articles on "Extension of the Church" to its regular agenda

1789 Commission of three ministers and three elders appointed to receive collections from classes and appoint missionaries to new American settlements

1792 Translation of the Rules of Church Government and Explanatory Articles by John H. Livingston

1796   Formation of the New York Missionary Society for evangelizing the Indians of the United States

1797   Formation of Northern Missionary Society to work with the New York Missionary Society

1800   Classis of Albany designates the missionary board of the Reformed Church

1806   Establishment of Standing Committee on Missions to be located in Albany, New York

1817   Formation of United Foreign Missionary Society

1819   Standing Committee on Missions transferred to New York

1819   Dr. John Scudder family sails for India under the American Board of Commissioners for Foreign Missions

1822   Organization of New York Missionary Society of the Reformed Dutch Church for extending the church in America

1824   Formation of the American Sunday School Union

1826   Merger of United Foreign Missionary Society and the American Board of Commissioners for Foreign Missions

1828   Formation of the Sabbath School Union of the Reformed Dutch Church

1828   Formation of Northern Board of New York Missionary Society and appointment of Schermerhorn as agent

1829   David Abeel sails for China under the American Board of Commissioners for Foreign Missions

1831   Formation of the Board for Domestic Missions of the Reformed Dutch Church which carried forward the work of the former New York Missionary Society and its Northern Board

1832   Formation of the Board for Foreign Missions of the Reformed Dutch Church to work in close cooperation with the American Board of Commissioners for Foreign Missions

1837   Formation of the Widow's Fund

1847   Second beginning—the migration of Van Raalte to Michigan

1850   Classis of Holland joins the Reformed Church

1854   Formation of the Board of Publication

1855   Establishment of Sustentation Fund for Disabled Ministers

1857   Secession of Graafschap and Polkton churches from the Classis of Holland and the Reformed Church in America to form a new denomination, eventually the Christian Reformed Church

1857   Separation of the Board of Foreign Missions from the American Board of Commissioners for Foreign Missions

1859   Brown and Ver Beck sail to Japan under appointment of Board of Foreign Missions

1862   General Synod dissolves the Sabbath School Board and places its work in the Board of Domestic Missions and the Board of Publication

1866   Chartering of Hope College, Holland, Michigan

1875   Organization of the Woman's Board of Foreign Missions

1882   Formation of Women's Executive Committee of the Board of Domestic Missions

1882   Establishment of Northwestern Classical Academy, Orange City, Iowa

1884   Establishment of Western Theological Seminary, Holland, Michigan

1888   General Synod appoints Committee on Systematic Beneficence

1889   Formation of the Arabian Mission by Cantaine, Zwemer, and Phelps

1897   Mission to the American Indians by Frank Wright

1916   Central College, Pella, Iowa, received into the Reformed Church from the Baptist Church

1919   Relationship established with Southern Normal School by Board of Domestic Missions

1923   Formation of the Minister's Fund

1925   Beginning of mission to Chiapas, Mexico, by John and Mabel Kempers

1935   Consolidation of the Educational Department of the Board of Publication and Bible School Work, the Department of Missionary Education, the Commission on Evangelism and the Department of Stewardship Education under the Board of Education

1944   Establishment of a Department of Evangelism by the Board of Domestic Missions

1945   Establishment of the United Synod Advance

1946   Woman's Board for Foreign Missions merged with the Board for Foreign Missions

1948   Mission begun in the Upper Nile

1949   Formation of the Stewardship Council

1951   Transfer of missionaries from China to Hong Kong, Taiwan, Singapore, and the Philippines

1951   Women's Board for Domestic Missions merged with the Board for Domestic Missions

1952   Women's work carried out by the Department of Women's Work of the Mission Boards

1954   Minister's Fund becomes the Board of Pensions

1960   Formation of National Department of Women's Work

1961   Formation of the General Synod Executive Committee

1967   Formation of the General Program Council, one board for the mission and program of the church

1970   Festival on Evangelism, Detroit, Michigan.

1972   Festival of Mission, Milwaukee, Wisconsin

1973   Family Festival, Estes Park, Colorado

1973   National Department of Women's Work renamed Reformed Church Women

1976   Jubilee, Slippery Rock, Pennsylvania

1980   Restructure of the General Program Council into the Divisions of Christian Discipleship, Church Planning and Development, and World Mission

NOTES

NOTES TO CHAPTER ONE

1. The various volumes in "The Historical Series of the Reformed Church in America" can provide the interested reader with more background on the lengthy period of Reformed Church history digested in this introductory chapter. In addition, books by the following authors (cited in the bibliography) may be helpful: Brouwer, Brown, Corwin, de Jong, Demarest, Eenigenburg, Hageman, Luidens, Smith, and Zwierlein.

2. A. J. F. Van Laer, ed., *Documents Relating to New Netherland 1624-1626* (San Marino: The Henry E. Huntington Library and Art Gallery, 1924), p 2.

3. Gerald F. De Jong has published an article on the "comfortors of the sick." Gerald F. De Jong, "The Ziekentroosters or Comfortors of the Sick in New Netherland," *New York Historical Society Quarterly*, 54: 339-359 (October 1970).

4. Edward Tanjore Corwin, ed., *Ecclesiastical Records of the State of New York* (Albany: J. B. Lyon, 1901), 1:53 (hereafter cited as *Eccl. Records*).

5. *Ibid.*, p. 34.

6. Frederick J. Zwierlein, *Religion in New Netherland* (Rochester, N. Y.: John P. Smith Printing Co., 1910), p. 86.

7. Corwin, *Eccl. Records*, p. 602.

8. *Ibid.*, p. 558.

9. *Ibid.*, p. 545.

10. *Ibid.*, p. 400.

11. *Ibid.*, p. 525.

12. *Acts and Proceedings of the General Synod of the Reformed Church in America* (New York: Board (later Department) of Publication, Reformed Church in America, 1848), p. 425. Future footnotes will use the abbreviation *MGS* (signifying the Minutes of General Synod) for the *Acts and Proceedings*. The footnote will give the appropriate year and page reference.

13. *Classis of Holland Minutes, 1848-1858*, (Grand Rapids: Wm. B. Eerdmans Pub. Co., 1950), pp. 36, 37.

14. *The Semi-Centennial Convention of the Board of Domestic Missions* (Newark: Board of Publication of the Reformed Church in America, 1883), p. 18.

15. Van Laer, *Documents Relating to New Netherland, 1624-1626*, p. 5.

16. Corwin, *Eccl. Records*, p. 56.

17. *Ibid.*, p 60.

18. *Ibid.*, p. 147.

19. *Ibid.*, p. 16.

20. Jonathan Pearson, *Two Hundredth Anniversary of the First Reformed Protestant Dutch Church of Schenectady, New York* (Schenectady: Daily and Weekly Union Stream Printing House, 1880), p. 73.

21. *Ibid.*, p. 74.

22. *Constitution of the Reformed Dutch Church* (New York: George Forman, 1815), p. 31.

23. *Ibid.*, pp. 32, 33.
24. *Ibid.*, p. 40.
25. *Ibid.*, pp. 52, 53.
26. *Ibid.*, pp. 149, 150.
27. *Ibid.*, p. viii.
28. *Ibid.*, p. 179.
29. *Ibid.*, p. 181.
30. *Ibid.*, p. 181.
31. *Ibid.*, p. 177.
32. *Ibid.*, p. 183.
33. *Ibid.*, p. 187.
34. *MGS*, 1784, p. 115.
35. *MGS*, 1786, p. 150.
36. *MGS*, 1788, p. 181.
37. *MGS*, 1791, p. 216.
38. *MGS*, 1794, p. 263.
39. *MGS*, 1800, pp. 308, 309.
40. *MGS*, 1804, p. 341.
41. *MGS*, 1809, p. 386.
42. Stryker Report, 1800 (RCA Archives, New Brunswick Theological Seminary, New Brunswick, N. J.).
43. *MGS*, 1814, p. 48.
44. *MGS*, 1819, p. 45.
45. *MGS*, 1820, p. 72.
46. *MGS*, 1821, p. 57.
47. *MGS*, 1822, p. 65.
48. *MGS*, 1828, p. 134.
49. *MGS*, 1830, p. 296.
50. *MGS*, 1830, p. 298.
51. *MGS*, 1831, pp. 383, 384.
52. John H. Livingston, *The Glory of the Redeemer* (New York: New York Missionary Society, 1799), pp. 42, 43.
53. John H. Livingston, *A Sermon Delivered Before the New York Missionary Society* (New York: T. & J. Swords, 1804), pp. 34, 35.
54. *Annual Report, American Board of Commissioners for Foreign Missions*, 1810-1858 (Boston: Crocker & Brewster), pp. 9, 10.
55. *Ibid.*, pp. 11, 12.
56. J. B. Waterbury, *Memoir of the Rev. John Scudder, M. D.* (New York: Harper & Brothers, 1870), pp. 22-28.
57. *MGS*, 1817, p. 40.
58. *MGS*, 1817, p. 40.
59. *MGS*, 1818, p. 37.
60. *Annual Report, United Foreign Missionary Society* (New York: J. Seymour, 1824), p. 6.
61. *MGS*, 1826, p. 61.
62. *MGS*, 1826, p. 61.
63. *MGS*, 1827, p. 75.
64. *MGS*, 1831, pp. 380, 381.
65. *MGS*, 1834, p. 327.
66. *MGS*, 1832, pp. 81, 82.
67. *MGS*, 1833, p. 225.
68. *MGS*, 1833, p. 227.

69. *MGS*, 1900, p. 757.
70. *MGS*, 1907, p. 26.
71. *Annual Report, Board of Domestic Missions*, 1907, p. 27.
72. *MGS*, 1832, p. 89.
73. *MGS*, 1832, p. 141.
74. *Annual Report of the American Board of Commissioners for Foreign Missions*, 1857, pp. 22, 23.
75. *MGS*, 1857, p. 235.
76. *Ibid.*, p. 236.
77. *MGS*, 1863, p. 335.
78. *MGS*, 1864, p. 490.
79. *Ibid.*, p. 490.
80. Bishop J. Leslie Newbigin cites the Amoy experiences of the English Presbyterian and Reformed Church missionaries as one of the initial thrusts for the conversations which culminated in the Church of South India.
81. *MGS*, 1859, p. 378.
82. *Annual Report, American Board of Commissioners for Foreign Missions*, 1847, p. XXX.
83. *MGS*, 1900, pp. 837, 838.
84. Theodore H. White, *In Search of History* (New York: Warner Books, 1978), p. 71.
85. Mrs. W. I. Chamberlain, *Fifty Years in Foreign Fields* (New York: Woman's Board of Foreign Missions, Reformed Church in America, 1925), p. 7.
86. *Ibid.*, p. 9.
87. *A Brief History of the Woman's Board of Foreign Misssons* (n. d.), p. 9.
88. *MGS*, 1957, p. 278 and 1958, p. 284.
89. *Annual Report, Women's Board of Domestic Missions*, 1910, p. 20.
90. *Annual Report, Board of Domestic Missions*, 1917, p. 8.
91. *Annual Report, Board of Education*, 1929, p. 15.

NOTES FOR CHAPTER TWO

1. William E. Leuchtenburg, *A Troubled Feast* (Boston and Toronto: Little, Brown and Co., 1973), p. IX.
2. Ludwig, Thomas and Myers, David, "Poor Talk," *The Church Herald*, Vol. XXXVI, No. 16, August 10, 1979, pp. 4-7.
3. Alexis de Tocqueville, *Democracy in America*, Volume I. (New York: A.S. Barnes, 1851), p. 341.
4. Will Herberg, *Protestant-Catholic-Jew* (Garden City, New York: Doubleday & Co., Inc., 1960), pp. 75-89.
5. William L. O'Neill, *Coming Apart*. (Chicago: Quadrangle Books, 1971), p. 317.
6. *Religion in America 1979-80* (Princeton, New Jersey: The Princeton Religion Research Center, n. d.), p. 21.
7. *Ibid.*, p. 29.
8. *MGS*, 1946, pp. 288.
9. *MGS* (directory), 1981, p. 112.
10. *MGS*, 1966, p. 490.
11. *Religion in America*, p. 16.
12. *Social Indicators III* (Washington, D. C.: U. S. Department of Commerce, 1980), p. 41.
13. Richard M. Scammon and Ben J. Wattenberg, *This U. S. A.* (Garden City, New York: Doubleday & Co., Inc., 1965), p. 20.

14. *Social Indicators III*, p. 43.

15. Scammon and Wattenberg, *This U. S. A.*, p. 91.

16. *Ibid.*, pp. 273, 102.

17. *MGS*, 1946, p. 313-324 and (directory) 1981, p. 12-19.

18. *MGS*, 1946, p. 243-287 and (directory) 1981, p. 24-111.

19. *Ibid.*, p. 65 (1981).

20. Leuchtenburg, *A Troubled Feast*, p. 125.

21. *Economic Report of the President*, (Washington, D. C.: United States Government Printing Office, 1976), pp. 178, 179.

22. *Ibid.*, p. 191.

23. *Social Indicators III*, pp. 409, 410.

24. *Ibid.*, p. 480.

25. *Markets of the Seventies* (New York: Viking Press, 1967), p. 9.

26. *Social Indicators III*, p. 491.

27. *Economic Report of the President*, p. 199.

28. *Giving in America* (Report of the Commission on Private Philanthropy and Public Needs, 1975), p. 63.

29. *Ibid.*, p. 10.

30. *Giving USA* (1980 Annual Report), (New York: American Association of Fund-Raising Counsel, Inc., 1980), p. 22.

31. *Giving in America*, p. 15.

32. *Ibid.*, p. 57.

33. *Ibid.*, p. 87.

34. *MGS*, 1946, p. 287 and (directory) 1981, p. 113.

35. Luidens, Donald, "Portrait of a Denomination," *The Church Herald*, Vol. XXXV, No. 18, September 8, 1978, pp. 4, 5.

NOTES FOR CHAPTER THREE

1. *MGS*, 1918, p. 541.

2. *MGS*, 1946, p 177.

3. *Ibid.*, p. 178.

4. *Ibid.*, p. 178.

5. A letter from Marion De Velder, director of the United Advance, "to all the Consistories and Ministers of the Reformed Church in America" (RCA Archives, New Brunswick Theological Seminary, New Brunswick, N. J.).

6. A brochure on "The United Advance in the Field of Evangelism" (RCA Archives).

7. *Ibid.*

8. A brochure, "Speak Unto the People That They Go Forward" (RCA Archives).

9. *Ibid.*

10. *Ibid.*

11. *MGS*, 1947, p. 180.

12. *MGS*, 1948, pp. 187-189.

13. *MGS*, 1949, p. 189.

14. *MGS*, 1950, pp. 180, 181.

15. *Ibid.*, p. 183.

16. *Ibid.*, p. 183.

17. *MGS*, 1952, p. 153.

18. *Ibid.*, p. 155.

NOTES FOR CHAPTER FOUR

1. *MGS*, 1951, pp. 174, 175.
2. *Ibid.*, p. 175.
3. *MGS*, 1953, pp. 195, 196.
4. *Ibid.*, p. 190.
5. *MGS*, 1951, pp. 180, 181.
6. *MGS*, 1954, p. 182.
7. *MGS*, 1958, p. 227.
8. *MGS*, 1957, p. 208.
9. *MGS*, 1953, p. 197.
10. *MGS*, 1971, p. 175.
11. *MGS* 1958, pp. 232, 233.
12. *MGS* (Appendix), 1955, p. 47.
13. *MGS* (Appendix), 1965, pp. 32, 33.
14. *MGS* (Appendix), 1968, p. 20.
15. *MGS*, 1960, p. 108.
16. *MGS*, 1953, p. 82.
17. *Ibid.*, p 97.
18. *Ibid.*, p. 243.
19. *MGS*, 1954, pp. 216, 217.
20. *MGS*, 1955, p. 216.

NOTES FOR CHAPTER FIVE

1. *MGS*, 1945, p. 222.
2. *Ibid.*, p. 226.
3. Andrews, Loring, "Unity in Program and Action," *The Church Herald*, April 11, 1958, Vol. XV, No. 15, pp. 4 and 22.
4. Andrews, Loring, "Unity in Program and Action," *The Church Herald*, April 18, 1958, Vol. XV, No. 16, pp. 12, 13, and 23.
5. *Ibid.*, p. 13.
6. *MGS*, 1958, p. 139.
7. The *Minutes of General Synod* for the year 1958 do not contain the details for the proposed amendments to the Constitution. The specific amendments can be found in: *Reports to the General Synod*, 1958, pp. 179, 180.
8. *MGS*, 1958, pp. 250, 251.
9. *MGS*, 1959, p. 143.
10. *Ibid.*, pp. 244-246.
11. *Ibid.*, p. 256.
12. *MGS*, 1960, pp. 333, 334.
13. *MGS*, 1961, p. 271.
14. *Ibid.*, p. 272.
15. *MGS*, 1964, p. 171.
16. *MGS*, 1961, p. 342.
17. A February 16, 1966, letter from the Rev. Donner B. Atwood to the Rev. Norman E. Thomas (RCA Archives, New Brunswick Theological Seminary, New Brunswick, N. J.).
18. *MGS*, 1961, pp. 350, 351.
19. *MGS*, 1962, p. 125.
20. "Minutes of the General Synod Executive Committee," January 26, 27, 1967, action 67-29.

21. "Minutes of the General Synod Executive Committe," June 10, 1964, action 64-67.

22. "Study Outline From the Subcommittee on the Study of Boards and Agencies," (n.d., RCA Archives).

23. *Ibid.*

24. *Ibid.*

25. "Minutes of the General Synod Executive Committee," November, 1964.

26. *MGS*, 1965, p. 136.

27. *Ibid.*, p. 137.

28. Memo to the General Synod Executive Committee from the Subcommittee on the Study of Boards and Agencies (October 12, 1965, RCA Archives).

29. *Ibid.*

30. *MGS*, 1966, p. 168.

31. *Ibid.*, p. 168.

32. *Ibid.*, pp. 181, 182.

33. Amended Proposal for Merging the Boards of the RCA, p. 48 (RCA Archives).

34. *MGS*, 1967, pp. 196, 170.

35. "Hay Report," February, 1968. p. 30 (RCA Archives).

36. *Ibid.*, pp. 14, 15.

37. *Green Book*, p. 3.

38. *Ibid.*, p. 7.

39. *Ibid.*, p. 7.

40. Draft of new Rule of Order for the General Synod Executive Committee (n.d., RCA Archives).

41. A letter from Mr. Arad Riggs, counsel to the Board of Direction, to the president of General Synod, Henry Bast (RCA Archives).

42. *MGS*, 1972, p. 273.

43. *Ibid.*, p. 274.

44. "Hay Report," p. 38.

45. *MGS*, 1959, pp. 130ff.

NOTES FOR CHAPTER SIX

1. *MGS*, 1969, pp. 200, 201.

2. *Ibid.*, p. 202.

3. *Ibid.*, p. 203.

4. *MGS*, 1970, p. 189.

5. "Minutes of the General Program Council," November 12-14,1969, p. 4 (RCA Archives, New Brunswick Theological Seminary, New Brunswick, N. J.).

6. *Ibid.*, p. 5.

7. "1980 Program Planning Budget of the General Program Council," n. d. (RCA Archives), pp. 1-98.

8. *Constitution and By-Laws of the General Program Council* (n. d., RCA Archives), 1969 edition, p. 4.

9. "Minutes of the General Program Council," April 15-17, 1971, pp. 6, 7.

10. "Minutes of the General Program Council," April 13-15, 1972, appendix (unpaged).

11. "Plan for Centers," (n. d., RCA Archives), p. 8.

12. *Ibid.*, pp. 11, 12.

13. *Ibid.*, pp. 13, 14.

14. Rottenberg, Isaac "A Festival of Evangelism What, Why, When, Where?" *The Church Herald*, Vol. XXVII, No. 6, February 6, 1970, p. 7.

15. Van Hoeven, Donald, "Festival of Evangelism Statement of Expectation," *The Church Herald*, Vol. XXVII, No. 7, February 13, 1970, p. 10.

16. Skinner, Thomas, "Evangelism: The Response of the Church," *The Church Herald*, Vol. XXVII, No. 17, April 24, 1970, pp. 12-16.

17. *Ibid.*, pp. 6, 7.

18. Mason, William, "For the Liberation of the Black Man," *The Church Herald*, Vol. XXVII, No. 18, May 1, 1970, p. 14.

19. Brouwer, Arie R., "Why Mission Festival '71?" *The Church Herald*, Vol. XXVIII, No. 19, May 7, 1971, p. 11.

20. Gatu, John, "Missionary, Go Home," *The Church Herald*, Vol. XXVIII, No. 37, November 5, 1971, pp. 4, 5, 20, and 21.

21. Miguez-Bonino, Jose, "The Present Crisis in Mission," *The Church Herald*, Vol. XXVIII, No. 38, November 12, 1971, pp. 12-14, and 20-22.

22. Mulder, Edwin, "What Did Mission Festival '71 Mean to You?" (his answer), *The Church Herald*, Vol. XXVIII, No. 37, November 5, 1971, p. 6.

23. Benes, Louis J., "Our Family Festival," *The Church Herald*, Vol. XXIX, No. 29, August 25, 1972, pp. 5-9.

24. Wagner, Carol, "Should I Go to Jubilee/76?" *The Church Herald*, Vol. XXXIII, No. 9, April 30, 1976, pp. 10, 11.

25. Stapert, John, "Jubilee 76," *The Church Herald*, Vol. XXXIII, No. 19, September 17, 1976, p. 25.

26. "Minutes of the General Program Council," November 9-11, 1971, pp. 25, 26.

27. "Minutes of the General Program Council," November 9, 10, 1972, p. 38.

28. "Minutes of the General Program Council," November 4-6, 1976, pp. 34, 35.

29. "Minutes of the General Program Council," April 16-18, 1969, p. 17.

30. *Ibid.*, pp. 17, 18.

31. "Minutes of the General Program Council," April 15-17, 1971, p. 9.

32. "Minutes of the General Program Council," April 13-15, 1972, p. 26.

33. "Minutes of the General Program Council," April 4-6, 1974, p. 24.

34. "Minutes of the General Program Council," March 29-31, 1979, p. 30.

35. "Minutes of the General Program Council," November 12-14, 1969, p. 10.

36. "Reformed Church Growth, Perspectives and Proposals," n.d. (RCA Archives), p. 15.

37. *Ibid.*, p. 18.

38. *Ibid.*, p. 15.

39. *MGS*, 1946, p. 177.

EPILOGUE

1. *MGS*, 1977, pp. 27, 28.

2. *Ibid.*, p. 28.

3. "Minutes of the General Program Council," November 13, 14, 1980, pp. 36-40.

4. *MGS*, 1979, pp. 31, 32.

5. *Ibid.*, p. 252.

6. "Minutes of the General Program Council Executive Committee," July 2, 3, 1979, p. 15.

7. Stapert, John, "Restructuring the Restructure," *The Church Herald*, September 7, 1979, p. 11.

8. "Minutes of the General Program Council Executive Committee," October 3, 4, 1979.

9. "Minutes of the General Program Council," November 1, 2, 1979, p. 41.
10. "Minutes of the General Program Council," March 20, 21, 1980, p. 5.
11. *Ibid.*, pp. 7, 8.
12. *MGS*, 1980, p. 226.
13. *MGS*, 1981, p. 252.
14. *Ibid.*, p. 253.
15. *MGS*, 1982, pp. 225, 226.
16. *Ibid.*, p. 226.

Bibliography

Acts and Proceedings of the General Synod of the Reformed Church in America, Volumes I-LX. New York: Board (later Department) of Publication, Reformed Church in America, 1771-1980.

Address and Constitution of the New York Missionary Society. New York: T. & J. Swords, 1796.

Alexander, Charles C., *Holding the Line* (The Eisenhower Era, 1952-1961). Bloomington and London: Indiana University Press, 1975.

An Address of the Board of Managers of the United Foreign Missionary Society to the Three Denominations United in This Institution. New York: J. Seymour, 1817.

Anderson, Rufus, *Memorial Volume of the First Fifty Years of the American Board of Commissioners for Foreign Missions*, 5th ed. Boston: American Board of Commissioners for Foreign Missions, 1862.

Andrews, Loring B. "Unity in Program and Action." *The Church Herald*, April 11, 1958 (pp. 4, 5, 22) and April 18, 1958 (pp. 12, 13, 23).

Annual Report, American Board of Commissioners for Foreign Missions. Boston: Crocker & Brewster; later T. P. Marvin, 1810-1858.

Annual Report, Board of North American (formerly Domestic) *Missions.* New York: Board (later Department) of Publication, Reformed Church in America, 1832-1968.

Annual Report, Board of World (formerly Foreign) *Missions.* New York: Board (later Department) of Publication, Reformed Church in America, 1832-1968.

Annual Report, United Foreign Missionary Society. New York: J. Seymour, 1818-1824.

Beaver, R. Pierce. *All Loves Excelling: American Protestant Women in World Mission.* Grand Rapids: Wm. B. Eerdmans Publ. Co., 1968.

Beaver, R. Pierce. *Pioneers in Mission.* Grand Rapids: Wm. B. Eerdmans Publ. Co., 1966.

Brouwer, Arie R. *Reformed Church Roots.* New York: Reformed Church Press, 1977.

Brown, Willard Dayton. *History of the Reformed Church in America.* New York: Board of Publication, Reformed Church in America, 1928.

Carroll, Jackson W.; Johnson, Douglas W.; and Marty, Martin E. *Religion in America: 1950 to the Present.* San Francisco: Harper & Row, Publ., 1979.

Centennial Discourses. New York: Board of Publication, Reformed Church in America, 1877.

Chamberlain, Mrs. W. I. *Fifty Years in Foreign Fields.* New York: Woman's Board of Foreign Missions, Reformed Church in America, 1925.

Church Herald, The, Volumes 1-36. Grand Rapids: Reformed Church in America, 1944-1980.

Classis of Holland Minutes, 1848-1858. Grand Rapids: Wm. B. Eerdmans Publ. Co., 1950.

Constitution of the Reformed Dutch Church. New York: George Forman, 1815.

Corwin, Edward Tanjore. *A Digest of Constitutional and Synodical Legislation of the Reformed Church in America.* New York: Board of Publication, Reformed Church in America, 1906.

Corwin, Edward Tanjore, ed. *Ecclesiastical Records of the State of New York,* 7 volumes. Albany: J. B. Lyon, 1901-1916.

Corwin, Edward Tanjore. *History of the Reformed Church, Dutch.* New York: The Christian Literature Co., 1895.

Corwin, Edward Tanjore. *Manual of the Reformed Protestant Dutch Church* (1st, 2nd, 3rd, 4th, and 5th editions). New

York: Board of Publication, Reformed Church in America, 1859, 1869, 1879, 1902, 1922.

De Jong, Gerald F. *The Dutch in America, 1609-1974*. Boston: Twayne Publ., 1975.

De Jong, Gerald F. *The Dutch Reformed Church in the American Colonies*. Grand Rapids: Wm. B. Eerdmans Publ. Co., 1978.

Demarest, David D. *The Reformed Church in America* (its Origin, Development and Characteristics). New York: Board of Publication, 1889.

de Toucqueville, Alexis. *Democracy in America*. New York: A. S. Barnes, 1851.

Economic Report of the President. Washington, D. C.: United States Government Printing Offices, 1976.

Editors of *Fortune*. *Markets of the Seventies*. New York: The Viking Press, 1968.

Eekhof, A. *Jonas Michaelius Founder of the Church of New Netherland*. Leyden: A. W. Sijthoff, 1926.

Eenigenburg, Elton M. *A Brief History of the Reformed Church in America*. Grand Rapids: Douma Publications, 1958.

Erskine, Noel Leo. *Black People and the Reformed Church in America*. New York: Reformed Church Press, 1978.

Fagg, John Gerardus. *Forty Years in South China*. New York: Board of Publication, Reformed Church in America, 1894.

First Ten Annual Reports of the American Board of Commissioners for Foreign Missions, With Other Documents of the Board. Boston: Crocker & Brewster, 1834.

Flowering Wilderness (Containing Twenty Articles by Various Authors in Commemoration of the Centennial Celebration of Reformed Churches in the West). 1947.

Giving in America. Commission on Private Philanthropy and Public Needs, 1975.

Giving USA (1980 Annual Report). New York: American Association of Fund-Raising Council, Inc., 1980.

Hageman, Howard G. *Lily Among the Thorns*. New York: The Half Moon Press, 1953.

Harmelink, Herman. *Ecumenism and the Reformed Church.* Grand Rapids: Wm. B. Eerdmans Publ. Co., 1968.

Herberg, Will. *Protestant-Catholic-Jew.* Garden City, New York: Anchor Books, 1960.

Iglehart, Charles W. *A Century of Protestant Christianity in Japan.* Rutland, Vt.: Charles E. Tutle Co., 1959.

Jubilee Commemoration 1853-1928 The Arcot Assembly and the Arcot Mission of the Reformed Church in America. Madras: Methodist Publ. House, 1931.

Kemp, Roger. "The Reformed Church in America and the Indian American." Thesis presented to New Brunswick Theological Seminary, 1970.

Kenney, Alice P. *Stubborn for Liberty: The Dutch in New York.* Syracuse: Syracuse University Press, 1975.

Latourette, Kenneth Scott. *A History of Christianity.* New York: Harper & Brothers, 1953.

Latourette, Kenneth Scott, *Tomorrow Is Here.* New York: Friendship Press, 1948.

Leuchtenburg, William E. *A Troubled Feast.* Boston and Toronto: Little, Brown & Co., 1979.

Levai, Blaise. *One Hundred Years With Christ in the Arcot Area* (n.d.).

Livingston, John H. *A Sermon Delivered Before the New York Missionary Society.* New York: T. & J. Swords, 1804.

Livingston, John H. "The Glory of the Redeemer." Sermon preached on April 23, 1799.

Lucas, Henry S. *Netherlanders in America, Dutch Immigration to the United States and Canada, 1789-1950.* Ann Arbor: The University of Michigan Press, 1955.

Ludwig, Thomas, and Myers, David. "Poor Talk." *The Church Herald,* August 10, 1979 (pp. 4-7).

Luidens, Donald. "Portrait of a Denomination." *The Church Herald,* September 8, 1978 (pp. 4, 5).

Luidens, John Pershing. "The Americanization of the Dutch Reformed Church." Ph.D dissertation, University of Oklahoma, 1969.

Marty, Martin E. *The Fire We Can Light*. Garden City, New York: Doubleday & Co., 1973.

Mason, A. D., and Barny, F. J. *History of the Arabian Mission*. New York: The Board of Foreign Missions, Reformed Church in America, 1926.

Merwin, Wallace C. *Adventure in Unity*. Grand Rapids: William B. Eerdmans Publ. Co., 1974.

Minutes of the General Program Council, 1968-1981. (RCA archives, New Brunswick Theological Seminary, New Brunswick, N. J.).

Minutes of the General Synod Executive Committee, 1961-1981. (RCA archives).

Mulder, Arnold. *The Peoples of America: Americans From Holland*. Philadelphia and New York: J. B. Lippincott Co., 1947.

Neill, Stephen C. *Christian Missions*. Baltimore, Maryland: Penguin Books, 1964.

O'Neill, William L. *Coming Apart*. Chicago: Quadrangle Books, 1971.

Pearson, Jonathan. *Two Hundredth Anniversary of the First Reformed Protestant Dutch Church of Schenectady, New York*. Schenectady: Daily and Weekly Union Stream Printing House, 1880.

Phillips, Clifton Jackson. *Protestant America and the Pagan World: The First Half Century of the American Board of Commissioners for Foreign Missions, 1810-1860*. Cambridge, Mass.: Harvard University Press, 1969.

Pitcher, P. W. *Fifty Years in Amoy*. New York: Board of Publication, Reformed Church in America, 1893.

Religion in America 1976. Princeton, N. J.: The Gallup Opinion Index, 1976.

Religion in America 1979-80. Princeton, N. J.: The Princeton Religion Research Center, 1980.

Social Indicators 1976. Washington, D. C.: U. S. Department of Commerce, 1977.

Social Indicators III. Washington, D. C.: U. S. Department of Commerce, 1980.

Smith, George L. *Religion and Trade in New Netherland: Dutch Origins and American Development.* Ithaca, N. Y.: Cornell University Press, 1973.

Strong, William E. *The Story of the American Board.* Boston: Pilgrim Press, 1910.

Tercentenary Committee on Research. *Tercentenary Studies: Reformed Church in America.* (No publisher: Published by the Church, 1928.

Te Winkel, Sarella. *The Sixth Decade of the Woman's Board of Foreign Missions.* New York: The Woman's Board of Foreign Missions, 1935.

The Semi-Centennial Convention of the Board of Domestic Missions. Newark: Board of Publications of the Reformed Church in America, 1883.

The World Mission of the Church. New York: The Board of Foreign Missions of the Methodist Episcopal Church, 1939.

Van Eyck, Wm. O. *Landmarks of the Reformed Fathers.* Grand Rapids: The Reformed Press, 1922.

Van Hoeven, James, ed. *Piety and Patriotism.* Grand Rapids: Wm. B. Eerdmans Publ. Co., 1976.

Van Hoeven, James. "Salvation and Indian Removal: The Career and Biography of the Reverend John F. Schermerhorn, Indian Commissioner." Ph.D. dissertation, Vanderbilt University, 1972.

Warneck, Gustav. *Outline of a History of Protestant Missions from The Protestant Reformation to the Present Time.* Edinburgh and London: Oliphant, Anderson and Ferrier, 1901.

Waterbury, J. B. *Memoir of the Rev. John Scudder, M.D.* New York: Harper & Brothers, 1870.

Wattenberg, Ben J., with Scammon, Richard M. *This U. S. A.* Garden City, New York: Doubleday & Co., 1965.

White, Theodore H. *In Search of History.* New York: Warner Books, 1981.

Zwierlein, Frederick J. *Religion in New Netherland.* Rochester, N. Y.: John P. Smith Printing Co., 1910.